Dedication

*This book is dedicated to the thousands of families
worldwide who relinquished their sons and other loved ones
to the uncertainties of this merciless war.*

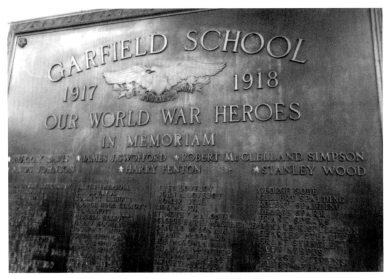

This plaque represents 213 families
from the Garfield School, that signed up to serve our country.
Some had four and five family members to register, some never made it home.

Front Cover:
Prather family, left to right: Aunt Anna May, Grandfather, Grandmother,
Joyce's mother; 2nd row Uncle Shannon, unknown, Uncle.
(Courtesy Joyce Kuechner)

Back cover:
Poppies (Photo by author); Marching soldiers
(From poster, courtesy Nancy Turner)

ISBN: 978-0-9857603-2-8

Printed by Walsworth Publishing Company, Inc. Marceline, MO.
Dennis Paalhar, Sales Representative

CONTENTS

CHALLENGES TO SOCIETY

AFTER THE WAR

INTRODUCTION

to Volume 2 of

"UNHEARD VOICES, UNTOLD STORIES"

To add to my introductory comments in Volume I, in my interviews I was not looking for exciting or heroic battle stories. Veterans rarely shared the details of horrific scenes with their families. I was looking instead for the average American soldier and his experiences. What kind of a man would volunteer to leave his family, cross an unknown ocean, and set foot on foreign land, all to risk death or be seriously wounded, for the sake of foreigners as well as for his countrymen. Those who were drafted, of course, were required to go to war or to face possible severe civil penalties.

But 2,500,000 young Americans from all of the 48 states put on a khaki uniform, learned to fire a rifle or aim an artillery piece to "save the world for Democracy," as their President Wilson declared. Most families were unaware of the terrible results that the ferocious fighting could have on a loved one. The effects of newly introduced weapons of World War I had never before been witnessed by either a private or a general. Use of machine guns changed combat strategies because the guns could kill hundreds of soldiers in merely a few minutes. For a man exposed to these bullets and to the shrapnel from a huge artillery guns, as well to poisonous gas, his efforts to survive became nightmarish.

However, when their soldier came home, the family and the veteran often tried to pick up life as it had been before he went off to war. Time had stopped for some men when they left the States, then started again on his return. Life continued as if he had not served in a war. Most men made adjustments to the necessary problems that were part of coming home. But for thousands more, their war experiences could not be forgotten. This was especially true if the veteran had been severely wounded or suffered from "shell shock." Their lives were changed forever, and integration into civilian life was difficult if not impossible.

These stories tell what the family remembers and what they have gleaned from the keepsakes or items the soldier brought home. Both stories and mementos are most likely also show the soldier would have wanted his life to be remembered. All World War I veterans have died. The last one alive was Frank Buckles of Missouri who died in 2011. Consequently, the stories, like the soldiers who lived them, have vanished with them into history.

Because memory is sometimes unreliable, or I was offered the "hearsay" of a grandchild or great niece or nephew, I checked all the details I could for accuracy. Some records were lost in a fire in 1973 at the National Archives Personnel Center in St. Louis, but there were other ways to verify dates and numbers. Frequently, I discovered unknown stories and facts and made them known to the relatives, which pleased them greatly. I realize that the next generation will have still fewer relatives who know with any accuracy the story of their World War I soldier. But, in many cases, traces remain in the memories and souvenirs preserved by younger relatives. My purpose is to bring life to these stories.

Now is the time to preserve as many stories as we can. Let me introduce you to a number of veterans and their history. Along with these narratives, I have also added information on a wide range of topics that provide more understanding about The Great War of which they were a part.

ROSTER OF VETERANS AND THEIR UNITS

LIST OF UNITS AND THEIR MEMBERS

Co. A, 16ᵗʰ Balloon Co., 5ᵗʰ Balloon Squadron . . . . Paul Ellis Allen

167ᵗʰ Reg. 42ⁿᵈ Division . . . . Luther Clyde Williams

134ᵗʰ Infantry, 34ᵗʰ Division . . . . Chester Amil Jensen

6ᵗʰ Illinois Regiment . . . . Clarence W.M. Moore, Augustana College Band

35ᵗʰ Division . . . . Sgt. Tirey Ford 129ᵗʰ F.A., Co. B
. . . . Sgt. Ernest E. Butrell, Co. H, 137ᵗʰ Inf.
. . . . Sgt. John Logan Rogers, 137ᵗʰ Inf.
. . . . Pvt. Isaiah Bowen, Co. M, 139ᵗʰ Inf.
. . . . Sgt. McKinley Wooden, 129 F.A., Co. D
. . . . Capt. Harry S. Truman, 129ᵗʰ F.A. Batt. D
. . . . Pvt. Howard Rodewald, Co. B., 154ᵗʰ
. . . . 1ˢᵗ Lt. William O. Jackson, 128ᵗʰ Machine Gun

92ⁿᵈ Div., Co. A, 1ˢᵗ Batt. 366 Inf. . . . . 1ˢᵗ Lt. William H. Clark

88ᵗʰ Division-Medical Depot . . . . John Meade Hunter

88ᵗʰ Infantry . . . . Brian Sweeney, 339ᵗʰ F.A.

142ⁿᵈ Infantry, 36ᵗʰ Division (Texas) . . . . Ed Johnson, Choctaw Indian

366 Inf. 92ⁿᵈ Regiment . . . . Wayne Miner

93ʳᵈ Regiment . . . . Henry Johnson

Quartermaster Corps . . . . Sgt. William Claude Tillotson

Co. F, 30ᵗʰ F.A. Co. . . . . Dowell Mowery Lentz

Co. L, 3ʳᵈ Provisional Regiment . . . . William George Alvamann

134ᵗʰ Machine Gun Bttn. 37ᵗʰ "Buckeye" Div. . . . . Capt. Harry Fouts Hazlett

2ⁿᵈ Regiment, 3ʳᵈ Division, "Rock of the Marne" . . . . Cpl. Peter Kraus

103ʳᵈ Engineers, 28ᵗʰ "Keystone" Division . . . . William Arthur Zirkman

Units Not Known
Henry Effertz, Sr.
Miss Louise Thompson
William Thompson
Robert Lambright, Sr.
Jacob Bachus
Dr. Ralph Albertson
Noah Gilbert Henley
Herbert Costa

British-Canadian Royal Air Corps
Capt. John Stanley Wood

354 Infantry, 89ᵗʰ Division
Shannon Alvin Prather

314ᵗʰ Engineers
Sgt. Edward Roche

S.A.T.C. Training Corps
Paul Wilde

41ˢᵗ Co., REC Battallion
Frank Wilde

489ᵗʰ Aero Construction
Raymond Pierson Jones

MARINES

6ᵗʰ Regiment, 4ᵗʰ Marine Brigade, 2ⁿᵈ Div.
Cecil Archle Ireland

NAVY

Great Lakes Naval Training Ctr.
Chicago, IL
William Waggoner, Jr.
Died of pneumonia

George Rodewald, Fireman 1ˢᵗ class
USS West Loquassuck

Henry Truhlsen, Apprentice Seaman

Yeomanettes
Marjorie Lewis

42ⁿᵈ Div. 117ᵗʰ Ammunition Train
John Meade Hunter
Pfc. Robert M. Simpson

117ᵗʰ Ammunition Train
42ⁿᵈ Rainbow Division
Fred Shields, Jr.

Jefferson Barracks, St. Louis, MO.
Maurice McDaniel

TIME LINE FOR THE UNITED STATES' PARTICIPATION IN WORLD WAR I

THE YANKS ARE COMING

GLASGOW	45000
MANCHESTER	4000
LIVERPOOL	844000
BRISTOL PORTS	11000
FALMOUTH	1000
PLYMOUTH	1000
SOUTHAMPTON	57000
LONDON	62000
	1025000

QUEBEC	11000
MONTREAL	34000
ST. JOHNS	1000
HALIFAX	5000
PORTLAND	6000
BOSTON	46000
NEW YORK	1656000
PHILA.	35000
BALTIMORE	4000
NORFOLK	288000
	2085000

LE HAVRE	13000
BREST	791000
ST NAZAIRE	198000
LA PALLICE	4000
BORDEAUX	50000
MARSEILLE	1000
	1057000

To Italy

This Map Illustrates Troop Sailings from American Ports to Great Britain and France

THE PRELUDE: 1914

June 28 – Archduke Ferdinand of Austria assassinated by Bosnian student terrorist.

July 28 – Austria declares war against Serbia. Austria fires first shot at Serbia next day.

August 4 – Germany invades Belgium and the world goes to war.

Month of August – War declarations against Germany are made by Russia, France, England, Belgium and a number of other countries.

THE ERA OF SUBMARINES: 1915

May 7 – Germany torpedoes and sinks *The Lusitania* and 128 American passengers are among the 1,198 passengers that die in the attack. More sinkings of ships by Germany occur during next two years including three American ships in March, 1917.

THE UNITED STATES BECOMES A COMBATANT: 1917

February – Britain intercepts Germany's telegram to Mexico asking them to invade the U.S. from the south. (Known as the "Zimmerman telegraph.)

April 6 – Congress declares a state of war exists with Germany.

June – Commanding General John J. Pershing and staff secretly depart for France, arriving safely with small contingent of soldiers, who became known as the "First Division."

June 5 – First time ever required registration of American males, ages 21-30, takes place.

September – First cantonment completed and basic training begins for what will become two million men to be transported to France to fight.

THE AEF BECOMES AN ARMY TO BE RECKONED WITH: 1918

March – Germany begins "Operation Michael," a last desperate effort to defeat the Allies before Americans arrive in large numbers.

June 6 – AEF Second Division and the Fourth Marine Brigade begin the attack to drive Germans out of strategic Belleau Wood.

June 1 – The AEF Second Division and Marines continue to Chateau-Thierry where they inflict a crucial defeat on the Germans.

July 1 – Allied campaign begins assault to capture Vaux, halting the German drive toward Paris.

July 15 – Germans launch final attack in the Marne River area, where the AEF's 42nd Division halt German advance.

July 18 – The AEF launches attack on the Marne River sector, suffering severe losses, but succeeds in defeating the Germans.

August – Third Division captures the salient at the Marne River held by the Germans for two years, and earn the title of "Rock of the Marne" for this difficult feat.

August 6 – French forces, with famed Moroccan troops, and American divisions achieve victory in the Marne sector campaign.

FINAL MONTHS OF THE WAR: 1918 – 1923

Meanwhile, AEF troops have been arriving at the rate of 200,000 per month and spent 4-8 weeks with experienced British and French soldiers in last training before seeing combat.

September – Pershing organizes American forces into one army under his command, with the French assisting, to attack the important salient of St. Mihiel, driving the Germans out in about four days. Simultaneously, Pershing and staff are planning campaign of the Meuse-Argonne which begins two weeks after capture of St. Mihiel.

Sept. 11 – Bombardment and attack on St. Mihiel begins. More than 500,000 AEF combat troops plus support are involved. Offensive includes for the first time ever the combined use of tanks, airplanes, artillery, and infantry. (Chronicles)

Sept. 26 – AEF troops smash the Hindenburg line at Cambrai. Other assaults made by the AEF include Montfaucon, Hill 304, and other sites in the Verdun sector.

Sept. 30 – Bulgaria surrenders to Allies and King Ferdinand abdicates.

Preparations for next campaign began before the capture of St. Mihiel, and the troops when victory was achieved, were immediately transported by trucks or marched as far as 200 miles to sites for the Meuse-Argonne offensive. A total of 1,500,000 AEF troops were placed under Pershing's command for this campaign.

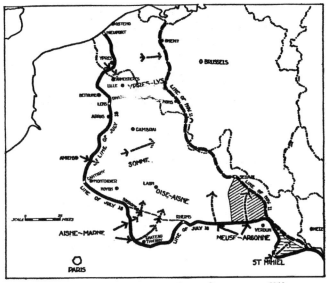

AMERICAN PARTICIPATION IN THE ALLIED OFFENSIVES OF 1918
PUBLIC DOMAINE

Oct. 4 – The Allied offensive begins to reduce the Kriemhilde Line, the eastern part of the Hindenburg Line that is four kilometers deep with barbed wire defenses. It proves crucial to ending the war.

Nov. 1 – Last phase of Argonne offensive begins and ends November 10. The entire Meuse-Argonne campaign has lasted 47 days, resulting in AEF casualties of 120,000, killed or wounded. (Ellis)

Nov. 11 – 11 A.M. – The Armistice begins. All firing is ordered to stop. In some instances this order was not obeyed (see story, "The Veteran's Best Friend," p. 141).

Nov. 12 – Preparations for discharge and transport home begin for some soldiers. A selection of 250,000 soldiers were assigned to serve as the Army of Occupation of Germany and stayed in Europe until as late as July, 1919.

AND SO IT ENDED: 1919 – 1923

June 28, 1919 – Treaty of Versailles is signed.

1920 – Also delayed in being discharged were some 5,000-15,000 Americans in Siberia and Russia, known as "The Polar Bears," who were part of the Allied group that guarded munition dumps in the former czarist Russia, and protected Russian citizens against the Bolsheviks and the White Army of the late czar.

1923 – Last AEF troops to be sent home consist of a small contingent of troops ordered to leave Europe in 1923 by President Herbert Hoover (U.S. Army Europe)

BASIC TRAINING: SOME FACTS AND IMPRESSIONS

THE ALPHABET AND WORDS YOU CAN'T UNDERSTAND ———-
Important things to Know and Then Forget – After Army Days Are Over

The most important thing to learn in army basic training are the commands such as: "a -ten-hut", "right face," "about face," "parade rest," "right dress," and finally, after hours of drilling, the command, "rest." None of these mean what they literally say. The "rookie" quickly learns that the drill sergeant and the first lieutenant have a supply of secret words in a code that only they know what they are really saying. But woe to the rookie who does a "right face" instead of "LEFT FACE," and ends up, tripping on his own feet as he turns, while knocking down his whole line of recruits in doing so.

"Rest" does not really mean, "take a break and have a smoke," nor does "right dress" mean you are wearing the proper attire. "Make it snappy," means to salute the officer properly, with the hand and elbow at correct angles, eyes in proper direction, and body stiff as a well oiled board. The "hard boiled" sergeant – wouldn't be so "boiled hard," if he did not have to instruct 50 or 60 recruits all day by yelling at the top or lowest part of his voice. In addition, the rookies don't understand Army English, and can't tell the difference between their right foot from the left. Especially those who wear a 9 ½ shoe and are issued a size 12 boot.

Basic training means just that. Forget what you never knew and learn what you possibly will never use again in your life. You will learn how to salute, march, run as a group, hold a rifle (or wooden stick as did the first recruits in 1917 when our rifles were shipped to our hard pressed Allies instead). After holding the rifle in one position, the rifle goes in this or that direction on a muttered command, three or four times, then finally back to home. If you are lucky, you will be standing on the back two rows where "Sarge" can't see you before your glance at your buddies to see which direction is the correct one.

It isn't all fun and games in Basic Training. There are a series of shots and inoculations, you know where. And after a case of measles (German, of course) appears in the barracks, you will wish there had been a shot for them – or mumps, chicken pox, or "The Flu."

Sooner or later, you will be issued your uniform and other essentials. The shirt may not fit, but your tent half will. The underwear will be wool although the month may be July. The campaign hat falls down past your ears while the socks would be a great fit on your baby brother. But sooner or later, yes, you will have traded, pleaded, bribed your way into looking presentable. Almost. Among the other items piled into your waiting arms are two pair or sets each (if it's cold weather) of winter breeches (trousers); winter coats; wool blankets; winter gloves; boots, flannel shirts; boot laces; and canvas leggings (commonly referred to as "puttees.") In addition, even if you are lost somewhere under the pile, you would be issued three pair winter drawers (underwear) and four winter undershirts.

Next, come a service belt, tunic jacket, steel helmet, hat cord, one half of a tent, a tent pole, haversack and pancho. In all kinds of weather you will wear one or sometimes two of the five pair of wool socks issued. To make the tent inhabitable, that means stand up all night, you are allowed five tent pins, which paired with a buddy's five tent pins, makes a complete tent using the two halves, two tent poles, and ten pins. As for how to do it, it's anyone's guess.

Next are eating utensils consisting of a canteen with cover, cup, knife, meat can, fork, spoon (often inserted in your puttees), pack carrier, first aid kit, and pouch. Weapons are assigned personally to you under your

Camp Funston, KS ; Men in Mess Line
(Courtesy of Douglas County Historical Society, Watkins Museum of History)

name and consist of a rifle, trenching tool, cartridge belt, bayonet, 100 cartridges, and a scabbard. Later a gas mask will be issued, especially if you are in France and had not received one earlier. All these garments, weapons and other important items when carefully packed into your haversack weighed only about 60-80 pounds. It's a light load for your back on a 20 mile march.

Finally, as the proud owner of these items, you become responsible not only for their security and your ability to have them readily at hand, but financially liable. So if is best to keep good watch on them and loan them out only in the direst of conditions or to your cousin. Don't trust a newly made friend until you have been under fire with him for several days in the trenches of France.In addition, you are assigned the task of washing and ironing your clothes, keeping your rifle clean, and washing your mess kit. (Sasse)

After being outfitted with the new khaki wool uniform, the civilian clothes were mailed home to parents who may not be expecting it. Dismayed by their arrival, Mom probably shed more tears, and Dad had to grit his teeth to keep from showing a similar emotion.

Then there were Duties. They involved the kitchen, latrine, and grounds. In the kitchen you do K.P., that is peel enormous pots of potatoes, then wash those enormous pots in which your meal was cooked. You may get to clean the latrine with, depending upon how many demerits you've earned—- a big brush or a small brush. You "police" the grounds, not giving tickets, just picking up trash and cigarette butts. It is good exercise and builds the body, while being good for the soul, says Sarge, who by the way, is NEVER referred to by that name. For some lucky Rookies, KP also involves chopping wood and hewing stone if a nearby quarry is available, and the building of the cantonment not quite finished when recruits arrived.

Exercise field is fun. You will have bulging biceps in no time, because "if it doesn't hurt, it isn't doing you any good." Ut oh, a whistle blows, drill time again. A bugle blows, no it's not Saturday night at the "Jigger Bigger." It's either time to get up or time to go to bed. It's important for you to remember which one. It makes a difference after a few days. Whistle blows. Out to parade field again.

Basic Training
(Cartoon courtesy Fred A. Sasse)

Finally, it's time to see the C.O.— at the C.P. or O. R. —and don't forget "Sir." A simple short word associated with a well executed salute. Can't be difficult. You say your piece, but not hearing a word the officer—The Oracle of Delphi – is saying. Be sure to say, "Thank you, sir." Then salute. About face, your hand knocks off an ink pot on the desk when you are completing the salute; your right foot steps into the wastebasket; you grab the closest thing, which happens to be the officer's right arm, and you call "Help" for your only friend in the world- Sarge.

Don't worry about fighting the Germans. If you can get out of the office without executing this scenario, you will be shooting Huns by the truckload.

If not assigned to nighttime guard duty, there might a nearby YMCA canteen where movies were regularly shown, or better yet, a vaudeville show to provide entertainment. Otherwise, it was card playing, story telling, letter writing, and such other activities as the barracks or tents allowed. (This is the scenario for the new recruit, as described by Sasse in his book, *Rookie Days*.)

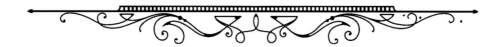

"A BRIDGE OF SHIPS" — THE CRITICAL SITUATION FOR SHIPS AT SEA

Commentary by Niel M. Johnson, PhD.

When the United States declared war against Germany on April 6, 1917, the U.S. Navy went right back to work. Actually, it was continuing its usual job of supplying the Allies with munitions, food, mules and horses, and other wartime essentials by using merchant marine vessels. No United States Navy vessels were employed. German submarines had been sinking a greater number of ships, including those of other neutral countries also, than had arrived safely in French or British ports. Somehow, despite the sinkings, enough ships managed to reach European shores with the necessary

Draftees from Illinois. Note the ID tag each one wore.

aid. However, the number of attacks by submarines was having a devastating effect, especially on neutral and privately owned vessels, and production of new ships could not match the number lost.

Meanwhile, almost two years earlier, in May, 1915, a major controversy arose when a large British passenger liner, the *HMS Lusitania*, was torpedoed and sunk near the Irish shore, by a German submarine. The British argued that it was not armed and was not carrying munitions of war. Its manifest, however, as divulged by *The Fatherland*, a periodical published by German-American propagandist, Georges S. Viereck, showed that it carried tons of rifle cartridges. Still, it was generally considered a passenger liner and not a warship. Casualties were huge: 1,201 passengers and crew died, including 128 American citizens.

As Dr. Johnson notes in his book, *George Sylvester Viereck: German-American Propagandist*, this tragedy persuaded many Americans who already had been skeptical of anti-German propaganda, that Germany was uniquely guilty of inhumanity and "schrecklichkeit" (terror) in the way it conducted war. Former President Theodore Roosevelt labeled it "murder on the high seas." President Wilson responded to the sinking by sending a series of notes to the German government that reaffirmed the right of Americans to travel on unarmed passenger ships of any nation on the high seas. He said Germany would be held to "strict accountability" for violating these traditional rights.

Later, following the sinking of the *SS Arabic* on August 19, 1915, which caused more American casualties, the German government agreed to order submarine commanders to give warning and assure the safety of passengers before sinking any passenger ships. With a few exceptions, the order held until February, 1917, when Germany declared all-out submarine warfare on any ship, neutral or not, that was aiding the British and the French. The stage was set for American entry into the war.

The debate continues today about whether the *Lusitania,* a ship carrying passengers, also transported suspected military items. Germany claimed it did carry suspect materiel, that they sank the ship on May 7, 1915, with no advance warning as already noted. Many American citizens wanted the United States to declare war on Germany after this sinking, and there was great outrage expressed when Congress refused to comply. President Woodrow Wilson was about to win the 1916 presidential election by campaigning on the slogan, "He kept us out of the war." He decided not to call for a declaration of war, even despite the tragedy of the *Lusitania* sinking.

Newspaper announcement

Some documents remain that claim to provide proof the ship's cargo included empty rifle clips, and that the ship carried three guns aft which were concealed from sight. In his book, *George Sylvester Vereck,* Dr. Johnson, relates an incident in which the Secret Service managed to take a brief case from a German purchasing agent, Heinrich Albert. The brief case contained written evidence that would partially support Germany's claim of the cargo manifest. However, American outrage at the loss of so many American lives outweighed any creditability Germany's protest might have warranted.

In August, 1914, there were 1,494 merchant vessels in the waters headed east to Europe. By the time the war ended, this had swelled to 2,113 vessels. One of the first official actions the United States did after declaring war in 1917, was to impound German merchant vessels stationed in U.S. ports. The weight of these ships amounted to about 629,000 tons and was valued at an estimated $100,000,000 in money of that time. This prize was the largest ever seized by a nation at war (Drinker.)

Within a few weeks, the United States naval forces were officially organized. Although the number of ships and sailors was small in May 4, 1917, some naval ships were already sailing in European seas. The first soldiers landed in France on June 27, 1917, a quick response to the call for American troops. All soldiers were Regular Army troops, having come from recent service on the Mexican border, Haiti or Santo Domingo. General Pershing arrived with them.

The voyage was planned in great secrecy due to security needs, but the Germans were vigilant and attacked on two different days. One sub was sunk and another one driven off (Drinker.) A great celebration was held when news came of the safe arrival of the General, his staff, and the first troops in France.

Activity was doubled at the embarkation ports. Ocean-going liners had to cancel regular runs. An armada of different types of ships was formed as escorts for troopships and merchant ships alike. Delivery of oil to Britain for military needs was essential, curtailing availability of oil to civilians. This shortage of fuel caused great hardships for the British civilians, especially during the winter of 1917, the coldest one on record.

The United States had some of its submarines based at the Azores Islands and also in Bantry

Bay, Ireland. In the States, construction had ceased on the big ships. The naval yards were instead turning out hundreds of destroyers, sub chasers, and merchantman ships. Two other innovations helped reduce the damage created by submarines. One was the invention of the hydrophone, a predecessor to radar, and the other was the depth charge. The sub chasers and destroyers were adept in pursuing and locating the attacking submarines.

To meet the urgent need for a massive number of new ships, a huge plant was built at Hog Island, located

Advertisement warning against traveling on the *Luisitania*.

beyond the city limits of Philadelphia, Pennsylvania. It was the largest such plant in the world and employed 30,000 men. Here the ships were assembled, rather than building them piece by piece. But there were almost 175 more ship building plants across America. Ships were made of steel, concrete, and the old standby – wood.

Opinions varied widely on which was the best material to use in construction, but the ship building program as a whole was a success. The industry had grown from a 1914 figure of only 37 steel shipyards with less than 50,000 men employed, to a 1918 figure of 171 plants with nearly 400,000 workers working in the yards. Even more men, about 250,000, were in ship building training when the war ended. (Ellis). America's success with ship building and the large number that remained seaworthy at the end of the war were other factors pushing her on the way to becoming a world power.

*(Title comes from the book, *Library of American History, America's Part in World War I.*)

SHIPS CARRY TROOPS SAFELY ACROSS THE ATLANTIC

Despite the constant menace of German submarines near the shores of Europe, over two million American troops were safely transported by ships of all types over the rough waters of the Atlantic.

Now, safely did not mean comfortably. Many troops spent hours and even days being seasick, standing at the rail of the ship, always clad in the uncomfortable life jackets. Some even had to sleep in them if a periscope had been sighted during the day. The possible watery wake of a torpedo

U.S. ships in convoy system
(Courtesy of Archives of National World War I Museum and Memorial)

aimed in their direction was good reason for the frequent life boat drills. But the United States had developed a method that kept their men safe in the waters.

Once the troopships entered the water, they were surrounded by destroyers and small swift boats like large yachts and small cruise ships, and later sub chasers and depth charges. These were added to the convoy of the large, slower moving ships and served as an outer fringe of protection against the vicious "unterseeboot," or U-boat. After the Battle of Jutland in 1916, an ill fated indecisive 20 minute sea battle of the dreadnaughts, giants of the waters, the Germans realized they would have to resort to a different sea vessel. The submarine was their choice and they produced them by the dozens.

The U-boats rounded the Cape of Good Hope of Africa sailing into the Indian Ocean, with some submarines venturing as far south as the waters of New Zealand and Australia. Some few crossed the Indian Ocean to haunt the ship supply lines from China and Japan. It was Japan's responsibility to be on the look out for an emerging periscope with possibly a fleet of submarines under it. In return, Japan desired the Pacific islands formerly "owned" by Germany. These islands became the spoils of war for that small island nation, as a result of her cooperation in monitoring the safety of the Allies in the Pacific Ocean. This was humiliating to Russia who had suffered an unexpected defeat in the Russo-Japanese war in 1905, when her great navy was destroyed by the oriental newcomers to the world's stage. In short, Japan was helping the Allies.

A couple of decades later, the Allies once again included those Pacific Islands on their targets to attack and wrest back in World War II at an even greater cost of lives than in World War I. The goals of nations can change over the years, and it is ironic, even tragic the actions the United States was forced to take some 20 year later.

NEW WEAPONS CREATE CHAOS, DEATH AND DESTRUCTION

Co-authored by Niel M. Johnson, Ph.D.

New weapons created the chaos, death and destruction that characterized World War I. Though called "The War to End All Wars," this war stands out in world history as the turning point in the lives of millions around the globe. The number of deaths and other casualties suffered by the military and civilians exceeded all previous totals of any war, the direct result of newly invented weapons. No one could anticipate the terrible cost in lives as well as property, amounting to billions and billions of dollars, sums the world had never before imagined.

Tag worn on uniform and Arrival Card, belonging to Shannon Prather
(Courtesy Joyce Kuecher)

Russia alone borrowed $187 million from the United States to finance her part of the war. Total costs for Russia will never be known because the accounting ceased during and after the Russian Civil War.

Big and Little Artillery

Artillery grew in size from the small Parrot gun of the Napoleonic Wars to a frightening German made monster. The "Paris Gun," the biggest gun used in the war, was designed to bombard Paris in 1918 so intensely, that the Germans believed the Parisians would immediately surrender. Because it weighed an incredible 256 tons, it had to be moved on railroad cars. Its barrel was 91 feet long, almost the length of a football field, and it could hit targets 75 miles away. Each shell weighed around 275 pounds, about the size of a very heavy man. Fortunately, its size limited its use. Immediately after the war, the Germans destroyed the two Paris guns that they had designed and built, including the plans and all equipment used in its manufacture. So it has never been replicated.

It is often confused with another German oversized gun called "Big Bertha." This gun was used in 1914 to attack and overwhelm the forts at Liege, Belgium. However, most of the deaths and injuries in the war were caused by smaller artillery guns. The French 75 mm howitzer was the favored gun by the Allies. The practice by both sides of incessant shelling for hours and even days at a time, not only struck fear among soldiers in the trenches, but the incessant noise was unnerving. In addition, the front lines usually were helpless to defend themselves from the shelling.

There were several types of shells the larger artillery guns used. The shrapnel was the most dangerous because when the shell exploded overhead, it released hundreds of small hot pieces of metal which spread out in large arcs. Soldiers were unable to protect themselves from the shrapnel which caused death as well as maiming the body. Sometimes when it rained frequently, the soldiers wore their water soaked great coats as a shield against small pieces of shrapnel.

Another unknown but quickly feared weapon was the newly designed German Maxim machine gun. The Allies had machine guns but none were as effective as the early German Maxim. The machine gun had been invented and demonstrated in the 1880's but had too many problems to make it useful. Even the 1914 gun, effective as it was, was too heavy to be moved by one man. Some of the larger machine guns required four men to move the weapon, although most guns could be handled by a two-man crew. This gun evolved from the Civil War's Gatling gun, a repeating firing machine.

The deadliness created by a machine gun crew hidden behind rocks, trees or bushes ended the daring and successful cavalry charges of past wars. The rate of bullets generated, as many as 200 per minute, in a constant stream, literally "mowing down" both horses and their riders. It made huge holes in the lines of advancing infantry men walking abreast toward the enemy. The British suffered their greatest loss ever in war to that date with 60,000 casualties on the first day alone at the Battle of the Somme in 1916. There were 20,000 deaths, and 40,000 wounded soldiers. Despite the high death rate incurred by hidden machine gun nests, it took several years before some British generals abandoned the cavalry charge, and changed the advancing formation of the troops. General Pershing required his AEF troops to move at their own pace, singly or in small groups. He respected the machine gun as the deadly killer it was. Still, AEF troops, mostly because of enthusiasm and lack of experience, suffered an unusually high rate of deaths in offensive movements.

The Tank

Most of the tanks broke down and became useless. But the American and British engineers kept improving the tank design. By 1917 the British had developed the Mark IV tank, nearly 500 of which were successfully used in the Battle of Cambrai. The French produced the better designed Renault FT-17 which required only two men to operate it. In addition, it had a revolving turret. This became the most widely produced tank and was the one American soldiers used in France.

The Submarine

A menacing weapon used under the sea created shock and horror when it was used to attack a surface ship. This was the German submarine, or Unterseeboot, or "U-boat" for short. Other than detecting a ripple on calm water caused by the periscope, the Allies had no way to determine the presence of the U-boat. This was used to great advantage by the Germans in sinking merchant marine ships bound for England or France with vital cargo. Ship losses up to 95% occurred during one month before the United States entered the war. The Americans formed convoys with protective destroyers and mine sweepers accompanying the merchant ships. The losses fell to a low of 5% most months for the remainder of the war.

Poison Gases

A more sinister and indefensible weapon existed in the use of poison gas, of which there were five types used in World War I. Thousands of Allied soldiers were first exposed to gas in April 22, 1915 at the Second Battle of Ypres. They had absolutely no protection against it, and the death and injury rates were high. The most serious damage to the human body was caused by mustard gas, used toward the end of the war.

On their first exposure to poison gas, when Allied troops saw low clouds hanging just above the battlefield, they became suspicious because of its green color. Troops, used to the heavy low lying fogs of northern France and Belgium, realized these clouds were not fog. They were lethal gas against which they had no protection. As they continued to be exposed time and again to this chlorine gas, they designed all manner of gas masks. Most were ineffective, and it was not until near the end of the war that an effective gas mask was made. The Allies also used gas, but learned as the Germans had learned, that a shift in the wind could cause the gas to change directions and blow back on them. While not always fatal, exposure to gas created painful lifelong lung problems, often making the veteran a permanent invalid if not dying younger than average. In 1925 in the German Protocol, international laws were approved which prohibits a nation from using poison gas. Still, some nations have in recent years used it despite the Geneva Protocol.

Barbed Wire

Added to the list of new weapons is "barbed wire." Ranches in the United States had used barbed wire for decades, but it was thin and easily cut. The barbed wire used in World War I was almost one-half inch thick and required heavy wire cutters 15-20 inches long to cut the wire. Sometimes artillery was used successfully to destroy the rolls of wire separating one army from another across "no man's land." However, at the war's beginning, British artillery was ineffective against the wire because the shells were not properly made. Workers in the munition plants had been replaced by untrained women when the men went to the Army. It took several months before the production of effective shells was resumed.

Hand Grenades

The hand grenade was perhaps the smallest of the new weapons, but its new design and ease in throwing made it popular from the start. The former hand grenade, called "a potato masher," consisted of a larger cylinder mounted on a wooden handle. It had to be thrown overhand and was much heavier. A soldier could carry only about six of these, whereas with the new "pineapple" or "apple", the British name, a soldier could carry a dozen or more. These were thrown like a baseball is thrown. Because so many American soldiers had pitched baseballs, they could throw the grenades better. The British developed the Marten-Hale grenade which could be fired from a special rifle or thrown by hand.

The Aeroplane

The last major invention to be mentioned, but the one that probably can be considered to have been developed the most, was the aeroplane (the European spelling) or airplane. It evolved from its invention in 1903 as a simple wooden box frame that was launched into the air, making a 20 second flight that covered a distance of only 15 feet. By the end of World War I, several planes were outstanding in their ability to fly. These included the German Fokker F.E.VII, the English Sopwith Camel, and the French SPAD. Planes now could climb up to 20,000 feet, but the oxygen in the air was so thin a pilot could not stay very long at that height. Oxygen masks had not been invented yet. Planes reached speeds of 150-160 miles per hour with gasoline capacity for 3-8 flying hours.

The Airplane Becomes A Weapon

Used only for observation purposes at first, they were unarmed. However, the pilots began carrying their own weapons, a pistol, or even large bricks or rocks which they threw at the fragile wings of their opponents. This led to arming the planes with revolving machine guns which, after the invention of the "interrupter gear" by the Germans, could safely fire without damaging the propeller. Later the planes carried a small load of bombs which were tossed over the side, hoping to find a target. Next, the Russians designed planes with two 260 hp engines that could carry bombs weighing one to two tons. From their initial tasks of reconnaissance and observation, planes became an effective offensive weapon to attack enemy planes and bomb cities. Life as a pilot was chancy, and in April, 1918, the British losses were 4-1 favoring the Germans. (www.airwar1.org.uk).

The average rate of 93 flying hours was recorded for English pilots before they either crashed in accidents, were shot down, or were grounded in need of rest. About 75% of all aviators lost their lives in the air forces, the highest death rate of all the services.

The Rifle

The rifle was among standard weapons that also saw improvements as the war progressed. The British Lee Enfield in the hands of an experienced marksman could fire its 10 bullet magazine in a minute. The German Mauser was popular but its clip held only five bullets, so the soldier was reloading more frequently. American soldiers used a modified Enfield Model 1917 with a clip of 10 cartridges.

The Flamethrower

A lethal weapon that was adapted included the "flamethrower." Although it had been designed and used for several years, it wasn't until February, 1915, when it was first used by the Germans against the French (Gilbert). The Germans had perfected the process of squirting a mixture of inflammable oil and gasoline under pressure. The nozzle of the pipe was lit but the flame extended less than 130 yards. The original purpose was to make the ground unusable by the enemy. Later, portable flame throwers were used by both German and French trained squads to clear out trenches, creating great fear and injury among those who were most vulnerable to attack.

Miles and Miles of Trenches

These were devised for defense against most of the new weapons. The trench system was first perfected by the Germans. Often there were six or more rows of trenches stretching hundreds of yards behind the "No Man's Land." In all, there were 35,000 miles of trenches from the English Channel to Switzerland. The length of the Front Line was only 466 miles, but many rows of trenches extended back from the front line. The simplest ones were dug hurriedly in advance of an expected attack and might be only five or six feet deep. Sometimes the soil was soft and easy to dig in, but it would collapse when hit by a shell, often burying the men standing there. The Germans dug many trenches in clay or limestone, requiring great expenditure of time and labor. They imported about 150,000 Chinese laborers to help with this work. The French also brought the same number of Chinese as laborers building airports or digging trenches.

The trenches were reinforced with lumber if available; otherwise, tree limbs or even stout branches were used. Sometimes when the trench was shallow due to a high water level or hard rocky soil, sand bags were placed on top for the men to shield their heads, or to reinforce the trench. The worst times were in winter and the rainy seasons. It was almost impossible to keep water or snow out, so the men's feet were constantly wet. This led to the dreaded infection, "trench foot," which if not treated quickly and properly, could result in amputation of the foot. The water, body lice, and rats, all conditions assigned to trench life, harassed soldiers on both sides, and often led to a collapse of morale or the condition called "shell shock" for the soldier or "neurasthenia" for officers. Today it is called "Post Traumatic Stress Disorder" for enlisted and officers alike. The medical profession is still learning ways to treat it successfully, but the rate of suicide today for American soldiers with PTSD is shockingly and sadly too high. (Bridger)

HENRY JOHNSON RECEIVES HIS MEDAL

Acts of bravery should be rewarded as bravery. Who performs it has nothing to do with the courage that spurred it. Private Henry Johnson was an African-American AEF soldier with the 369th Infantry Regiment "Harlem Hellfighters," assigned to the French Army for combat duty in World War I. For Private Johnson, justice was finally achieved, nearly 100 years after his act of valor was performed.

Henry Johnson
(Courtesy of Joelouis Mattox)

The act took place during an attack by a German squad against Henry's listening post in "No Man's Land" between the trenches on the night of May 15, 1918. Henry Johnson and his fellow soldier, Private Needham Roberts, also a member of the 369th defended their listening post in a life struggle fight using rifles, grenades, and a knife in what became hand-to-hand combat. Needham was severely wounded, as was Johnson, but despite his 21 wounds, Henry protected them both until help arrived.

As a result of their wounds, neither man ever served in combat again. Hospitalized for a time, Henry nevertheless was unable to recover his health enough to lead a normal life. He resorted to drinking, separated from his wife and children, and died penniless at age 38. He was buried in Arlington National Cemetery, but the family did not discover the location of his grave until decades later.

Shortly after this desperate struggle that night, the French government rewarded his actions with the Croix de guerre avec plume (with palm), the highest French award for valor. It is similar to our American Congressional Medal of Honor. However, it was not until 1966 that the United States awarded him the purple heart posthumously for his injuries. Then in 2002 he was recognized as a recipient of the Distinguished Service Cross.

Now, the injustice has been finally corrected, due to the persistence of his friends and admirers in pursuing his claim for years. In early June, 2015, President Barack Obama awarded both Pvt. Henry Johnson and a Jewish soldier, Sgt. William Shemin, with the honors they should have received years ago. Some critics have claimed "discrimination and bigotry" prevented them from being honored with the awards in their lifetimes.

(A story in Volume I of *"Unheard Voices, Untold Stories,"* told about the combat actions of Henry Johnson and his partner, in defending themselves from almost two dozen or more Germans.)

WHICH ONE OF US GOT HIM?

Two young American soldiers saw an enemy sniper perched above them in a tree, as they crouched in the shadows of the big rocks which hid them. Here was the first German soldier they had seen, and each one was reluctant to be the first to shoot. So they agreed to count to three and then fire their rifles.

"1, 2, 3." They both fired at the same time. One of their bullets hit the German sniper, and down he fell from the tree. The Americans were inexperienced, not realizing that if the German had seen them first, he would not have waited to count. But, according to Brother Anthony W. Effertz, Order of St. Francis of Kansas City, Missouri, his grandfather wasn't ready to claim the bullet as coming from his gun.

The grandfather, Henry Effertz , Sr., and his buddy each claimed "the other one" had shot the German. "You're the good shot!" "No, I don't think it was my bullet." Regardless of whose bullet hit the German, he was dead when he hit the ground.

Their natural reluctance to shoot an enemy changed quickly as Henry and his buddy fought on the front lines all the time they were in France. Henry learned there were numerous reasons to shoot the enemy. For one thing, there were places where they couldn't drink water from the local ponds or wells. The French farmers claimed the Germans had poisoned them. So they waited until the engineers tested the well, then drank or departed, thirstier than ever as they marched to the front lines. Soon Henry's helmet had dents from deflected bullets, but luckily for him, none caused any injury.

Gas masks were issued and used. Many times, to escape the murderous bullets of German machine guns, they fell "on their bellies" as they crawled through grassy fields.

Two more stories about Grandfather Henry have surfaced recently, according to Brother Anthony. One involves Henry in the Argonne sector when he was under machine gun fire crawling across a vast wheat field to his trench. The gunfire was so intense it ripped big holes in the knapsack he wore on his back. Another story was when he and his buddy were incredibly thirsty, and for just a swig of water from another soldier, they had to pay $5.00 to the water toting soldier. Five dollars!

That was a large amount of money, almost one-sixth of a month's pay of $30.00.

This last story lacks some essential details to make it credible, but Brother Anthony claims, "If Grandfather said it, you'd better believe it!"

One story remains with unanswered questions. It was about fighting at the Second battle of the Somme. Or did his grandfather fight? Father Anthony said his grandparents would look at each other when the Somme was mentioned and laugh. His Grandmother would threaten Henry when she was mad at him. "Someday I'll tell the little kids what you did in France." But she never told.

His grandfather lived to be 101 years old. He had perfect teeth and his hair was still its natural black color. A logger from Northfield in southern Minnesota, he at age 29, married Angeline Bachus from a neighboring county, when she was just 16 years old.

He rode a horse or drove a buggy to court her. (See story "The Soldier No One Knew," p 28)

They had 13 children and at times, all the family had to help with the dairy farm. But about what happened in France at the Battle of the Somme, Brother Anthony is still mystified and shakes his head.

Grandfather Henry was born in El Mino, Wisconsin, near Assumption or Green Hill, Wisconsin. The family made a video tape of Grandfather Henry in 1994, which remains a priceless memory of their World War I veteran grandfather.

AMERICAN LEGION POST NAMED AFTER 20 YEAR OLD SERGEANT

Tirey J. Ford (Courtesy Tirey Ford American Legion Post 21)

To honor a local 20-year-old AEF veteran fatally wounded in Charpentry, France, the American Legion decided to charter American Legion post in his name. Thus was the beginning of The Tirey J. Ford American Legion Post #21, the largest Legion post in Missouri. Sergeant Tirey Ford, despite the personal danger of enemy artillery fire, stayed with his artillery gun firing until finally a well aimed German shell killed him and put his gun out of action on September 29, 1918. He was with Battery C, 129th Field Artillery, 35th Division at Charpentry. Commanding the nearby Battery D was Captain Harry S. Truman, who years later was to become America's 32nd President.

For his "gallantry in action," Ford was awarded the Silver Star posthumously on June 3, 1919.

The Silver Star is the United States' third highest medal. What the citation does not state was the high price the Silver Star cost Sergeant Ford in performing that act of gallantry. It was the third day of the offensive to take Montfaucon, and the 35th Division was supported by the 110th Engineer Battalion and the other gun batteries. The two opposing armies attacked and counterattacked several times during the day, which had begun without the usual important artillery support from the 60th Division. The 60th artillery had been unable to get its guns into position because the heavy rain had made a morass of the roads. At the end of the day, the 35th had exhausted not only its food supply and physical strength, but most critically, its stock of ammunition.

Sergeant Ford, the son of Independence, Missouri, stockman, Hugh W. Ford, had served with General Pershing two years before in the National Guard action on the Mexican border in June, 1916. He had graduated from Independence High School as president of his class in 1914. He had prominent forebears, being a grandson of a Judge Adams and a great-grandson of James R. Abernathy, a former editor of the Paris (MO) Mercury newspaper.

Ford had trained at Camp Doniphan, Oklahoma, with a group of 200 Independence men who formed Company C of the 129th F.A. and shipped to France as part of the 35th Division. A letter detailing his death was written by an Independence officer, Lt. C.C. Bundschu, to Ford's father, commenting that "It was quite a blow to every man in Battery C, for he was a fine fellow and liked by everybody. Captain Marks said he had lost his best sergeant." Ford's last words were reported to be, "Captain, I am going over the top."

He is buried at the Meuse-Argonne Cemetery and Memorial in France. He was first buried immediately, according to Lieutenant Bundschu, by "comrades in an orchard in a town captured by us. We have it definitely marked on a map."

The Tirey J. Ford Post has more than 1500 members, making it the largest post in Missouri. It has been committed to the service of the community and veterans since its inception. Examples of its early activity included awarding a prize to the school "having the largest percentage of its total enrollment at Tuesday 's {Armistice Day, November 11, 1919, parade." The winning school was Noland School of Independence. Another event occurred in May, 1920, when the post held Memorial Day services, with veterans of the Civil War and Spanish-American War participating. The Rev. James Small, chaplain of the 110th Sanitary Train in France, delivered the address and Mayor William McCoy, a veteran, presided.

Ford was born August 25, 1898 in Monroe County, Missouri, to Hugh and Ellen Adams Ford. Mrs. Ford preceded her son in death in 1905, and his father died in 1926. Ford had a brother who was serving at the Great Lakes Naval Training Camp during the war and also a sister, whose names are unknown.

HONEST AND FAITHFUL SERGEANT

"Honest and faithful" reads the enlistment record of Sergeant Ernest E. Butrell, Lawrence, Kansas, who enlisted May 5, 1917 as a volunteer before the first draft was held June 5, 1917.

Sgt. Ernest E. Butrell
(Courtesy of Wincel Jehle)

He served in the 1st Kansas Infantry from his enlistment to October, 1917, when as a member of Company H, 137th Infantry, he saw the tough action for which World War I was known. It was at the Meuse-Argonne offensive where he was wounded September 27, 1918. His daughter, Wincel Jehle, Baldwin, Kansas, tells his story.

Sergeant Butrell probably considered himself fortunate to be trained by battle experienced British and French instructors at Camp Doniphan, Oklahoma. At this time, there were not enough American Regular Army instructors to train the influx of volunteers and the nearly 700,000 draftees who flooded the newly established camps in 1918. When war was declared in April, 1917, the American Regular Army stood at merely 130,000 men. From this number, General John J. Pershing was to build an army of more than four million men in less than two years.

Sergeant Butrell departed from Camp Mills, New York, on April 27, 1918, although one record reports the date of 25th. He probably received more training in a quiet sector of the Vosges Mountains in southern France. One unit from his division made a raid on a German position bringing back five prisoners. At St. Mihiel the division was held in reserve which meant spending time in pup tents during the celebrated French rains. Then began the rough trip in 200 French trucks across the ruts that were called roads to the area of Grange-le-Conte, a wooded area east of Beauchamp, where they went into action on or about September 26.

An artillery barrage early that morning announced the beginning of the AEF assault on Germans situated in the Argonne sector. That was where Sergeant Butrell received a gun shot wound and was gassed. Here his combat days ended, and after his recovery, he was transferred to the Third Indiana A.G.O. where he served under General Pershing, according to family stories. He completed his term of service and returned to the states nearly a year after his wounding, to be discharged November 4, 1919, at Camp Meigs, Washington, D.C.

There he received a $60.00 bonus that was part of the full amount of $125.52 accompanied by the silver Victory button issued to overseas veterans. A single man when he had enlisted at the age of 22 ½ years, Sergeant Butrell gave up the hard earned rank of "Sergeant" for the civilian title of "Mister." He exchanged the khaki uniforms he had worn for two years for civilian clothing, new or old, from his days as a Kansas farmer. "Farmer" also probably sounded mighty good to the "Sarge."

Described on his record as being of "excellent character," Mr. Butrell married and raised a family near Baldwin City, Kansas. He died at what could be considered an early death, possibly from having been gassed, on May 7, 1953, at age 56, and was buried at Oakwood Cemetery, Baldwin City, Kansas.

THE SOLDIER NO ONE KNEW

An old fading photograph of four World War I soldiers was passed around at a reunion of the Effertz family of Minnesota a few years ago. Three men were immediately identified, but none of the 40 or more family members recognized the fourth soldier. Brother Anthony Effertz, Order of St. Francis (OSF), who tells the story, was disappointed. Surely someone there would know these four army buddies and could attach a name to the solemn face of the young soldier in his brand new uniform.

Later an aunt came over and said, "Let me see that photograph again." She peered at it and then with a smile announced, "That's young Jacob Bachus." Brother Anthony Effertz asked, "Bachus? Who ever heard of that name before?"

"That's your mother's young brother who died in the war. He lived in a different county and would never have met your family before he went overseas. Maybe he met your father and the others in training camp.

"Your mother didn't meet your father until after he came home from the war. She would have been too young before to start courting." The aunt had seen young Jacob's photograph of him wearing his uniform. The aunt explained, "The photograph was hung on the wall of the home of your grandmother before your mother met your father." She and Brother Anthony's mother were close friends, but the friend, Angeline Bachus, didn't want to talk about her Jacob, her dead brother.

Satisfied, Brother Anthony and the others continued their reunion. When it came time to leave, he and his mother followed his brother and his child in another car. The brother had said, "I'm going to take another road home. It's off the highway and will be safer from all the holiday traffic." So down an unfamiliar road both cars traveled.

Along the way, the brother called Brother Anthony on his cell phone. The child had to use a bathroom. They drove on looking for a convenience store, but there was no store. In fact, there were hardly any houses in this rural area of Minnesota.

Finally they found a few houses clustered together and an outhouse attached to a closed rundown gasoline station. Brother Anthony decided to get out and stretch his legs. He wandered around the deserted yards. Grass and weeds grew almost to his knees. He came to a small memorial stone, and out of curiosity, looked closely at the carving. The words were fading. They read, "This is in dedication to those who lost their lives in defense of our country." It was erected by the county and underneath were six names. Jacob Bachus' name was the last one.

(Brother Anthony is from Kansas City, Missouri.)

FROM PRIVATE TO COLONEL — MAKING THE MILITARY INTO A CAREER

One of the earliest men to enlist in the Army after Congress declared war on Germany was Isaiah Fredrick Bowen, who joined April 12, 1917. Isaiah said he enlisted because he wanted to get away from farm life with its stubborn Missouri mules and irritable horses. He also probably wanted a break from his newer job as a store clerk.

He was assigned to Company M, 139th Infantry, 35th Division, which was made up mostly of Missouri and Kansas men. He was only 19 years old and had worked as a general store clerk in his hometown of Clarksdale, Missouri. To the pride and yet the dismay of his parents, as well as siblings and a new girlfriend, Gladys, he soon left to become a "Rookie," the name given to new recruits.

His records show he did not have to qualify in marksmanship as he already knew how to shoot a rifle, and also, firing a rifle was not required in his job description. Somehow, despite his farm experiences, he managed to avoid working with horses, something he was tired of doing. He was labeled "Not mounted," meaning he would not be required to ride horses.

But Isaiah, as a member of the 35th Division, served in some of the most active fighting sectors, including St. Mihiel, Meuse-Argonne, Verdun, and the Argonne sector. His discharge paper says he was entitled to wear two gold chevrons, indicating one year of overseas service. The 139th regiment lost the highest number of men of any regiment. It was claimed to be due to poor leadership. Historians and military experts still debate this charge. It equally could have been caused by lack of training and lack of experience in battle. Many units were shipped overseas without the soldier having actually handled a rifle, knowing how to take it apart if it jammed, and most importantly, how to shoot it.

According to military records, a major in his unit was gassed in the Argonne which may have been where Isaiah and his buddies also were gassed. The gas was loaded into the artillery shells the Germans used. When the shell exploded, the gas was released, exposing everyone within a certain area. Sometimes several hundred men could be affected by the constant shelling of cylinders containing gas. Despite the warning of bells or klaxons, sometimes it was difficult to quickly don the uncomfortable gas masks.

His granddaughter, Maura Landry, Lawrence, Kansas, remembers her grandfather talking about the "yellow cloud that slowly crept across the battlefield and, like a gigantic python, slithered into the trenches." This was mustard gas which immediately settled in the mucous areas of the body: eyes, nose, mouth, lungs and other organs. She wonders if this may have contributed to his early death by emphysema, although he had "smoked like a chimney" for years.

She also recalls him telling about how it felt "to live in a trench knee deep in mud, waking up to find his buddy next to him… dead from being shot, bombed or frozen." But he never mentioned other possible experiences," crawling out of trenches, and over barbed wire making his way across 'no man's land' which was "peppered with bomb craters, strafing by machine gun fire to shoot at some faceless stranger only to crawl back over dead and wounded men to the trench from which he began."

The 35th Division was relieved on September 30, 1918, after five days in what was called the "greatest battle in American military history" until then, declared General William G. Hann, commander of the 32nd Division. (Wright) He was referring to the Battle in the Argonne sector. The division's men captured 12 German officers, as well as 900 men of lower rank and many pieces of artillery in this battle.

PORTRAITS-
Of Veterans You Should Know
MEET ---
I. F. (ICK) BOWEN

Reported by Carl Castel

The colorful military career of Isaiah F. (Ick) Bowen is a story of two World Wars; a saga of St. Joseph's historic Tank Company and a history of the Officer's Reserve Corps in St. Joseph. It covers a period of more than thirty years in time and halfway around the world in space. And "Ick" is still pretty much of a young fellow.

This career got under way on April 12, 1917, when he enlisted in Company M, 139th Infantry, 35th Division. He participated in three major campaigns in France and was discharged after having served 25 months.

The old blue serge suit felt pretty good for a while, but in 1921 civilian Bowen became Sergeant Bowen in the newly organized 35th Division Tank Company of the Missouri National Guard. The following year he was commissioned a second lieutenant. He attended every encampment of the National Guard except the one held in 1934.

In 1940 the company was federalized and became part of the 194th Tank Battalion. It was transferred to Fort Lewis, Washington and in 1941, the company commander, the late Captain Spencer Canby and thirty of its personnel was ordered to the Philippines. Captain Canby and many of his men lost their lives on Bataan.

Promoted to Captain, "Ick" took the remainder of the company and a headquarters detachment to Alaska in September, 1941.

His feelings may easily be imagined when in February, 1942, his association of more than 20 years with his company was broken by his assignment as tank adviser to the commanding general in Alaska. The company was the first tank unit to go overseas in World War II and the first to operate in Alaska. With its 7 officers and 126 men, it was the only organized military unit to leave St. Joseph during the war.

"Ick's" next task was a complete reconaissance of Alaska. This was done for the establishment of communications and army posts and required seven months to accomplish. His last Alaskan assignment was the command of the army post at Galena, 40 miles South of the Arctic Circle.

After 43 months of Alaskan duty he returned to the States for reassignment. He attended Infantry school at Fort Benning, Ga., for two months and later was assigned to the last infantry batallion to be trained in War II. He was discharged on Christmas Day, 1945, with the rank of Lieut.-Colonel.

The colonel is a long-time member of the American Legion and his civilian job is that of managing the club of the Macdonald-Dugger-Duncan Post. He retains his reserve commission and is executive officer of the 511th Reserve Composite Group, which is comprised of all types of ground units in Northwest Missouri.

"Ick" and the Mrs. live at 2621 Ashland avenue in St. Joseph. Their only child, Darlene is employed in New York City.

Newspaper article (Courtesy Maura Landry)

The removal of the division from the front lines saved them from having to participate in the next big offensive planned for the French city of Metz. It was scheduled to begin November 12. The 35th Division had been moved from the First Army and merged with the newly formed Fourth Army. The Armistice was signed November 11, fortunately cancelling what would have been another huge slaughter of men on both sides.

Isaiah's granddaughter, Maura Landry, told two family anecdotes she remembers. One tells how Isaiah and three other soldiers secretly left the trenches to look for something to eat. They hadn't had a real meal in days. Meals were delivered on an irregular basis at night because of the constant shelling on both sides. Also the roads had become mud holes from the rain and snow, and army trucks could not get through to the troops with food supplies. The kitchen wagons dealt with the same problems as they endeavored to supply the men with one hot meal and coffee per day.

Many times the shelling from the Germans made delivery of food too dangerous to attempt, or the men would have to wait for hours until the bombardments ceased. By then food would be cold and almost unedible, no matter how hungry a soldier was.

The four men found an "empty farm house, bleak and war- ravaged, and an abandoned potato field. They built a small fire hoping no one could see it and roasted potatoes." Those were the best potatoes they would ever eat in a lifetime. If they had been caught by the military police, those potatoes might have been the most costly as well.

She gave more details about his being gassed in the trenches. It was mustard gas. It settled in the snow banks and pools of water and would stay there undiscovered for days. The colder the weather, the longer the gas lingered. This is one reason why mustard gas was so feared. Death could come immediately or after painful lifelong symptoms developed, such as prolonged coughing of mucus and blood. The gas created excruciating pain until death came. It was the worst of the five types of gas the Germans used. Many soldiers could not quit the smoking habit, born from days of boredom from their weeks in the trenches. They also smoked to calm themselves when in perilous situations.

Isaiah was discharged May 18, 1919, in St. Joseph, Missouri, but he liked military life and soon enlisted in the National Guard. An undated newspaper clipping shows him in the uniform of the National Guard. Known by the nickname, "Ick," he had been promoted to sergeant. In 1921 his unit became the newly formed 35th Division of the Missouri National Guard. He trained and attended maneuvers for the next 20 years. When the United States declared war on Japan in December, 1941, "Ick" realized as a reservist, he would be one of the first to be called up for this new war, World War II. Once again, Ike was among the first to join the ranks of the fighting men.

In 1942 he was assigned to Alaska and promoted to captain. There he served as tank advisor to the commanding general in Alaska. This was the first tank unit to go overseas in WWII, and it operated in Alaska. Isaiah was flown around Alaska looking for evidence of a possible Japanese invasion. Because the Aleutian Islands extended near Japan, the United States Army feared the Japanese might try to land troops on other islands, as they did on Attu and Kiska islands.

Isaiah told his family about one tragic mission. He was accompanied by two soldiers on a flight over snow covered mountains. The pilot noticed the wings were so badly iced up that the passengers would need to bail out and abandon the plane. Being the commanding officer, "Ick" made sure the two soldiers jumped. Just as he was readying to jump, the ice shattered and fell off the wings. The pilot was able to land safely with Ick aboard. The bodies of the other two soldiers were never found in the icy wasteland, despite many desperate rescue attempts. One wonders how Ick's decision may have influenced him the rest of his life.

After serving four years of World War II, Ike was finally discharged on Christmas Day, 1945, as a Lieutenant Colonel. He kept his reserve commission with the 511th Reserve Composite Group of northwest Missouri units. He also volunteered to help the American Legion.

In his lifetime, "Ick" had a remarkable service record. He had served in both theaters of war, the European and the Pacific, with a military career extending over a period of 30 years. He had been disappointed when he was assigned to Alaska and separated from his tank company. However, that change of orders may have saved his life, as many in his unit were assigned to the island of Bataan in the Philippine Islands. The islands were captured by the Japanese and were the scene of the infamous Bataan Death March led by the Japanese. Only a fraction of the Americans captured by the Japanese survived the march and the subsequent inhumane prison conditions.

Lt. Col. Isaiah Fredrick Bowen died in 1970 at the age of 72. His life had been one of lifelong military service for his country, both in the ranks as a sergeant, and in command as a colonel. A true patriot.

A MODEL "DOUGHBOY"

William O. Jackson, Butler, Missouri, was a "model doughboy" in several interpretations of the phrase. First, he enlisted early, on April 28, 1917, in the Missouri National Guard as a private just a few weeks after Congress had declared war against Germany. He was assigned to Company B of the Second Infantry Regiment, where he rapidly rose to the rank of Second Lieutenant on April 30, 1917, and two months later on June 28, 1917, was promoted to First Lieutenant. His story was shared by Linda Rappell, her uncle by marriage. She lives in Overland Park, Kansas.

At some later date, the Missouri National Guard was integrated into the 35th Division, consisting mostly of men from Missouri and Kansas. The 35th Division trained at Camp Doniphan, Oklahoma, spending seven months learning how to become soldiers. During this time Lieutenant Jackson was transferred to the 128th Machine Gun Battalion and was trained in the use of that weapon. (Pypes)

Because it was early in the war, the United States did not have enough experienced sergeants or officers to provide more specific training, so British and French instructors were sent to Camp Doniphan. There they provided specialized instruction on how to use the bayonet, the hand grenade and the gas mask. This knowledge would be invaluable some months later when the soldiers arrived in France on May 10, 1918. The division fought a few skirmishes in the Gerardmer sector in July and August, 1918, and later was designated to serve as a reserve force in the St. Mihiel assault. But the Germans were less formidable there and the St. Mihiel salient was captured in an easier than expected campaign.

The real test for the Division began in the Argonne Forest on September 26 which lasted until October 1, and then later at the Somme-Dieue sector until the Armistice took effect on November 11, 1918. To reach their assigned sector, the Division was transported by 200 trucks, a grueling and uncomfortable trip requiring several days in the over crowded vehicles. The condition of the roads, the congestion of civilians, trucks, ambulances, artillery guns made movement slow to a crawl at times. Food was often hard bread and cold "gold fish," as the canned salmon was named.

Lt. William O. Jackson
(Courtesy of Linda Reppell)

Once they arrived and dug in slots for the guns, the rain began and the temperature dropped. Attacks and counterattacks were accompanied by the blasts from the heavy German machine guns, which had the advantage of the Argonne terrain, rocky and heavily forested. Nevertheless, the AEF's actions resulted in the hard worn gain of one and one-half miles. Adding to these conditions, the Germans used gas which affected many troops, including Colonel Clad Hamilton of Topeka, Kansas, who had to be moved to the rear. Total gain for the 35th Division over the four days was 6.25 miles. More than 900 Germans with 12 officers were captured along with many pieces of artillery. (Wright)

At this time the 35th was relieved by the First Division and after some days at a rest camp, the Division moved to the Verdun sector and relieved French troops. To the great respite of the 35th Division, their last night under fire and in the trenches was November 6. But the end was not in sight, as a few days later they were assigned to the Second Army which was preparing for an offensive near the city of Metz, an important transportation hub. Fortunately for both sides, the Armistice was signed before the offensive took place.

It was not until April 23, 1919, that the 35th Division returned to the United States. According to official reports, the Division experienced 1,480 deaths, 6001 wounded and 167 captured with most of the losses occurring in the Argonne campaign.

Of great pride to Lieutenant Jackson, and certainly to his welcoming family, was the entry of March 24, 1919 in Lieutenant Jackson's Officer Book by Major Westley Halliburton, 128th Machine Gun Battalion: "This officer has rendered faithful valuable and intelligent service as supply officer. For a period of two months he acted as adjutant and personnel officer. As acting adjutant during the Meuse Argonne offensive Sept. 26-Oct 1 he displayed great personal courage and an extraordinary indifference to enemy fire remaining cool and resourceful under the heaviest enemy fire. He attended machine gun school, receiving grade of very good..."

The action the Major was referring to was written about in a book by Edward Lengel, *To Conquer Hell – The Meuse Argonne 1918*. Lengel described the actions of those days where the engineers were digging trenches with the machine gunners placed nearby. The two groups were "the last line of defense… in preventing a complete German breakthrough." Overhead, German planes had spotted the machine gunners and engineers and soon heavy artillery began blasting their site with dangerous high-breaking shrapnel and causing "clouds of acrid, yellow smoke, blurring the view from our sweating engineers."(Pypes)

A number of officers were wounded but noncoms took charge and directed the troops in a steady fashion. The wounded were wrapped in blankets and placed safely in old German dugouts. It was also during or about this time that a Sergeant Edwin Wiggins, Carthage, Missouri, courageously led his men "to a threatened portion of the line. He walked back and forth directing the work of constructing emplacements, and organized a group of infantrymen, who had been separated from their units to assist. He was killed just as the work was completed." He was awarded the Distinguished Service Cross for his actions. It is not known if he and Lieutenant Jackson were acquainted but it is quite possible as Carthage and Butler are in the same area of Missouri and both men had been in the same unit for more than a year.

But, what about the other role of "model" that Lieutenant Jackson portrayed? The town of Butler petitioned for funds to erect a statue of a doughboy in their town. Finally, the funds were available and a sculptor selected, but who would be the model? William Jackson was available, a handsome looking man in uniform, who had made a name for himself in the war. So Jackson donned his former uniform with gas mask kit and helmet, cleaned up his rifle and served as the model. A photographer took pictures from several angles and positions which were then sent to the sculptor.

No special medals accompanied this officer's report, but perhaps Lieutenant Jackson's recognition was realized when he depicted the fighting man from the AEF as a statue. It stands today on a corner of the Bates County (MO) Court House among a statue of a soldier from the First Kansas Colored Regiment with a bronze tablet relating their fighting against Union troops. Large stones slabs are engraved with the names of hundreds of Bates County men and women honoring their participation in more recent wars. A small stone wall is engraved with depictions of vehicles and planes used in more recent wars. On an adjacent corner is a stone monument erected in honor of the Disabled American Veterans.

Post Script:
William Jackson's career as a leader and role model for men continued as he completed his law studies in 1926 and served as prosecuting attorney for Bates County. After serving as an assistant attorney general for Missouri, he returned home to Butler to set up a successful law practice. In 1954 he was appointed Circuit Judge of Bates County, Missouri, a position which he held until his death on December 7, 1967. The Missouri sent House Resolution No. 13 in his honor to his widow, Mrs. Iva E. Jackson, and family.

William O. Jackson continued in service to his home town, state and nation until the day of his passing, a genuine model for younger men to admire.

"FEED MCKINLEY GOOD . . . HE IS ONE OF MY BEST SOLDIERS . . ."

McKinley Wooden and Battery D as interviewed by Niel Johnson for the Truman Library

In an oral history interview in February, 1986, Sergeant McKinley Wooden remembers the people in his small town of Walker in southern Missouri "were talking war, war, war" when Wilson went to Congress with a war message. Wooden quickly decided to sign up to do his part. He arrived in Kansas City, Missouri, on April 7, 1917. He says he knew nothing about the Army, except there were infantry, artillery, and engineers. While deciding what branch to enlist in, he spent six weeks of training in the Rahe Auto and Tractor plant at Eleventh and Locust Street, Kansas City which he says "was one of the best things I ever did." On June 11th he walked into Convention Hall and enlisted in Battery D of the Second Field Artillery, which was then part of the Missouri National Guard.

Captain Harry S. Truman
(Courtesy Harry S. Truman Presidential Library.)

He recalls that while in training at Convention Hall, and being billeted there, he and about sixty others went out one night to rough up some drivers of the Shaw Taxi Cab Company. One of the Battery D members had earlier been beaten by a taxi driver, and his buddies decided to get revenge. The taxi drivers saw them coming and dispersed into a hotel, where the trainees could not go. He says, "We just milled around there in the street, and Morris Reilly, a second lieutenant, came along. He blowed his whistle and lined us up in the street, and marched us down on 15th Street in front of a vacant lot and gave us hell. Well, the next morning old Captain (Charles B) Allen called up on the carpet in Convention Hall. There are seats all around up above, and then a floor down the middle, you know. He lined us up there and Colonel (Karl D.) Klemm came in with his swagger stick, hot damn. Of course, they called us to attention; they came in, and he (Klemm) stood and directly said, "All of you men that were in the fracas down at the hotel last night, one step forward, yoho." . . . Oh, he laid us out—you've disgraced the uniform, you've disgraced the flag, you've disgraced the organization." Oh, he just laid us out. And he said, "I'll tell you (that if) this thing ever happens again, I'll court martial every damn one of you." Then, he left. In later years, Reilly told Wooden that he was under pressure from the Colonel to identify three or four who were ringleaders, but he replied that there were no ringleaders; they were all in this together. That way, he avoided anyone being court-martialed.

On August 4th, the battery was mustered into the Regular Army as Battery D, 129th Field Artillery regiment, 60th Field Artillery Brigade, of the 35th Division. From Kansas City they entrained for Ft. Sill in Oklahoma. He remembers that "The dust would blow from the south one day and from the north the next day . . ." He recalls buying "candy bars and stuff like that" from the unit's canteen, but did not know at the time that Harry Truman and Eddie Jacobson were running it. He recalls that Klemm was the first commander there, but he was sent for further training, and was succeeded by Colonel Robert M. Danford. He says the boys liked Danford, but did not care for Klemm. He notes that Klemm was a West Pointer and came from a rich family in Kansas City; he speculates that Klemm looked down on the "poor" fellows in the battery. (At one point, he describes most of his battery mates as well educated and coming from "good families," while he was a "poor boy, and they just kind of adopted me.") Danford apparently was succeeded by Rollin Ritter, a West Pointer whom Wooden says told the battery that he was there to "straighten out" the battery and "if there was any trouble they'd get it right here." He lasted 90 days or less, according to Wooden. Captain John H. Thacher was in charge when the battery went overseas, although Captain Truman was assigned to succeed him.

Wooden recalls that the outfit entrained for the east coast in April, 1918, but he says he still was not acquainted with Truman. Truman had left in advance, and went through Kansas City. Wooden and his mates went through St. Louis on their way to New York. From New York harbor they embarked on the English ship, *Saxonia*, which had been a freighter. "We were 16 days crossing the pond" he says. "There was quite a convoy of us, and the Navy had big battle wagons all surrounding us, you see. They landed in Liverpool, and after two or three days, they "got on a little old boat, the *Viper*," to cross the Channel. In early morning they disembarked at LeHavre, France just in time to notice a train coming in with wounded from the front, which Wooden notes, "was our first taste of war."

At first, they were quartered out of town, in the "dirtiest place you ever saw," a result mostly of coal dust and cinders. They then got on a train and went to Angers, farther south. There were 43 men squeezed into a "40 and 8," which meant that the maximum load was supposed to be forty men. At Angers they were let off, and then walked out into the country for six to eight miles to a bowling alley. They were quartered there for two or three days, and then walked back to Angers where they "unloaded guns and caissons and stuff like that. We didn't have any lunch. That night we figured on having to walk back to camp. But as I say, we had nothing to eat and one of the men said, "If you buy a bottle of that white wine, it's just like a meal."

"Well, I bought a bottle of that white wine and I drank about half of it. It didn't taste good and I gave it to somebody else. Well, about that time, a truck company came along and was going to take us back. The truck beds were about that high. We got in there and after I drunk that white wine on an empty stomach, and that truck started to rolling, things went to going around, like that. I saw I was going to fall out, so I sat down right in the corner. When we got back to camp, I got out and the cooks had a hell of a good supper for us. So I had supper and I went to bed, and the boys never did know I was about half drunk. To this day, they say, "Well, you never did drink anything in the Army nor smoke anything, did you?"

Like Truman, Wooden was assigned to the French artillery school at Coetquidan, Napoleon's old artillery range. The rest of the battery would join him there later. Wooden says that is where he first met Truman. Wooden's duty was to attend to maintenance of the guns and keep them in operating condition, as he had been trained also to do at Ft. Sill. Of the 3.2-inch guns used at Ft. Sill, Wooden says they were "not worth a damn." Presumably, it was in France that they were supplied with the superior French 75-mm gun. Wooden notes that it was on July 11th, 1918, when Captain Harry Truman first addressed the battery. He says the Captain told them, "I didn't come over here to get along with you fellows; you're going to get along with me." When the men came back to camp, "I said to an Irishman, "What do you think of the new captain, Mike?" He said, "Ninety days! Ninety days!"

Wooden recalls that the next evening, Truman "sent his orderly down for me to come to his tent. I went up there. "Well", he said, "I'm going to promote you to chief mechanic." I said, "Thank you , sir. I'll do my best." He said, "That's all I expect." Just like that. But that started a friendship that lasted for 54 years. . . I just went ahead and did my business and took care of the guns on the range and everything else. We were firing about every day then. . . ."

Two or three weeks later, the battery pulled up to the front. Wooden says, "There was a quiet sector up there in the Vosges Mountains. So the brigadier general wanted to start a little excitement, and we moved one night from our position. That was all day, it was cloudy, and they couldn't observe us at all from a plane. That day for lunch, all we had were two crackers and a spoonful of syrup. That night, the regiment fired 3,000 rounds. It had been going on about 15 or 20 minutes. Harry was standing back of the guns, about from here to those cars out there. He motioned to me. I had never spoken to him since he promoted me. I walked over there. He said, "How's our guns performing?" I said, "Perfect, sir." "That'll be all, (he said)." Wooden says these shells were gas, chlorine.

About the episode that has been labeled "the Battle of Who Run," he speaks of a "bitty old squawky, hard boiled fellow," describing the sergeant who was late getting the horses up to where the battery was receiving German shelling. The sergeant yelled "They've bracketed us; everybody run." Some of them did. Wooden says he did not, nor did "Skinny" (James T. McNamara,) gunner of the number four gun, who fired back. After they got back to camp, very early in the morning, "the cooks had a wonderful dinner for us. . . . They had a wonderful meal. We lined up and I came along with my mess kit. Harry was standing there. He said, "Feed McKinley good. . . . He's one of my best soldiers." I'd rather that he wouldn't have said it (to avoid the appearance of him bragging.)"

McNamara figured the range and elevation for firing. He sat on the right of the gun's breech. The number one man sat to the left. Wooden's recollection is that there was a crew of five for each gun. The battery was also divided into sections, with about sixteen men in each section, to handle a gun, caisson, and horses. He had responsibility for the caissons, but a stable sergeant handled the horses. He indicated that his duty especially was to make proper adjustments to the recoil mechanism of each artillery piece. According to Wooden, the firing of 3,000 rounds "wasn't much of a strain on those guns," but when they got up into the Argonne, "That was a different deal." Regarding meals, he recalls having prunes, "and anything you would want in a field ration."

Within a short time after their first combat in the Vosges, the battery moved to Kruth, and then started toward St. Mihiel. The battle was initiated on September 11th. Battery D was, at first ordered to the front, and then the orders changed, and they were directed toward the Argonne. They traveled at night to avoid detection as much as possible. In the daytime they hid in the timber and other places of concealment. He remembers the night they reached

Nancy was "the most miserable night I ever put in my life. . . . It was raining and foggy and you could hear the guns, you know, and we were all worn out. Oh boy, that was awful." Battery A led the regiment and the other three batteries were lined up in alphabetical order. Each battery was equipped with four guns.

There was more marching, to get to the Argonne forest. Troops were moving up every night near the front. "Some of them were the infantry, and the machine guns would come on by us, you know. So I had a guy with me, and we had stretched a little old tent there in the brush. He had never been in action at all before. So the Germans commenced firing over us, just anywhere. I heard a shell come over. He said, "Is that us or the Dutch?" I said, "Dutch." He said, "Goodbye." He took out. The boys had dug a trench behind each guy about three feet deep and they're a pretty safe place, unless they made a direct hit on you, you know. So I got up. They weren't coming very fast, and they were going way on over us. I put on all my clothes, got my gas mask and my gun, and walked out and thought I'd get into that trench. Hell, they were lined up, and there wasn't room for a mouse in there. So I sat down on the trail of a gun until they ceased firing. One shell lit (sic) pretty close to us. We had a cook by the name of (Lee A.) Heillman, and he had rigged up a stovepipe, twisted some sheet metal you know, and a piece of shell hit that, and knocked it down.' He came running down and said, 'Goddamn, they shot the stove pipe down.' But that bombardment didn't last very long.

"But the night of the 26th day of September, as I recall, twenty minutes to eight, the fireworks started. And I mean to tell you that it was the greatest artillery battle the world had ever seen up until that time. They'd fire those guns and then they'd pour a bucket of water down the muzzle and it'd come out the breech just a steaming, you know." He says they never used wet gunny sacks to cool the gun tubes.

At one point, near sundown, a German plane came over their position. What did Captain Harry do? "He moved us back about 100 yards, and to our right about 200 yards, right in a little cut in the road, a chat road. The muzzle of the guns just swung right over the bank, the trail of guns set back here. It wasn't fifteen minutes until they just shot that orchard all to hell. If Harry hadn't done that, there might not have been a one of us left." Wooden notes that "the main thing of the artillery is getting the location."

"Well, we were up there, I don't know how many days, in the Argonne, when the 35th Infantry Division was relieved. They marched right back by our guns and them old boys would pat those old 75's on the muzzles and say, "Boy, they're all right." They kept us there for four days to support the artillery of the 1st Division. . . . They couldn't get their artillery up because of the muddy roads. We finally got a letter of commendation from the major general of the First Division for backing them up." He adds that the battery was relieved late one night, and they were to go through Varennes, but had to wait for the end of an enemy barrage against that town.

The interviewer, Niel Johnson, then mentions a letter that Harry Truman wrote to his cousin, Nellie Noland, on November 1, 1918, in which he says that the commanding general of the 35th Division had a written commendation to him for the "Best taken care of guns in the brigade." The general recommended that the twelve other 75-mm batteries follow his example. Truman wrote, "My chief mechanic is to blame for it. He knows more about a 75 than the manufacturer, but as usual in such cases, the CO gets the credit. I'm going to endorse it and give him the credit and file the copy." Wooden would get a copy of that with the two or three endorsements, including that of the commanding general of the 35th Division.

A direct hit on an Austrian 77 mm gun
(Public Domaine)

Wooden recalls that on November 11th, in the morning, the battery fired 150 rounds in support of the infantry. At twenty minutes after ten o'clock, "Harry came along. His office was down in the chat road about 100 yards. He said, 'McKinley, look here.' He pulled out a piece of white paper about as big as my hand. It said, 'Please cease firing on all fronts 11/11/11, General John J. Pershing.' Prettiest piece I ever saw in my life. He went up and told the rest of the battery. We weren't firing. The French battery there did; they fired right up until 11 o'clock, and there was not need of it.

"Well, sir, it was the damnedest feeling you ever experienced when that stopped. Words can't express it. Just a few hours before you were killing people, and all of a sudden, France was at peace for the first time in four years. Well, we just stood around there and looked at one another. Finally someone said, 'Why don't we go home.' "

Wooden notes that after you were in France for six months, you were entitled to a ten-day furlough. After the war was over, Truman provided passes to Wooden and seven other Battery D members who planned a trip to southern France. They gathered at the Varennes railroad station which was "all shot up." Waiting for the train, they made a meal out of canned tomatoes. They took window sash and doors to burn and warm the tomatoes. Their destination was Laberbeau. "It was right in the mountains on a beautiful place. You could run around in your shirt sleeves in December." On their way, they subsisted mainly on sardines, purchased at "some little town," when the train stopped. They found, too, that sleeping overnight on a lurching train posed a challenge. In Laerbeau he drew quarters at the Richelieu Hotel. He remembers there was a bath house there that had a hundred tubs. When he went down to breakfast, "the French serve everything in courses. Guess what the first course was. . . . Two damn sardines." They now were able to take a bath every day, and there was a stand with fruits they could enjoy. They were there about ten days,

150 mm German gun captured by the AEF's 77th Division
(Public Domaine)

before returning to the place where they were stationed. Their final destination would be the homes they had left in April, 1917.

It is obvious that McKinley Wooden had acquitted himself well as a valued member of Battery D and the 35th Division of which it was a part. In later years there would be correspondence between him and "Captain Harry," including during Truman's Presidency. His papers are in the Truman Library. Wooden also was able to take part in some of the Battery D reunions. From this interview and other evidence, it is clear that he viewed his old battery commander with respect and admiration.

HONORING THE KEYSTONE DIVISION

The bright red insignia of the Keystone 28th Pennsylvania Division was dominant in many important battles in France from the time of the Division's arrival in May, 18, 1918. After only two short weeks of training with the French, the 28th Division immediately went into combat, side by side with experienced French troops to learn the hard, and sometimes fatal, ways of how to fight the Germans.

28th Infantry Division Patch
(Public Domaine)

William Arthur Zirkman, a corporal in the 103rd Engineers, which was assigned to the 28th, would have been among those advancing ahead of the infantry, repairing roads and bridges, and clearing small clumps of trees to allow the advance. He might also be locating tall bushes or rock formations where machine guns could be concealed, or find a tree 30 to 40 feet tall to build an observation post. His story is told by his grandson, Paul Laedlein, of Coronado, California.

The 28th was one of the divisions designated as an attack division. It was necessary for the engineers to remove obstacles or make essential changes to terrain before the 28th Division could advance in the offensive that started July 1, 1918. The objective was to take Hill 204 in the Marne sector. By capturing this objective, the Division would contribute to the defeat of the Germans' Spring Offensive, their effort to make a final, desperate last push in the war. The 28th fought continuously August 6 and 7 near the line on the Vesle River, not far from the crucial town of Fermes. In that town Zirkman and others had been gassed earlier on June 9, 1918 with mustard gas, the most poisonous of all gasses used. The 28th captured and held this site until September 8 when they were relieved by a French division.

Their "training" had also included the horrific battles at Chateau-Thierry with the Marines and the 2nd Division. Later in September, after weeks of relieving various French and AEF units, the 28th joined the huge massing of AEF troops preparing for the ambitious final drive in the Argonne. All the while, they also engaged in aggressive patrolling and frequent extensive raids near Thiacourt.

It is recorded that as of May 15, 1919, the 28th Division had 2,531 troops killed in combat; 13,746 wounded; and 726 captured as prisoners of war. In the usual AEF division of 25,000 to 27,000 men, those numbers amount to more than 60% casualties. (Ellis) This high figure is a result of their assignments as a "point" unit. In recognition of their bravery, 58 Distinguished Service Crosses were awarded to men of the Keystone Division, an indicator of their heroic actions. (Brief History of the 28th "Keystone" Division)

Several units of the Division originated as a national guard unit as far back before the American Revolution, and that proud tradition continues today. The 28th Division was honored with special commendations from General Pershing on August 28, 1918, for valor near Fismes and Chateau-Thierry, and again on December 19, 1918, for their actions in the Meuse-Argonne campaign. William Arthur Zirkman, a corporal age 21, was among those who lived up to the Keystone Division's proud traditions established 150 years ago.

HE SURVIVED A TERRIBLE WOUNDING

Despite being severely wounded in World War I, Chester Amil Jensen returned to civilian life and led what many would consider a "normal" life. He married, raised a family of six children, and was a prosperous Nebraska farmer. Upon his return to the States, he found a bride in a teacher named Nina Amber Kinkaid, who had boarded with Chester's brother and wife on their Nebraska farm during World War I. The wedding took place shortly after his discharge May 19, 1919, from Camp Dodge, Iowa, just a few days after his 24th birthday. One of his sons, Gerald E. Jensen, Kansas City, Missouri, tells his father's story.

Chester was one among several thousand Nebraskan farmers who trained in Deming, New Mexico, and was assigned to Company C, 134th Infantry on October 21, 1917. He was born on a farm near Wakefield, Nebraska, on May 8, 1895, one of three boys in his family all who attended a one room schoolhouse. His parents, Mads Peter and Minnie Jensen, were both of Danish descent. The brothers, Carl and Chris, both registered for the draft but little is known about any service they might have performed.

Chester was wounded August 28, 1918, in the left arm by shrapnel and lost the use of most of the muscles. This was several months after he had arrived in France on June 24, 1918. His unit may have been in the drive to halt the Germans' crucial last effort to reach Paris, as his record shows he participated in the Aisne-Marne, the Oise-Aisne and Meuse Argonne campaigns. The inexperienced American troops fought side by side with experienced French soldiers in this Salient, where the artillery barrages were especially vicious. He was discharged from the service in June 29, 1919. No record is available of where and how long he was hospitalized in Europe, but the late date of his return in May 21, 1919 to the States would seem to imply a lengthy recovery.

For his injuries, Chester was awarded the Purple Heart, and later qualified for a disability payment of $15.00 per month. This would have been about half of his regular pay as a private. He and Nina bought ten acres of farm land near Coleridge, Nebraska. He used the land as pasture for several cows while Nina tended a large garden raising vegetables for the family's use.

Chester died in 1988 at age 95, having moved to the Veterans Home in Grand Island, Nebraska, in April 6, 1984. His son, Gerald, recalls as a child, seeing his father's uniform, helmet, and gas mask and playing with then. Unfortunately the mice also played with the uniform, chewing up much of it. The mice also found several other items tasty and likewise took bites of them. Gerald now regrets the family had not taken better care of his father's belongings. The helmet however, is now in the safe hands of Gerald's older brother.

Gerald and other family members admire their father's combat service and how he managed to live a successful life as a father, husband and farmer, despite his severe injuries. He was a hero in their eyes.

A BRAVE MAN TO THE END

In the span of his career, starting as a coach of high school students, then advancing a few years later to a captaincy in the Ohio National Guard, Major Harry Fouts Hazlett lived a life requiring courage and leadership. He began as head coach of both the football and basketball teams at McKinley High School in Canton, Ohio. He moved from coaching high school players to coaching a semi- professional football team, the Canton " Bulldogs" of the "Ohio League," a forerunner of the National Football League.

However, for still unknown reasons, he was fired after he "benched Canton rookie Jim Thorpe," not allowing him to play in the first game of the 1915 league title game. The reasons for Hazlett's dismissal are not clear, but Thorpe, the Bulldog's quarterback, in a show of loyalty, left the team in protest, only to be hired later as the team's new coach. Fortunately for Thorpe, he led the team to victory and the title, and excelled as an athlete himself in the 1936 Olympics in Germany.

As for Hazlett, his dismissal provided him an opportunity to make a life career change that demonstrated his skills as an army commander, when he decided the next year, 1916, to join the Ohio National Guard with the rank of captain. This was in time to take part in the futile Mexican expedition chasing the bandit, Pancho Villa, who had crossed the Texas

Major Harry Hazlett WWI and as Major-General in WWII
(Courtesy of Carole Babcock)

border and attacked some Americans. The chase was cancelled before the bandit could be caught because the United States declared war on Germany in April 6, 1917.

As one of General Pershing's experienced officers, Hazlett was in an early group of soldiers who went to France with Pershing. Hazlett served with the 134th Machine Gun Battalion of the 37th "Buckeye" Division, eventually being transferred to command the 135th Machine Gun Battalion from October, 1918 to January 1919. He left an extensive diary, which his granddaughter, Carole Babcock, and her husband, Terry, who live in Denton, Texas, have shared. Portions are quoted as follows:

Tuesday, 5 June, 1918 – "Red (the nickname of his younger brother, Walter) left today. Last tie with home is broken now. God but it's hard to go when it comes to the last." He sailed overseas on the *Leviathan* in a "secret" departure. He commented that "only a few million people saw her leave…a destroyer was waiting to escort us. Also a plane and dirigible." "Destroyer circles the ships all the time… abandon ship drill is now daily routine." The ship carried almost 1400 men. (This was one of the first transfers of AEF soldiers to France, and great care was taken, especially with General Pershing aboard, to provide as much protection as possible.)

"Ship stopped to take in starboard mine sweeper, port one having been lost," he comments.

A few days later, the "men bathed on deck with fire hose… nearing sub zone, orders to sleep with clothes on tonight." June 21 – "a convoy of four destroyers joined us," and the next day they entered Brest harbor in France. During the training school Hazlett was assigned to attend, a trench mortar exploded during an exhibition killing two or three men.

Real military action started for Hazlett on 25 Sept when the artillery barrage began at 2:30 A.M. The men went over the top at 5:30 A.M. They were assigned to fight alongside French troops, while overhead "the Bosche avions knock down 4 balloons." The unit crossed "No Man's Land," "some job for transportation. Hard fighting in Bois Montfaucon. Captured 6 M.G. & field pieces. Lost my horse." This was part of the campaign of St. Mihiel where the inexperienced AEF incurred great losses.

Rain and cold weather continued the next few days and food supply problem was "serious" as trucks can't get through on the muddy roads, although "ambulances are beginning to." The division was relieved on October 1, and they finally got the "first sleep since drive began" on September 25. The unit moved to Paigny-sur-Meuse, requiring two nights of marching. Men, vehicles, and guns usually moved at night to stay out of the sight of the ever roving daytime German scouting planes. Finally he got a hot meal of waffles at the YMCA in nearby Toul and (in heavy type he remarked: **"Found bullet hole through my gas mask."** There were more days of marching with men lacking (the) proper clothing and hot meals. Many are sick and trip is hard."

Fri 11 Oct – Hazlett was relieved as DMGO* and sent to the 135th. He manfully wrote, "Have tried hard to please certain parties, but it can't be done." The next day he took command of the 135th, writing in his diary: "great to be in command of something again." (*Division Machine Gun Officer)

Tues 14 Oct – Another "Hurry up relief with fool orders issued piecemeal." He added, "The unnecessary hardship enforced on our troops by ignorance or carelessness is an outrage." His frustration was becoming obvious, and despite efforts to locate their relief, Hazlett's helplessness and concern for the wellbeing of his men and animals were about to reach their limit. One messenger could not give the correct pronunciation of the French town and no maps were available, so the Americans were unable to communicate with the French.

Still, there was more movement north toward Ypres, the scene of great bloodletting battles earlier in the war. "Animals in bad shape from lack of food…"A wagon of forage meets them. They continued the "cleaning up" process of looking for stray German outfits or stragglers. The towns they pass were "badly damaged but not demolished. Hun dynamited a fine church here for pure cussedness."

Thurs 31 Oct – Drive began at 5:30 A.M. with 5 minutes of preparation. "Many refugees coming back out of battle (are) gone, many wounded and sick among them. Pitiful sights." The next day they were able to move kitchens and supply company…French setting battery barnyard (?) so not likely much sleep."

In entry after entry Major Hazlett repeatedly commented upon the hardships of his men and animals. Rarely is there a personal complaint. It is as if he knew these mistakes were integral to war, and it was his responsibility, as commander, to make the best decisions, given the circumstances. He even pitied the civilians they met on the road and expressed indignation at the useless destruction the Germans had made of their houses, furniture and personal belongings. He wrote of days of witnessing damage and injury.

Sun 3 Nov – Reported "Heavy shelling all night and today. Hun avions busy with B.G.? (and) shell towns. Dug woman and two kids out of wrecked house last night. Woman and little girl infirmed. Two other children dead. Large number of refugees wounded. Hun shelled dressing station severely today. (Note: These latter two actions, shooting women and children and firing at a first aid station, are severe violations of international law.)

The next day he found "Relief coming, Hun busy with artillery & planes. Dug man out of earth where he had been buried by a shell. (Hazlett doesn't say if the man survived.) Ambulance station wrecked by shells. Relief completed but 1 platoon lost. ..Some sleep and pancakes."

Tues 5 Nov – "Rained all the way to Meulbeke. Good billet and stables. Miller found lost Platoon...

Wed 6 Nov – "Cold rainy day. Supper at Geul Lassetts (?) this evening. Fine time, my most pleasant day in France or Belgium. Letters from (home)... Rec'd word McCook died 7th Oct. ANOTHER good soldier and gentleman gone." At last, he had a relaxing and enjoyable few moments.

Two days later the war tempo picked up as the "Bosche M.G. fire made the reconnaissance of the Escaut river dangerous." The next day he had difficulty locating the Brigade Headquarters, but "Hun falling back and attack set for morning of 11 Nov. Ordered for 1A." (He doesn't explain what 1A means.)

Sun 19 Nov – Barrage 5 to 7. French slow crossing river. We got two bns (battalions) over before dark on foot bridges. Wagon bridge put in during night. Artillery and M.G. only resistance."

Mon 11 Nov – "Order to cease firing at 11 A.M. Does it mean real "fin l' guerre?" (the end of the war)(a la fin de le guerre) "One terrific explosion there at (3:25 P.M.) Comfortably fixed at Brewery at Aspen."

The next date was a week later and simply said, "Started forward and moved to Dickele."

Thur 21 Nov – "Change of orders and we are not going to Rhine. Returned to Aspen. (What cheering there must have been.) "Welcome everyone," he notes.

It would be pleasing to think that the trip going home went smoothly, but for the 135th and many other units, the road to French harbors was paved with more trials and troubles, including serious ones. Such a time was when a number of men from Company B marching through "No Man's Land" were poisoned by the mustard gas, which still was lying in holes and deep ridges, became active. The atmospheric conditions had allowed for the gas to be released. This resulted in some extremely sick men who had to be hospitalized. There would be no trip soon to the waiting boats for them. In large amounts of exposure, the gas can cause death.

A proud time for the unit came when two of its men were presented with Distinguish Service Cross medals and other soldiers were awarded Belgian medals honoring their brave actions. A concluding dinner at a chateau made a good story to tell their families, as well as more complaints about the continuous soaking rains during marches.

Perhaps as a reward for all they had endured, the day of their last hike started out bright and sunny, but it was not to last, for later, the onslaught of hail, snow and rain chased the sun away. The men cheered up when told there "was a bunch of mail waiting." Harry Hazlett ends his journal here with this good news.

The career and life of Major Hazlett continued to be interesting and challenging. He taught at the University of Akron and the University of Dayton as Professor of Military Science and Tactics. He attended the Army War College in Lawrence, Kansas, and in 1933, he published a paper, "Procurement and Processing during the Voluntary Enlistment Period of Initial Mobilization." From 1935 to 1936 he was an instructor there.

In World War II, he served as Commanding General of the Replacement and School Command. He also moved on to command the 86th Infantry Division. He later served as Post Commander at Yokohama, Japan, until 1947, and retired to California, as a Major General. He is buried in Arlington National Cemetery.

Major General Harry Fouts Hazlett could look back on his life of service to his country with pride. A career that started coaching high school boys culminated with commanding hundreds of soldiers in two of the most important wars in history. A brave man to the end.

BALLOONING — A HIGH RISK ASSIGNMENT

Balloon Pilot Wings
(Public Domaine)

Huge airships referred to as "balloons" were used in large numbers by both the Allies and Central Powers. The AEF had 69 balloon companies by the end of the war with 6,811 men serving as crewmen, while the Germans had almost double the number with 115 companies. There were several types and shapes of balloons used for different purposes. One kind of balloon was called a "captive" balloon because it was anchored to the ground by long cables. Two observers would climb into the basket which hung about 20 feet below the balloon and the balloon would be raised. The observers' job was to monitor enemy troop activities and numbers, as well as sizes and kinds of large artillery.

Each balloon had to be launched in large areas free from ground obstacles that blocked the view of the observer in the balloon. Those obstacles included large clumps of trees, deep ravines, and hills. Previously, scouts on foot or the cavalry were used to reconnoiter the enemy, but balloon pilots could see farther and obtain more exact information.

The occupants, high up in the basket, provided a tempting target for daring enemy planes. However, if the balloon was low enough, when enemy planes swooped down for a" kill," the balloon's protective ground troops could use rifles or even pistols to bring the plane down. Later, antiaircraft guns, mounted in the back of trucks, provided better protection for the balloon. The job of a balloonist obviously was one of the high risk assignments as they tried to stay at least 1,000 feet above the ground.

Other types of balloons included ones with "tails" wrapped around the end and balloons with what looked like wings on each side. They were filled with hydrogen usually and were highly flammable. Huge ground winches raised them hundreds of feet in the air. This depended again upon

Ballooning- Observers of the 14th Balloon Company about to ascend. Note the parachute container on the side of the basket. (Courtesy of the Balloon Section of the American Expeditionary Forces.)

the availability of open ground space with lack of trees or forests and the absence of enemy planes. On one occasion described from a height of 3,500 feet, the two observers could "see a man on the ground 5 miles away, a vehicle 10 miles away, and a train coming 30 miles away." It was their job to confirm where artillery projectiles fell, the number of enemy planes shot down, and the condition of the terrain. Also they reported if there were any sites, houses, trenches, or dugouts that might be useful for the AEF or where German troops might be hiding.

Descent in basket parachute from burning balloon. (Courtesy of the Balloon Section of the American Expeditionary Forces.)

The balloonists wore parachutes and in emergencies, could climb out of the basket and open the chute, although its bulk sometimes made for slow exits. Even then, the safety of the balloonist parachuting down to earth was problematic as a parachutist floating down slowly made a good target for the enemy airplane. Another potential hazard of ballooning was if the cable broke and the balloon drifted away. There was no way to control its direction or speed. A serious accident occurred in one training incident at Fort Sill, Oklahoma, when deflating the balloon. The balloon caught on fire and unfortunately two men were killed and several injured. (The Doughboy Center, 43rd Balloon Company.)

Another danger of fire could happen when deflating the balloon. In one situation, the balloon caught on fire, killing two men and injuring several others. Tempting as it might be, pilots became wary of trying to shoot down balloons, because if the plane was too close, and the balloon caught on fire, the plane might catch on fire also from the nearby flame. A Belgian pilot, Willy Coppens, shot down

A German balloon landed in the woods and was captured by AEF.
(Courtesy Signal Corps Photos.)

35 balloons, the most of any pilot, and was called the "balloon buster." He was lucky and had no accidents. Loss of balloons was high during the Meuse-Argonne campaign when "21 balloons were destroyed by either enemy planes or shells." ("Jumping from WWI Observation Balloons...")

Balloons played an important role in the Battle of the Somme in 1916 when the French and British fought became what became known as the bloodiest day of the war. The balloons used were oblong shaped with 30,000 c.f. (cubic feet) capacity. This new design eliminated the rolling of balloons when hit with gusts of air. The interior was filled with air-filled balloonets instead of metal brace planes used for stability. The balloon remained fairly steady and did not drift. It could ascend to 5,000 feet when needed to be beyond the range of enemy planes. It rose with a wind velocity of 65 feet per second.

The 308th Engineers repairing shelled roads. American observation balloon in the distance, and French artillery are scattered about the field of Bethincourt near division headquarters on the road between Cuisy and Montfalcon. October 5, 1918.

(All photos are Courtesy of Signal Corps Photos).

When it was discovered that ordinary bullets from a machine gun, or the pistol that pilots often carried, would not penetrate the skin of the balloon, new bullets had to be developed. These were explosive or incendiary and easily pierced the balloon's fabric and exploded inside, starting a fire.

When an enemy plane appeared, the balloons, if possible, lowered their height to below 1,000 feet. At that height, the planes were subject to ground fire and except for the most adventurous pilot, the plane gave up its pursuit.(First World War Balloons.)

The AEF lost 48 balloons with an unknown number of crew during the war. Of that number, German planes had shot down 35 balloons. German antiaircraft guns downed 12 more, and one balloon broke its cable. (United States Army Air Service.) Still, the adventure of flying in a balloon was a temptation many young men could not resist. Their daring actions provided more reasons for flying as a means of conducting war.

A free balloon (not attached with cables to the ground) with, in the rear, are showing the fins of a Zeppelin.
(Courtesy of "The Balloon Section of the American Expeditionary Forces.")

The Drachen about to ascend.
(Courtesy of "The Balloon Section of the American Expeditionary Forces")

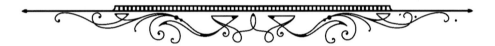

FLYING? IN A BALLOON?

Paul Ellis Allen's military service took place mostly from a height of more than 1,000 feet above the ground. No, he wasn't a spotter in a tree or a pilot flying low over the meadows. He was a member of the elite Company A, 16th Balloon Company, 5th Balloon Squadron. Perhaps he wondered why he, a CPA (Certified Public Accountant) in civilian life had been assigned to being a "high flyer." But, he may also have reasoned, if that's where the AEF wants him, then that's where his duty takes him. Besides, ballooning was a relatively new method of combat, and was perfect for an adventuresome spirit like Paul.

He enlisted in the regular army April 16, 1917, at Ft. Logan, Colorado. His granddaughter, Charlotte Allen-Colvin, Overland Park, Kansas tells his story. Paul was unusually tall for an American male at that time. He stood six feet, three inches. The average American male was five feet, eight inches. Paul's height would have probably kept him out of the aviation corps because airplane cockpits were small. For a balloonist, however, there was enough space between the basket and the balloon for Paul's height. He was even able to wear a parachute, which was standard procedure for balloonists. For pilots, again, the cramped cockpit prohibited the use of a parachute.

Balloon companies were another innovative weapon created by World War 1. Paul's company originated in Omaha, Nebraska. It was one of the last balloon companies to be activated and shipped overseas before the Armistice ended the war. He trained in San Antonio, Texas, and arrived in France on June 16, 1917, soon after America declared war on Germany. He was promoted to corporal on June 10, 1918, and served in the 22nd Aerosquadron Signal Corps.

It was a proud day when balloon observers could cooperate with their artillery to create a devastating bombardment of properly aimed shells. Later, the infantry recognized the usefulness of balloons in photographing the terrain and the lines of enemy trenches.

At this time, balloon companies were assigned to infantry outfits, creating confusion in addresses and locations of the balloon company members. Paul's official discharge says he had no overseas duty, but it is documented that balloonists from Companies A,B and C were released to English flying corps. Also, the family recounts a story of Paul marrying a French girl. They moved to the States, but the marriage did not work out, so the bride returned home. There were no children from this marriage.

Moreover, records of the 22nd Aerosquadron Signal Corps show the unit reassembled in France after having been assigned to other infantry units. They went on to Gulnes, Issoudun, Orly, Toul and finally arrived at Saint-Berain on or about September 20, 1918. The unit stayed there until after the Armistice. So the marriage to the French woman could have taken place, considering how often the 22nd was split up and assigned temporarily to British or French flying corps.

Paul later married Mary Magdeline Bruno of Council Bluffs, Iowa. They had one son, Paul Ellis, Jr., Charlotte's father. Grandpa Paul was born in Lamar, Oklahoma, and died in 1954 at about 69 years of age. He had led a military life of adventure and daring. But despite the danger of flying balloons or planes, he and airplane pilots proved that conducting warfare in the air was going to play an important role in future wars.

In the prophetic words of Brigadier General Billy Mitchell in November, 1918:

"The day has passed when the armies on the ground or navies on the sea can be the arbiter of a nation's destiny in war. The main power of defense and the power of initiative against an enemy has passed to the air."

YOU'RE A RAILROAD MAN NOW

When Lawrence Andrew Felling, St. Joseph, Missouri, signed up for the army on April 9, 1918, he was a 21 year old grocery store clerk for R.L. McDonald Company. He may have had no idea that his former job of clerking might be useful in the new regiment the Army was initiating. This is another one of the Army's amazing stories of the use of "Yankee Get Up and Go." When they needed an American gauge train track unit— none being available in France—they would build one!

And to build the train track, they had to create an Engineer Company to provide the labor, the experience, and the materials. Felling was sent to Camp Grant, Illinois, for his basic training. Camp Grant was an Engineer's Training Camp, and word arrived that the previous company which was supposed to go to France, had been commandeered by the British. What could the Americans do? They would build their own engineering company and send it to replace the lost unit. They recruited men from Camps Devens, Taylor, Dodge and Funston who had some experience in railroad work, construction work, and engineering. They were to have a total of 49 officers and 1,589 enlisted men.

Felling's assignment changed from the First Missouri Engineer Battalion to the 32nd Engineer Battalion. For several months while the men were learning to lay and repair tracks, build platforms and supports, the officers were exchanging a flurry of letters to the Quartermaster for supplies, to the Recruitment Department for more replacements, and finally to General Pershing. He, in a word, said something like, "Hang it all. You'll get what you need, now get busy."

Despite the activity, it was still a few more months before the 32nd shipped out to France where they were scattered all over the country, filling in where replacements were needed. All, that is, except Company C, which was kept intact. They began to build the regular gauge rails that would fit the American-made locomotives and railcars shipped to France. France and other European nations had narrow gauge railroad tracks and could not use the American made machines.

Army railroad programs began in 1917, and were quickly organized when Samuel Felton, president of the Chicago & Great Western Railroad, consulted with the American Chief of Engineers and later the French Ambassador. Nine Engineer Regiments were organized and sent to France to begin building miles of track, storehouses, yards, and supplying all other needs of the industry.

Finally, the office clerks typed out memorandum after memorandum until most details were agreed upon. (They don't specify yet which type of underwear the men were issued.) Meantime the soldiers were either drilling on cold campgrounds, bedridden in quarantine barracks with mumps or the flu, or performing general duties.

Again the question arose of taking the best and most experienced men for the 32nd, thereby leaving other Engineer Companies with less able soldiers. Also to be considered was that an engineer had to be skillful with a rifle also. After months of debate, a letter outlining what was to be required of an engineer was sent with the statement that the "action would be referred to the Commission of the General Staff."

It was late in 1917 when the 32nd was officially organized in response to the special needs for men skilled in locomotive car repairs, train operation, and as superintendents. The other Engineer Companies had different responsibilities including road and bridge building, digging trenches, reconstruction of outposts and other duties. Differences of opinions often arise when a new project is evolving and this was no exception. Officers disagreed upon duties of the men, what type of repair and construction equipment they would need, even whether they should be sent in winter or summer underwear.

A higher officer recommended that recruitment of "locomotive engineers, firemen, conductors, brakemen, bridge carpenters and etc." be instituted. Nowhere did it mention jobs as a grocery clerk. But by now, Felling was promoted to Private First Class, so he must have had other qualities that stood in his favor.

Finally, on June 15, 1918, the Engineers set sail for France with a full strength of 52 officers and 1,942 men, including one chaplain and a dentist. They embarked from Hoboken, New Jersey, on the well travelled troop transport ship, *Leviathan.* It should be noted that 20% of the soldiers had experience working on railroads and 42% were from "the trades." Some of the men previously had been transferred out because of lack of physical ability or other disqualification.

Men came from a background of miners(60); draftsmen, surveyors, civil and mining engineers (77); house and bridge skilled carpenters (141); skilled machinists(48); blacksmiths (19); and section men and foremen, skilled (174). This is only a partial listing but indicates the efforts to select men who would fit more easily into their role of workers in the "Standard Gauge Railway Construction," as the unit was officially titled.

Another difficulty, a serious one, that was not resolved until late in the planning, concerned motor transportation. No longer was the army dependent upon the four-legged animal. The requirements for 15 two ton Pierce Arrow trucks; 4-five passenger Dodge touring cars; 6 Trailmobile water carts, 300 gallon capacity; 26 Indian motorcycles with side cars; and 6-¾ ton delivery trucks. These were in great demand by all the military units and more letters, telegrams and phone calls were necessary to obtain the full list of vehicles.

Then came the notice that rifles would be supplied to only 10% of the men because they were railway and forestry troops. It had been the Army's practice not to supply labor battalions with weapons. "… noncommissioned officers…would be armed with revolvers and pistols."

This resulted in a cable from General Pershing himself stating that the men would be working in "a zone of fire" and should be equipped accordingly. Taking away their rifles would seriously affect their morale as they would be unable to defend themselves if attacked. There had been recorded incidents where the engineers were needed as back up fire support for their infantry.

The approval of musical instruments for a regimental band was obtained immediately without any controversy, as were requisitions for photographic equipment, and field desks.

The portion of the report available to the author ends with this proud statement:

"The 32nd Engineers, 1,665 men and 49 officers, reached here {Camp Upton} tonight. Every man pledged came; no illness, no AWOL. You cannot beat that record."

(Author's note: The underwear problem was solved by this ruling: If the troops embarked before April 30, they would be issued winter underwear. If the transporting occurred after that day, the underwear would be cotton.)

Companies A,B,C, and the Det. of Sanitary Detachment, composing the 1st Battalion, proceeded to Camp Pontanezen, France, to perform construction work. In July they began grading bank installation, trench, and concrete work in connection with camp addition repairs. The Battalion participated in the July 4th parade at Brest, marching 10 miles to arrive there. A few days later they joined the 32nd Engineers at a rest camp. The Regiment had been assigned to work in a large area of the SOS. Company C, of which Felling was a member, had been building barracks and buildings to house the Stevedore Camp at Bassens. Some men were sent to LeCourneau.

In August a group of 68 engineers from Company C supervised the work of 1,000 prisoners and 2,000 AEF troops who worked on yard and dock construction at San Loubes. Other Company C men remodeled a building at Bordeaux University to be used as a central office for AEF officers stationed in Bordeaux, which is on the western coast of France. Company C men continued in this area through September and into October at San Loubes with the extra help of 2,000 more prisoners and 2,000 AEF laborers.

Private First Class Felling served overseas until June 9, 1919, when he was discharged soon after. He married Rose Ellen Felling, raised three children, and died November 27, 1952. He was buried in Mount Olivet Cemetery in St. Joseph, Missouri. This story is related by a granddaughter, JoAnne Walsh Stovall, Prairie Village, Missouri.

"HURRY UP AND WAIT"

The above old army phrase sums up the military career of Private Raymond Pierson Jones. A sophomore at "Rose Poly," in Terre Haute, Indiana,* Raymond enlisted October 24,1917, six months after the United States declared war on Germany on April 6, 1917.

Raymond was interested in flying. It was new and exciting, especially when compared to the infantry. In order to become a pilot he had to sign up in the aviation section, which then was a part

---
* Institute of Technology in Terra Haute, Indiana.

of the Signal Corps. The United States did not have a separate flying section. (See story about balloons, p 46, 49). He boarded a train for Jefferson Barracks at St. Louis, Missouri, the next day with $20.00 in his pocket. (In today's dollars, that is approximately $350.00) (Measuring Worth) For many men in 1917 that was a large amount.

Private Raymond Pierson Jones
Courtesy of Maj. Gen. Thomas P. Jones

Raymond spent his spare time writing letters home. He had mixed feelings about his decision and was not sure if his feelings were due to being excited or feeling homesick. His mother saved many of the letters, and his son, Major General Thomas Pierson Jones, Retired, tells this story using the information from those letters.

Basic training started with inoculations for typhus and a vaccination for small pox. Unfortunately, for Raymond as was proved later, there were no preventative injections protecting against measles, chicken pox, and mumps. As sore as his arm was after the first round of shots, Private Jones may later have wished for more shots against those three diseases. Outbreaks of these latter common diseases were prevalent in the crowded conditions of barracks, both in the States and in France, as well as on troopships sailing across the Atlantic.

Call after call came for the 240 recruits of his group to ship out from the basic training camp. Time after time, it was canceled. Finally, a few days after Jones had written a letter home on November 19, 1917, a unit of 800 aviation men got the final order to head for Kelly Field, Texas. Going by train from Jefferson Barracks, Missouri, the men were met by groups of local people in small towns cheering and waving at the young soldiers. Private Jones said he wanted to take a stretch at some stops, but, unlike many other troop trains, this train required that they had to stay on board.

He commented with curiosity on one scene he saw from the train. Born on his grandmother's farm in Indiana with its tall corn fields, he was amazed at the huge cotton fields of Texas that seemed to stretch for miles. Even more unusual were the workers picking the cotton. They were African-Americans, called "colored" in those days. Indiana had few or none, and he was impressed by them. His knowledge of the world outside Indiana was rapidly broadening.

At Kelly Field, located near San Antonio, the men lived in tents, and were afflicted by the frequent Texas dust storms. The men from Jefferson Barracks were told their next stop would be San Diego. Excited to see some more of America, when the word, "cancelled" came, their hopes were quickly extinguished.

Instead, there was more waiting this time for "trade tests," vocational and aptitude. Raymond spent Thanksgiving at Kelly Field with turkey and all the trimmings. It seemed strange to Raymond that in Texas in November, he could walk outside in shirt sleeves, while folks at home on Indiana would be bundled up against the northern cold.

In high school Raymond had been an enthusiastic football player. The annual hometown Thanksgiving game with Wiley High School vs. Garfield High School was always a big event. He was anxious to know about who won the game and all the details of the game. He wrote his mother to save the newspaper for him. Football games in small towns were often the town's biggest events of the year.

Bad news once more. Not "cancelled" but "lost" was the word this time. The Army had lost his injection record, so Private Jones rolled up his sleeve and grimaced. Sore arm again. A bigger loss was his missing pay record. So it was a letter to Mom for some money.

After relaxing and enjoying some off time, Private Jones had his trade tests on December 11 and an assignment for his first guard duty. Two hours on, four hours off. Then, at last the word came. Assignments. His was to the 64th Aero Squadron at Camp Morrison, Virginia. Again the train ride. This time through the marshes of Louisiana, where he saw flocks of wild ducks. He wished for his shotgun so he could hunt those ducks.

The trip took six days due to minor breakdowns along the way. The 12 hour layover at Memphis, Tennessee, was the hardest to endure, sitting in the station or in the train on side rails. Worse was yet to come. In crowded conditions an infectious disease has a choice of many victims. Measles was the disease this time.

This delayed trip called for the need for relief from anxiety and inactivity. One of his letters described what young men with pent up energy can do with cores of apples flying everywhere. This event began after six days of being "cooped up" on the train. Finally the train came to a halt at Camp Morrison, Virginia, a crossroads town just seven miles from Newport News, a shipping port for European bound ships. It was a new camp and muddy from winter rains and snow. The future aviators cut wood, removed stumps, and dug sewer lines. In short, they finished building the camp they would live in for the next few months,

On Christmas Day his letter commented on the big turkey dinner they were served. "It was the only thing that seems like Xmas." He tried not to sound down hearted, so he added that he took out a $10,000 insurance policy and an allotment for his mother. But for 25 men from his squadron, army life had proved not to their liking. They took "French leave," that is, left the camp. They would be charged with desertion if they were caught, he was told.

The next news was good. He was finally paid. The bad news was "wait again." His unit and his equipment were shipped out, but he was sick with a cold and the army would not take a chance of it spreading to other soldiers. Therefore, he was transferred to the 73rd Aero Squadron. Then came a quarantine for chickenpox. Luckily, he managed to get a furlough for a short visit home then. When he returned, his unit had been renumbered as the 485th Aero Construction Squadron on February 1, 1918. It was another change of his address to send home to the folks.

Because one of the lieutenants believed the 485th would soon be shipped out to England where better training was available, the officers did not provide much training at Camp Morrison. The few experienced American officers lacked adequate training in aviation themselves. They opted to wait for English instructors. Instead, the unit was to be shipped directly to France, and training in England was off the schedule. Another "hurry up and wait" had occurred, but this was not one to joke about.

This time the order was the real thing. The unit left the States on March 4, 1918, on the former German ship *SMS König Wilhelm II*, arriving two weeks later at St. Nazaire, France. This was one of the busiest ports to disembark American soldiers. From there, Private Jones' unit went to Romoratin, Loir-et-Cher, an airbase under construction. It was called the Air Service Production Center No. 2, which was the second base built for Americans. This indicated how small the U.S. air corps was. The unit did general construction and erected a steel frame building. The Center may also have repaired balloons.

But for Raymond Jones, the aviation training and work he had enlisted to obtain, was delayed by yet another setback. This time it was a case of the mumps. After his recovery, he was transferred to another squadron, the 489th Aero Construction. In France the 489th was detailed to construct barracks and other buildings on many of the small airfields in France.

Raymond's letters contain several interesting stories. One story was when the AEF Commander General John J. Pershing asked all his soldiers to write their mothers a letter for Mother's Day. The YMCA supplied stationery and gave each soldier a flower.

The other story tells how the squadron celebrated July 4th by challenging a French camp down the road to a baseball game. It was to be played by the best players in one squadron from each army. Perhaps some Frenchmen might have thought it unfair, because baseball is a popular American game. Unfortunately, for the letter reader, Raymond doesn't say who won. As for helping the French celebrate their National Day (Bastille Day) on July 14, he was on guard duty and could not participate. Another disappointment.

He also had a story about guard duty which goes like this: One night he was positive he saw a German trying to enter the camp. There was a dark shape down the hill, but oddly, it never moved. Next morning he found out why. It was an old abandoned wheel barrow. If he told others this story, there must have been plenty of laughs.

Luckily, after the Armistice was signed, his squadron was among the first to leave. So "hurry up and wait" was out of the picture now. It probably was "hurry up and pack, we're leaving." He was discharged February 28, 1919, at Camp Zachary Taylor, near Louisville, Kentucky. Instead of returning to college, he ended up in the lumber business, later as president of Armstrong-Walker Lumber Company in Terra Haute, Indiana.

He joined the American Legion in Terra Haute, but his work limited his ability to participate. He said he didn't "have any war stories to swap," but his experiences with "hurry up and wait" make for some good retelling, his son, Tom Jones, says. Raymond Jones followed in his mother's family tradition of military service which extended back to her great- grandfather, Moses Pierson, a soldier in the American Revolution. Other Pierson men served in the Civil War. Raymond's son, Tom, was a career army officer.

Catching the mumps, being exposed to measles, and then chickenpox, gave Raymond some anxious days, creating many impatient delays in fulfilling his ambitions to become a pilot.

But somehow, he escaped the dreaded Spanish flu. That is one piece of luck for Raymond. His patience was tested; he saw much of a different part of the United States; and spent months on French soil. Some men would say he had good luck, but Raymond might heartily disagree. He would have grinned and said, "All's well that ends well." And his career in the army finally ended well for him. He died July 23, 1959, at age 63.

CHASING PANCHO VILLA, THEN THE GERMANS

Private Robert Lamar Lambright, Sr. and the United States Army couldn't catch Mexico's Pancho Villa in 1916, so they turned their attention to chasing Germans in 1917. Led by the famous General John Pershing in both pursuits, the Americans would face a larger and more ominous enemy in far-off France. This time they were successful. Robert, who had enlisted in the army at the young age of 16, was convinced he had had enough of Army life by the time the Armistice was signed on November 11, 1918. His son, Robert L. Lambright, Jr., Raymore, Missouri, recounts his father's adventures.

Lambright learned the rudiments of soldiering as a member of the 88th Division, which pursued Pancho Villa, a famous Mexican bandit, who had crossed the United States border to attack an American town. But Lambright learned that being a soldier in France required training for a different kind of fighting than endless riding a horse across desert sands. On Armistice Day, November 11, 1918, Lambright was still in a special training camp in France. Faced with the battle fields of France, he may have believed his young age and need for extra training was a lucky break for him. He never had the experience of living in the trenches or being battered by huge enemy artillery. He was 18 by then and was finally the legal age to become a soldier.

After the war he returned to his home in Bogalusa, Louisiana, where his family had moved from Mississippi in 1905, and went to work in a paper mill. He later attended West Point for one year, when General Douglas McArthur was the Superintendent. Lambright was enterprising and played baseball to earn money. Unfortunately his baseball skills did not help him to learn algebra. He had to drop out. He never had any steady education, but somehow with "luck and pluck," he finally graduated from Mississippi State College. Once again, playing baseball paid his way through college. There was no GI Bill then. Just a strong arm and a good catching glove was all Robert needed to pursue that college degree. He had both and he accomplished his goal.

Note: The raid on Pancho Villa was of a punitive nature because Villa had crossed the United States border and attacked the New Mexico town of Columbus. President Wilson ordered American troops to find and capture the wily Pancho Villa and bring him to trial. This action almost caused a diplomatic crisis between the Mexico and the United States.

An important side effect for the Americans in this pursuit, it was the first time the United States used trucks instead of animals for hauling. Many maintenance problems occurred due to the desert conditions encountered in Mexico, but General Pershing had the vision to recognize the inherent value of vehicle transportation. He used trucks to a large extent in France, especially to supply troops and to move them long distances. General Pershing may not have caught Pancho Villa, but he caught an idea that was more useful. It was the usefulness of an army truck.

MIDWEST MAN TAKES TO NAVY — BUT NOT THE WATER

Why would a young man from Nebraska, a Midwestern plains state, choose to enlist in the Navy during World War I? Perhaps he wanted to see the world's oceans, or maybe he was tired of endless prairies. Whatever the speculations, Henry Truhlsen's reasons for joining were lost over the years. Not even his son, Dr. Stanley Truhlsen, Omaha, Nebraska, knows, as he tells about his father's experiences.

Henry Truhlsen
(Courtesy of Dr. Stanley Truhlsen)

Henry had worked in Chicago a few years before the war and liked Lake Michigan, so perhaps he wanted to see bigger bodies of water. But in 1910 fate beckoned, and Henry returned to his home in Herman, Nebraska. Henry's mother sent a letter urging him to come home as there was a good business offer available. His father had decided to sell his share in a hardware and furniture store located in Herman, population 400 inhabitants.

Henry accepted the offer and also enrolled in a correspondence course in embalming. As was the practice in learning a new profession then, he was mentored in his studies by an undertaker in the adjacent town of Blair. Henry passed the course and received his state embalming license. The store's name was changed to include Henry's latest training and became "Truhlsen Brothers Hardware-Furniture and Undertaking." The inventory included coffins, of course.

When in 1917 the United States declared war against Germany, the United States Navy had only 53,000 sailors. Immediately, Congress authorized the recruitment of 34,000 new sailors. Here was Henry's opportunity to see something besides Nebraska prairies.

He signed up in the U.S. Navy on February 13, 1918, at age 28 and headed for the Great Lakes Naval Training Center in Chicago. There he learned seamanship including how to fire the large caliber guns on ships. When offered to be trained as a radio operator and learn the Morse code, he accepted. He was off to Boston, Massachusetts, for six weeks more education. His pay sheet recorded his pay as $32.67 per month, which was the rate for his rank.

From that income, he incurred some interesting but typical deductions. There was one payment to a hospital fund for 15 days at 20 cents per month for a total deduction of 30 cents. (There was no explanation on whether he had been hospitalized and for what, possibly the flu?) He bought a Liberty Bond for $10.18 and paid a war risk insurance premium amounting to $13.40. The payments added up to $23.88, leaving a balance of $9.79.

While he was at radio school, his fiancée in Nebraska, Lola Marshall, suffered a ruptured appendicitis and almost died. Henry was greatly relieved when she recovered from what was a serious illness in the days before antibiotics. Henry was discharged from active duty on February 15, 1919, and the couple were married on November 26, 1919. They had three children, Stanley being the oldest, with two younger sisters.

Among Henry's papers is a faded three-page typed copy of a letter from President Warren G. Harding. In the letter the president pleaded with the Navy Department to take action to preserve a Naval Reserve for future national defense. The navy of a large country could hardly be competitive with only the original 53,000 sailors it had on active duty when the United States declared war. The pre-war seagoing merchant marine consisted of 624 steamers and 870 sailing vessels and schooner barges. By the war's end, despite the loss of tonnage and ships caused by German submarine activity, the Americans through a tremendous building program, finally had a merchant marine to be proud of. (Ellis)

In the Battle of Jutland, which was anticipated to be the naval battle of the century, the Germans used 99 combat ships to engage the Allies 151 combat ships. The battle lasted about twenty minutes due to an unanticipated heavy fog, that mixed with the smoke from the numerous guns of the 250 ships being fired furiously, and resulting in both sides suffering huge losses. The outcome was considered a draw, since neither side would admit to losing. However, the Germans returned to base and directed their attention to building numerous submarines that would deal a precarious blow to the Allied shipping until the United States entered the war.

Henry served in the U.S. Ninth Naval Reserve until he completed his four years of service including two years active duty and two years in the reserve. He was discharged September 30, 1921. The reserve unit was exactly what President Harding had envisioned as necessary for defense, thus the two extra years reserve duty required of Henry and other recruits.

Henry returned home without having sailed on even one of the seven seas. But he was content in Herman, a busy rural town with two banks and two farm equipment businesses. Henry got along well with his fellow businessmen and served on the Village Board. He even was elected mayor as well as becoming a member of the school board, Village Board, and numerous other civic posts. Not forgetting his duty to his country and those who served,

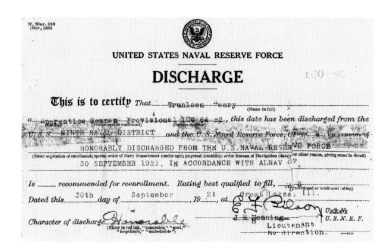

.Henry Truhlsen; discharge paper from Navy
(Courtesy of Dr. Stanley Truhlsen)

Henry and other veterans formed an American Legion Post. In the early 1920's they built a community hall which all the citizens used. Organizing these veteran groups was common in the post-war years.

Along with his business activities, Henry delivered the rural mail during World War II. At various times he was on the local school board and was elected the town mayor again. In his off hours from work, he played baseball with the local club, and later organized and coached a boys' softball league. One small player, in a burst of admiration, wrote on Henry's office window: "I LIKE KIDS." He lived a busy and civic minded life.

Henry died in 1970. Born on April 20, 1891, he was almost 80 years old. He was buried in Herman, Nebraska, his birthplace, his hometown, and the "land that he loved." No oceans for Henry, just good old Nebraska prairie sod.

ALMOST A TANKER

Expecting to be trained as a member of a tank crew, Frank Lawson enlisted August 7, 1918. He was sent to Camp Pike, Arkansas, for basic training and assigned to the 41st Company, 11th REC Battalion. The tanks were the newest weapon to be used in some offensives and were credited as contributing to the overwhelming Allied victory seizing St. Mihiel from the Germans in September, 1918. British and French tanks were used by the AEF because the United States had not yet produced a workable model. The more successful tanks were the small and speedy British Whippet tank and the French Renault T-17, a two man tank. (Jarymowycz)

However, mechanical problems often plagued the tank corps and disabled tanks faster than the German artillery or machine guns could. At St. Mihiel, for example, only three of the 49 tanks were put out of action by German fire. Still, the tank had many admirers, as well as critics, among the military, and as history reveals, it was the German Panzer tank that provided one of the biggest military challenges to the Allies in World War II.

However, for Frank, serial number 4264820, described on his draft registration as having gray eyes, brown hair and a dark complexion and standing 5 feet, 7 inches, his career as a tanker ended shortly after the signing of the Armistice with the Central Powers. He was discharged Dec. 29, 1918, at Camp Pike, and went home to his wife who lived near Lebanon. He was 24 years old.

He and his wife had four children including Steve, Bruce, Lois, and Harold. Frank lived until February 29, 1980, when he died in Shawnee Mission Hospital, Shawnee Mission, Kansas. He is buried at Chapel Hill Memorial Cemetery in Kansas City, Kansas. This story was told by his daughter-in-law, Bonnie Lawson, Overland Park, Ks., who married Harold. She was with her father-in-law when he died.

A REGIMENT WITHOUT A BAND?

"Can't be true." What a crazy idea!" "A disgrace." These comments and stronger ones would have been declared in the World War I era by grizzled old veterans and brash young recruits alike. A good marching band uplifted the spirits of weary front line troops, enlightened the foot-sore soldiers marching to a camp 20 miles down the road, and calmed men whose days and nights had been filled with the shrieking noise of artillery bombardments. They were in need of the soothing melodies and harmonies of a military band.

In camps, the band members were assigned to their own barracks and to scheduled practice times each day. They also were instructed in first aid techniques and expected to assist in the aid stations in combat zones. They might be excused from reveille and roll call in some regiments if they had played a performance the night before. In some camps, the band was allowed to perform music off the posts, but if it meant competing with local bands, then the privilege to perform was withdrawn.(Sasse)

In pre-world War I days it was not unusual that a local band would be commandeered to consider being the official regimental band. Such an event happened on August 13, 1916, when twenty members of the Greater Galesburg Band, Galesburg, Illinois, enlisted and became the official band of the 6th Illinois Infantry Regiment. This was a National Guard unit and they were assigned to the Headquarters Company.

However, almost a year later, when war was declared against Germany, orders to mobilize were received. After two weeks in camp, the official rules were announced that all married men and those with dependents were exempted from service. This was probably good news for some but for the band, it meant ten less members including the band leader and assistant band leaders. This was when the Augustana College Band of Rock Island, Illinois, was recruited.

As a soldier, the life of a musician in a regimental band could involve long hours spent in parades, regimental reviews, assisting the bugler at guard mounting, and playing at all special occasions. Their uniforms and dress, as well as the condition of instruments, had to pass the sharp eye of their sergeant. Uniform "spit and polish" was the rule. But to the real musician, being in a regimental band was the ideal slot for a military musician.

HOW MANY OF THESE SONGS DO YOU RECOGNIZE?

There's A Long, Long Trail A-winding
Mother Macree
Love's Old Sweet Song
Till We Meet Again
Pack Up Your Troubles
Boola, Boola

Goodby, Broadway
Beautiful K-K-Katie
Round Her Neck She Wears A
    Yellow Ribbon
Hail! Hail! The Gang's All Here
Over There

These songs and many more were popular with World War I soldiers and sung around camp fires and while marching to keep their pace the same and their spirits up. Singing and band music also helped dispel loneliness and boredom, as well as helped to dissolve feelings of anger or frustration. "So sing a song, any song, just sing," was good advice in 1917-1919 for the uniformed AEF man. (Sasse)

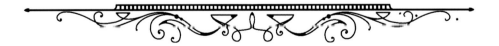

Augustana College Band as the 123rd Regimental Band, 1917
(C-L378). Special Collections, Augustana College, Rock Island, Illinois)

THE PROUD MEMORY OF A MUSICAL BAND OF BROTHERS

Co-authored with Niel Johnson, Ph.D.)

This is a condensation of "A Musical Band of Brothers: The Augustana College Band in World War I," a non-fiction story by college alumnus V. Rodney Hallberg of Cheyenne, Wyoming. His father-in-law, Theodore Lenz, was a member of the band, and came out of the war with a disability. This article is about a remarkable band, armed mostly only with musical instruments while serving in the war theater. The portions with quote marks are the words of Mr. Hallberg.

The narrative begins with a scene in northeastern France in the late summer of 1918 as envisioned by Hillberg. He writes…"a group of tired American soldiers needing a break from the long weary march to the front lines, shuffled off the line of march into an open field. Red poppies, blooming in the shell-cratered fields littered with debris of damaged homes and farm buildings, struggled vainly to conceal the ugliness of the war-ravaged area.

"The mood of the soldiers matched the depressing countryside as they shrugged off heavy field packs and stretched out on what little grass they could find for a welcome rest." Fourteen months prior, these men had been students, at least one of them studying for the Lutheran ministry at Augustana College and Theological Seminary in Rock Island, Illinois, founded in 1860 by the Lutheran Augustana Synod.

Their 14 months of soldiering had included times of anxiety, as was to be expected. They remembered April 7, 1917, the day that 33 of them started on a band tour. The day before, Congress had declared war on Germany. The band consisted of scholars and an athlete; writers and a newspaper manager; an organist and several composers; a German speaking student; debaters and the usual talented musicians. The Augustana band had a reputation for excellence among Midwestern colleges. As events turned out, one of the most useful of the members was Theodore Lenz who spoke German, which he had learned in his home environment. He played several musical instruments and created art work for the college yearbook.

They were two days into the concert tour when Band Director Harry Kalquist was handed a telegram from the commanding officer of the 6th Infantry of the Illinois National Guard. It contained a surprising request. The officer asked the band to cancel the rest of its tour and return home to offer services as the regimental band. Shocked, pleased, yet curious and cautious, the band members had to make one of the most meaningful decisions of their young lives. We may conclude their answer was, "Yes, we will serve."

The Illinois regiment had been placed on active duty in March, but most of its regular band members for various reasons were ineligible or unable to serve, leaving the band, which was the heart and soul of a regiment, seriously depleted. Why the Augustana Band was requested to replace them has not been ascertained to this day, other than it had a most competent director and many talented players. The college granted permission and each man was given a passing grade in all his courses. The band was sent off with a rousing farewell concert on April 17. A newspaper reported, "Words cannot describe the feelings of the student body at that moment." The original 33 was whittled down to an enthusiastic group of 26 dedicated young men because some Augustana men were physically or otherwise unable to enlist.

AT CAMPS LOWDEN AND LOGAN

Basic training began at Camp Lowden, near Springfield, Illinois, where the men set up their tents with eight men and one noncommissioned officer per tent. Basic training included more than daily tuning of instruments and practicing marches for parades for these 26. Their day began at 5:30 a.m. when they marched around the camp playing reveille. There was the daily band practice, then learning first aid and hospital work which would be their jobs when the battles are raging. The afternoon schedule consisted of the band marching drill time, and at 6 P.M. the band played "Retreat."

Some nights the band played in a dress parade, and everyone went to bed by 10, tired but with martial sounds of music in their heads as they fell asleep. On Sunday mornings, the band marched around the many buildings that made up a training camp holding as many as 40,000 troops at one time. The band played "Onward Christian Soldiers" as a call to urge men to come to the church services. Sunday afternoons the band usually played concerts for visitors and occasionally a performance at local churches, fraternal groups and Red Cross programs.

123rd Regiment Field Artillery Band: The last photograph taken in front of the Catholic Church in Besancon just before leaving for the active fighting front.

In September, 1918, the band embarked for Camp Logan, Texas. More intensive training came with the new camp. The players were issued rifles and taught how to use them. They fired at targets from trenches spaced at 100 yards, 200 yards, and 300 yards. Soldiering was becoming more realistic. They still had the usual band practices and marching drills. By now, some of the band members were commissioned as officers, or left for Officers Training School. The band and life itself were changing, as the events of May, 1918, proved. That is when they boarded trains for the long circuitous trip to the east coast where ships awaited troop passengers.

DEPARTURE FOR EUROPE

At Hoboken, New Jersey, on May 26, the regiment marched up the gangplank onto an old wooden beam British vessel, the *HMS Scotian*, scarcely large enough to hold the regiment of 3,000 or more. The ship was in a convoy of 13 ships. To counteract, if possible, any homesickness or seasickness, the band, now conducted by Ray Houdek, played daily concerts. On the second day the band played its first military funeral for a soldier who had died on board the ship.

No submarine attacks or other unfavorable incidents occurred, and the convoy landed at Liverpool, England, after a 12 day trip. The men were greeted warmly by local people, who offered them cigarettes and refreshments. Then on June 12 the men reached the port of LeHavre, France, where after a day of rest, they boarded the famous French 40 and 8 railcars. Finally they reached their destination, Fallerans, France, a small farming village. In their spare time, some of the band helped the locals in the fields with the harvest. The war had taken all the able -bodied Frenchmen and it was up to the women, old people and children, to do the farming.

More practicing and performing, more medical training and drilling occurred until July 29, when the regiment arrived at a French artillery camp for final training under experienced French and British soldiers. One wonders what the veterans thought of these young men who proudly and carefully carried musical instruments around the campsite.

The locals and the experienced soldiers learned the value of those instruments when the regiment celebrated American Independence Day on July 4 and Bastille Day on July 14, the French equivalent observation of their independence, with concerts and celebrations involving American patriotic music.

ASSIGNMENT TO THE FRONT

The day of departure came August 22 when the regiment was ordered up to the front. The band, playing its final concert, opened with the "Star Spangled Banner" and closed the religious ceremony at the Besancon Catholic Church by playing the French national anthem, "Les Marseilles." The priest took their picture, showing their precious instruments which then were packed into a French military van. The newly named 123rd Field Artillery Band thought they might never see their beloved instruments again, but fate was not that unkind.

The rains came and made giant mud puddles out of the roads, creating almost impassible routes for the heavy 155mm howitzers and caissons to move to what was considered a quiet sector near Toul. German aircraft dropping bombs gave an unwelcomed greeting. From Toul, the regiment, a unit of the 58th Field Artillery attached to the valiant and experienced 1st Division, began the difficult trek to the St. Mihiel salient where it became an important role in its capture.

The roads were crowded beyond belief. Constant rain and German artillery shelling made the days miserable. All movement and traveling had to be done at night where the dark forests made the sky seem even more black. In addition, the klaxons sounded "gas alarms" while flares lit up the sky like fireworks. To make matters even worse, on the night of September 12 the men were shrouded with a thick fog, so penetrating they could not see the man ahead of them. Each man kept his free hand on the shoulder of the soldier in front to avoid getting lost.

Then at 1 A.M. the artillery from both sides began a barrage. It was a battle of sound and light such as the Augustana men and all other AEF soldiers had never seen before, and hoped never to see again. But it was the beginning of the end for the capture of St. Mihiel on September 13. The Germans, realizing their impending defeat, either surrendered by the scores or retreated. One of the band members, Elmer Swanson, was gassed and sent to Toul and Dijon to recuperate. He eventually was assigned to another band, so he had played his last concert with his band brothers a few days previously.

IN THE MEUSE-ARGONNE CAMPAIGN

The 123rd and its band, as part of the First Division, began the 200 mile trip to the Meuse-Argonne front. Again the rains. Again the struggling and dying horses and mules that were hitched to artillery weapons and their caissons. Again, there was a lack of sleep and food, much less a hot meal. It was reported that men fell asleep while standing in line at traffic jams. But good news for the musicians! Their instruments somehow had arrived and were recovered by their owners. They tuned up and turned on the music, exhausted as they were. As was to be expected, the martial music revived the spirits of all listeners for a while.

Then the reality of another campaign set in. Heavy bombardments killed men and horses. For 18 days the regiment was situated near "Hell's Alley," a deep and wide valley, where they received uninterrupted shelling from the Germans. Finally the 123rd entered the cross roads of the villages of Very and Cheppy, a destination for the wounded whose stretchers filled the streets. This time the band members utilized the first aid training they had received. Some served as medics, others were stretcher bearers, still more dug "bomb proof" dugouts and gun emplacements, or installed camouflage. Band members filled in as kitchen police and laborers; wherever a hand was needed, a band member was there.

This was the time Ted Lenz, the German speaking member, had looked forward to. His language skills were much in demand for interrogating prisoners. But misfortune lay ahead for him. In one of the bombardments, he was riding in the back of a truck when a shell landed in front of the truck, causing it to crash. Lenz was thrown from the truck and his back severely injured. He became a lifelong disabled veteran.

THE CONCLUSION

The end of their war time adventure for the last of the Augustana band members came in June, 1919. Many had been dispersed in other directions previously. In 1919 the remainder of the band played their last parade in Chicago in the presence of Illinois Governor Frank Lowden and General George Bell, commander of the 33rd Division, to which the band had been transferred earlier.

The director, Ray Houdek, then pronounced, "The band was no more."

Yes, no more than a memory, but what a proud memory! Augustana College will always honor these men and their band for their distinguished role as the United States 123rd Artillery's Regimental Band of World War I.

HE CARRIED STRETCHERS AND BARITONES

World War I caught up with musician Noah Gilbert Henley in a "big" way. He carried a large brass baritone band instrument during his tour of duty in the AEF, until he was diagnosed with a heart murmur and received a medical discharge. Band members were also expected to learn how to carry stretchers, that being their main duty assignment. Carrying a wounded soldier from the battle field required the strength and stamina of four men usually, especially when the ground had six to twelve inches of mud. The bearers had to stand upright, which made them a good target, so most of the carrying was done at night. Lack of light added to their problems, as well as avoiding as much movement as possible of the stretcher. The slightest jolt or bump often was agonizing to the injured, and sometimes they died of shock from pain.

Noah's only son, Richard Henley, Kansas City, Missouri, tells the story of his father exchanging a handsome civilian band uniform for a dull khaki one. Noah had played the baritone on river boat bands in the St. Louis area after receiving his Bachelor of Music degree in 1912 from Washington University, St. Louis, Missouri. He played the large "um pah pah" in the army band, with the 4/4 rhythm of a march replacing the engaging and energetic music of the Charleston or Rag Time.

And what happened to his initial assignment as a stretcher bearer? His diagnosis of a heart murmur, not detected when he was drafted, prevented him from fulfilling that strenuous duty. To his pleasure, he was still allowed to carry and play his big baritone and blast out a big "um pah pah" for many weary soldiers.

(For an interesting book about young American ambulance drivers and their stretcher bearers, see *Gentlemen Volunteers*. It is listed in the bibliography.)

MARTIAL MUSIC GOES BACK THOUSANDS OF YEARS

Some of the earliest frescoes and relief carvings depict men playing instruments encouraging their soldiers in the fight. Scenes from Abyssinians and Babylonians show the importance of music during warfare. It might be used for signals, for triumphal parades, or simply to while away the lonely nights of soldiers in camps miles from their homes. The ancient Romans in 200 A.D. standardized 43 signals that a musician had to learn. It was usually a drummer or a horn player, although the horn might be a giant conch shell or a ram's horn.

The drum was introduced to standardize the rate and rhythm of marching, and also signaled the commands for each time of the day. The drummer was later replaced by the bugler as horns became more developed and better metals used. Some bands played during combat, and the present day bands of the 101st and 82nd Divisions have received decorations for such activity. American generals from George Washington onward have recognized the importance of band playing to inspire and encourage soldiers.

General Custer designed a band mounted on gray chargers to lead his cavalry into battle. Such an occasion included the 1868 battle of Washita. For Custer's band, the players had to be skilled horsemen as well as musicians. American band players have performed many acts of bravery, and 32 members have been awarded the Congressional Medal of Honor. One such feat was the American band member scaling the wall at Peking in the Boxer Rebellion of 1900 and inspiring his soldiers to follow him and defeat the Chinese.

Finally, an official school for band leaders was authorized by Congress in February, 1920, at Fort Jay. General Pershing had been a great admirer of marching music and recognized the morale boost a good band could give. Often, civilian bands were "enlisted" as regimental bands (see story, page 61) Pershing doubled the size of military bands from 28 players to 48, and the rest is history. ((A History of U.S. Army Bands…)

SONG WRITER 'SINGS OUT' COMMANDS AS A SERGEANT

'Hup, two, three, four...' shouted out Sergeant John Logan Rogers to his young recruits as they learned the basics of marching as a squad. Later that evening, perhaps, they may have gathered around a piano singing another of Sergeant Rogers' inspiring war songs.

SERGEANT WRITES PATRIOTIC MUSIC IN SPARE HOURS

SERGEANT JOHN L. ROGERS.

(Courtesy of Veda Rogers)

Kansas City's John Logan Rogers, was a well known songwriter who rose from a private in the Kansas National Guard to sergeant during his service in the AEF. Single and 30 years old, he enlisted in early 1918 after a year's deferment due to his prior National Guard years. His story is told by his son, Bruce Rogers, Kansas City, Missouri.

During the time he trained recruits at Camp Doniphan, Oklahoma, he wrote several songs including 'Goin' Over." A March 14, 1918, newspaper article called it "the Sammees' goodby song" and 16,000 copies were sold the first few months after it was published. "Sammees" was the first nickname given for American soldiers, coming from the nickname "Uncle Sam." But "doughboys" caught on and remained the familiar name for the rest of the war. It competed with "Yank" in popularity.

Because Sergeant Rogers had trained during weekends in the National Guard at the Robinson Gym, University of Kansas, Lawrence, Kansas, he received an assignment as a non-commissioned officer at Camp Doniphan, Oklahoma. Many Missouri and Kansas "rookies" were sent there. He didn't stay at Camp Doniphan long before he was shipped out to France. This was evidenced by his signature on the card that each soldier was required to sign upon arrival. It read, "THE SHIP ON WHICH I SAILED ARRIVED SAFELY. The family has the card.

A member of Company M, 137th Infantry, 35th Division, Sergeant Rogers and the 137th were sent to the Vosges Mountains in France by way of the famous box car trains called "40 & 8." For a while there was little fighting. Then the nearby 139th Division was attacked by the Germans in early August, perhaps as retribution for some earlier AEF raids in which Germans were killed or captured.

On September 30 the 139th Division commander, Colonel Clad Hamilton, and others were gassed. It is perhaps during this time that Sergeant Rogers was exposed to gas also. This was the beginning of the combined AEF forces' effort to take the St. Mihiel Salient which had been held by the Germans for three years. General Pershing finally seized the opportunity to use all

(Courtesy of Veda Rogers)

his units-- tanks, airplane, artillery and infantry-- to force Germans from the Salient. This was the first time in warfare that all four forces had ever been used as a fighting unit.

Sergeant Rogers was one of the 71,345 men gassed in the war who survived. There were an estimated 1,462 estimated soldiers who did not. Those numbers are not entirely accurate. Some of the deaths occurred because the troops had previously suffered from influenza and were in a weakened condition when exposed to gas. Also tuberculosis was rampant in Europe then, and some doughboys who were gassed, caught the disease and died. Lastly, sometimes death came years later after the war ended because the lungs had been damaged by the gas. (Pierson-diary of a waggoner)

During the capture of the Salient, the 35th Division gained 10 kilometers or 6 1/4th miles. They were ordered to rest a few weeks before being transferred to the Meuse-Argonne sector where they fought until November 6. That was their last night on the front lines. AEF losses were the heaviest in the Meuse-Argonne fighting with 1,500 dead; 6001 wounded; and 167 captured.(Pipes Family)

After the Armistice on November 11, the unit was stationed in the Le Mans sector, and finally shipped home in late April, 1919. Sergeant Rogers was hospitalized in Arkansas where he recovered his health. While he was recuperating in the hospital, he met and married Lela Owens McMath. She had a daughter from a previous marriage, who became known later as "Ginger Rogers." Sergeant Rogers was proud of Ginger's success in Hollywood in the late 1920's. When he died in June, 1960, she sent a huge spray of mums that totally covered the piano in his hometown church, the Quenemo Federated Church. The card read: "From your daughter who loved you."

After his discharge from the hospital, he made Kansas City his home. John continued his song writing. One song, "Baby O'Mine," was written for Ginger pre-1920. Mrs. Veda Rogers, his daughter-in-law, used the song as a lullaby for the three children born to her and Bruce, his son, and later her grandsons.

But no songs reached the heights of popularity of his hit war song, "Goin' Over." The chorus goes:
> "We're go-ing, we're go-ing, we're go-ing right on ov-er.
> We are on our way to France. We're go-ing, we're go-ing, we're go-ing right on ov-er,
> For now we have our chance. We're man-y and we're mighty, keen and ver-y fight-y,
> We'll make the Fritzs dance the tune of Yankee Doo-dle-Doo." (repeat)

It was advertised: "For Sale at all Music Dealers or Send 15 cents to ..."

One questions if his men knew they were in the company of a famous song writer. Or more importantly perhaps, a sergeant who later would be a step-father to an even more famous and glamorous movie star. They would have tagged him as special indeed.

TRY IT
CHORUS.
We're go-ing, we're go-ing, we're go-ing right on ov-er. We are on our way to France. We're go-ing, we're go-ing, we're go-ing right on ov-er, for now we have our chance. We're man-y and we're mighty, keen and ver-y fight-y, we'll make the Fritzs dance the tune of Yankee Doo-dle-Doo. We're——
(Also arranged for orchestra.)

NO EXEMPTION FOR HIM — HE CHOSE THE RIFLE

When William Henry Burmester filled out his draft registration card on June 5, 1917, at Hudson in St. Croix County, Wisconsin, he noticed that the blank #12 asks that if the man claimed an exemption from the draft. If so, he was to specify it. William filled in "defective fingers." What that indicated is unknown now, but evidently it was not serious enough to disqualify him from becoming a rifleman.

William was 22, single, lived at home and helped his father with the farm. His future brother-in-law, another William but with the last name of Alvermann, signed up at the same time. So did a number of young men from nearby Glenwood City, Wisconsin.

This story is told by William Burmester's grandson, Steve Burmester, of Knob Noster, Missouri, about the two friends. The men were assigned to the 29th Company of the 161st Depot Brigade, Camp Grant,

William Henry Burmester
(Courtesy of Steve Burmester)

Illinois, as noted on a large group photograph made early in their service. Steve has the original in his possession. From Camp Grant after basic training, the two friends were assigned to the 342nd Infantry for a few months. They sailed for France, arriving September, 1918. Afterwards, their assignments took them in different units. Burmester stayed with Company A of the 55th Infantry, part of the 7th Division.

Steve has another photo of his grandfather, taken in Domfront, France, on May 24, 1919. This one also was with the remaining men of Company A, 55th Infantry plus new ones who had replaced the dead or wounded. In the background there are road signs indicating the routes to the sector of Mayenne and the city of LeMans. These locations are in northern France and probably indicate they are departing France.

The Seventh Division, to which William and his future brother-in-law were attached, began training and re-equipping immediately after arrival in France. Their destination would be the Meuse-Argonne sector, where fierce fighting was expected. This overseas training in France was necessary because the men's training in the States had been brief. It had been important to ship the troops to France as quickly as possible to impress the Germans that U.S. troops would overwhelm them in vast numbers. So the AEF had been recruited and briefly trained in the States, and the most important training would be done in France by experienced French and British soldiers.

Sometimes, however, the raw recruits were unfortunately thrust into fighting before the appropriate training had been accomplished. The 55th Infantry was held in reserve, so they had the extra training for dangerous situations.

From October 10 to November 9, 1918, the 55th Division held a defensive position in the area, but the next day they went on the offensive for the two days before the Armistice took place on November 11. The 7th Division as a whole suffered 1,546 casualties. Three men became prisoners of war for a brief time.

During the two days of combat the 55th Division engaged in, the fighting must have been severe because numerous acts of heroism shown. There were 30 Distinguished Service Crosses awarded for their brief but perilous period on the front. (Ellis)

Grandfather Henry Burmester
wearing his German uniform
(Courtesy of Steve Burmester)

The last months in France were spent with additional training, and also probably some belated leave time was granted, as this division was not one of the units assigned to the Army of Occupation of Germany. On February 24, 1919, William was assigned to two Guard Companies until his discharge on May 17, 1919. Despite the change, one could expect that many of the men's letters expressed boredom and impatience at the long delay in returning stateside to be discharged.

Steve has his grandfather's two shoulder patches of a red circle with the black hourglass in the center, along with a collar brass insignia that has a numeral "55" over "A" with crossed rifles in addition to the photographs. Moreover, he has his last pay book and his identification tags with the number 3751083.

He is proud of his grandfather, who at age 22, with "defective fingers," left his plow and horses behind to serve his country despite all the dangers of the battlefield that waited for him and his company.

An interesting twist to the story was recently remembered by Steve. He found a copy of a photograph of his father's grandfather, Henry Burmester, wearing a German uniform. Prior to his immigration to the United States, in the early 1900's he had been drafted at age 21 into the German army, as was required by German laws. At that time, physically able German men had to serve part time in the army until age 45, but Henry was not involved in any combat because he had immigrated before World War I started. Steve comments, "It must have been a little strange for Henry to (later) send his own son, William, to fight against the army that he, Henry, had once served in Germany," (see story "The Two Williams," p. 73.)

TWO WILLIAMS SAW THE WAR — BUT NOT TOGETHER

As was often the situation, good friends or relatives joined the army at the same time or nearly so and usually went through the trials of boot camp together. Then they usually were assigned to the same regiment or at least, division. Such was the case with William George Alvermann and his future brother-in-law, another William with the surname of Burmester. Both were of German ancestry, both were farmers and single, and both from the region of Glenwood City, Wisconsin.

William George Alvermann
(Courtesy of Steve Burmester)

However, William George enlisted July 23, 1918, at Hudson, Wisconsin, a month after the other William had signed up. Both trained at Camp Grant, Illinois, as documented by the three foot long company photo now in possession of the Burmester family. William G. was born in Macon, Missouri, in 1890, yet for some reason he migrated to the north, where he was "self employed," while working for a small town in Wisconsin, according to his draft registration.

The two friends were later assigned to Company E, of the 342nd Infantry until October, 1918. However, because William G. had contracted the influenza on the ship going over to France, once they arrived , this was when they parted. It took William G. a long time to recover from the flu. When he did, he was placed in a provisional regiment along with other AEF soldiers who likewise had been separated from their units, which had moved to other stations by then.

William G. was assigned to Company L, 3rd Provisional Regiment until February, 1919. Perhaps his health was too precarious for combat. Family stories tell about him being around dead bodies much of the time, so he may have been assigned to a Graves Registration unit, recovering, identifying and reburying fallen soldiers. It was often unpleasant work, because many bodies were decomposed, torn into pieces, and putrefied. It also may have reminded him of the immense loss of men as a result of the war.

His friend was serving with Company A, 55th Infantry Regiment, 7th Division. (See story, "No Exemption for Him p.71)

When William G. was discharged July 2, 1919, he returned to Wisconsin and he and his buddy married each other's sister. William G. married Helen Burmester, and William A. married Anna Alverman. Their farms were close to each other a few miles north of Glenwood City, Wisconsin. They remained lifelong friends, and when William George's wife, Helen, died, he move to live with his son, Walter, in St. Paul, Minnesota.

The 1930 census details that the family had no radio, that he and his wife owned their own home, and that he could read and write but had not attended school. He died in 1981 and was buried in Glenwood City, Wisconsin.

After sharing many experiences in the AEF, both men also shared the worry of having their sons, Walter Alvermann and Arthur Burmester, also serve in the army in World War II in the European theater.

Another interesting twist to the story concerns William Burmester's father, a German immigrant, who previously had worn a German uniform as a member of the German army before World War I started (See story p. 72).

FRED A. THOMPSON, A SCOTTISH STONEMASON, TAKES UP RIFLE, PUTS DOWN TROWEL

Although his draft registration card says Fred was "natural born an American," his grandson, Gene Cramer, Kansas City, Missouri, recalls stories of Fred telling about his early days in Scotland. Now, Gene wonders, was that really the native land of Fred's birth or stories Fred had heard from others.

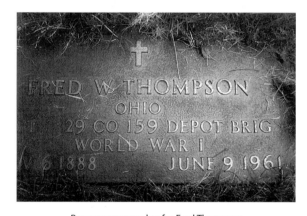

Bronze grave marker for Fred Thompson
(Courtesy of Gene Cramer)

Or perhaps Fred had even lived his early years in Scotland. A mystery with perhaps no answer. Fred's military records are missing, along with thousands of others. Nearly all Army records were burned in an accidental careless fire in 1973 at the National Archives in St. Louis, and Fred's have not yet been replaced. So where he fought in France and in what unit or division are unknown.

True to the traditional image of a feisty Scotsman, Fred sometimes had difficulty with others in his crowd. His headstone states he was in Company 29, 159th Depot Brigade. Men were assigned to depot brigades for several reasons, usually while they were awaiting assignment to another unit. Some official state records show that Fred was born June 16, 1888, and his place of birth is listed as Jewett, Ohio. He married "Tiny," the nickname given to his wife who was Gene's grandmother.

But an earlier marriage to Carrie W. Groves of Harrison County, Ohio, is recorded in Ohio records. That is another mystery in Fred's colorful life.

As a civilian, he was a brick layer and a stonemason. Many houses and churches in Kansas City he helped to build are still standing, attesting to his skill and expertise. He often had disagreements with the Brick Layers Union's prohibition on how many bricks he was allowed to lay in one day. Fred could lay a higher number of bricks or hew more stones than the Union allowed. The Union wanted to spread out the work as much as possible. Fred wanted to speed up the job, as well as show off his unusual skill.

But disagreements often didn't matter to Fred. He was discharged as a sergeant, so he must have agreed with the right people at the correct time to achieve that rank. Depot brigades often employed soldiers who showed the inability to perform a job, had a lack of English speaking skills, and for various reasons were unable to get along with others. But none of those reasons were why Fred spent his last days of the war there. He was there, waiting to be discharged.

Fred and Tiny divorced after some years, and Tiny remarried. Gene remembers how many wonderful stories he heard from his unusual grandfather, a Scotsman, a stonemason, and a sergeant. But for Fred A. Thompson, like most soldiers, his war stories were not the "telling kind" to a family. So for Gene and other family members, Fred is almost a "legendary" person. His mysteries make him a most interesting character.

THE ROCK OF THE MARNE AND GREAT UNCLE PETER KRAUS

Gassed and severely wounded in World War I, Corporal Peter Kraus, 2nd Regiment, Indiana, spent the remaining years of his life in a veterans' home. Corporal Klaus had volunteered for the 2nd Regiment, Indiana National Guard in 1917. They trained at Camp Shelby, Mississippi, from where they were shipped overseas. The unit later was incorporated into the Third Division of the National Army.

His nephew, Joe Baltewiez, Chicago, Illinois, recalls hearing about the physical suffering his great uncle endured, most likely from mustard gas the Germans used in great quantities in the Meuse-Argonne area. That was where Corporal Kraus' unit fought the last few months of the war. He previously had been wounded in the crucial Second Battle of the Marne, known as the "Battle of the Rock of the Marne." The Marne was an important river which flowed among huge rocks which made excellent sites for hidden machine guns. The river also curved and wound around clumps of trees and more rocks, making it difficult, if not almost impossible to attack the Germans who had built cleverly disguised gun shelters.

In addition to the overwhelming odds of facing some of Germany's most experienced troops, the AEF also had to attack across the strange configuration of the land extending into the Marne River. It made a three sided shape, or salient. The Third Division launched successful attacks by using successive waves of troops and gradually wiping out the machine gun nests. By the end of the day, July 15, 1918, the well planned offensive of Germany's General Ludendorff had failed, and the German drive to Paris was halted.(Eisenhower)The Third Division designed an unique shoulder patch of four blue stripes alternating slantwise with three white stripes. This design refers to the river and its rocks, and the division earned the nickname of "Rock of the Marne."

The campaign for Chateau-Thierry that began the next day was a continuation of the Marne battle, and it was here that Peter Kraus is believed to have been promoted to corporal. He also was wounded by shrapnel in the later Meuse-Argonne campaign and was awarded the Purple Heart. He was later discharged from an evacuation hospital in France because of his injuries.

The family story is that he liked to drink, and it became "his hobby." After preparing the drinks, he would often be the last one drinking. This drinking habit, along with being gassed, and having had TB as a child, may have contributed to his early death on April 24, 1943 at age 48. Large amounts of mustard gas would kill the soldier within a few days. Small amounts, which is probably what Corporal Kraus was exposed to, caused painful damage to mucous parts of the body such as lungs and throat, and weakened the immune system.

He was born August 15, 1895, in Chicago, and is buried in the Holy Cross Cemetery in Calumet, Illinois. His parents were Polish immigrants and had eight or nine children. The record is not clear. Corporal Kraus never married.

He helped his unit earn the title, "Rock of the Marne,"contributing with his actions and his being gassed. His family has always honored his courage.

AN UNUSUAL DIVISION EARNS AN UNUSUAL SHOULDER PATCH

As the first organized division in Europe, the AEF First Division rightly earned its title as "First." However, the Second Division had its own unusual origin of name with the distinction of being the only AEF division that was formed on foreign soil. This occurred at Beaumont, France, in October 26, 1917, in response to the need for troops in the Belleau Wood sector. In collaboration with the 4th Marine Brigade (composed of the 5th and 6th Marine Regiments), the men of the Second Division and the Marines would capture Belleau Wood after a fierce and bloody encounter with the Germans in July, 1918.

2nd Infantry Division

They proceeded to more ferocious fighting at Chateau-Thierry, Soissons, the battle of the Aisne River, and then completed the circuit of well known battles, by fighting their way through Aisne-Marne, Blanc Mont, St. Mihiel, and the final campaign at Meuse-Argonne.

An early incident in the first days of combat told by the Marines demonstrated their determination and courage. A Marine order to "hold the line at all hazards," was followed by a command from the French commander to dig a trench line several hundred yards behind them. The Marine commander, General James Harboard, bristled and replied: "We will dig no trenches to fall back to. The Marines will hold where they stand." (Freidel)

The many days spent on the battlefield resulted in high casualty numbers, with the Second Division experiencing 1,964 killed and 9,782 wounded. The Marines suffered a similar large percentage of causalities. In doing so, however, they had advanced a total of 60 kilometers (about 38 miles), captured 228 German officers, along with 12,000 soldiers, 343 pieces of artillery and 1,350 machine guns. The Second Division ended their days overseas as part of the Army of Occupation (AOG) of Germany, stationed in the Rhineland, returning home in mid-1919.

Numerous medals from several nations were awarded to many troops for their important part in defeating the Central Powers. (Sasse). History was made when two Marines were each awarded two of the Congressional Medals of Honor. They were Major Gen. Smedley Darlington Butler and Major Daniel Joseph Daly. The Second Division received a total of seven Congressional Medals of Honor, the fourth highest of all the divisions. (Ellis)

Take a look and see for yourself. Just as the organization of the division was exceptional, so was the design of the shoulder patch.

COULD HE HAVE BEEN A CHOCTAW CODE TALKER?

Several mysteries surround the background of Ed Johnson, Choctaw Indian of Broken Bow, Oklahoma. One mystery is his exact birth date and place of birth. His obituary gave October 25, 1894, as the date he was born. Another record showed his birth as October 3, 1896, at Eagle Town, Oklahoma. His Social Security record used 25 October 1896, while the date on his draft registration card was October 26, 1895, birthplace listed as Ft. Towsand, Oklahoma.

Ed Johnson
(Courtesy of Mark Johnson)

Some confusions or inaccuracies are to be expected to occur on military records of the more than 4 million men recruited within 18 months from the time the United States declared war April 6, 1917, on Germany, until the last man was signed up in November, 1918. But these two inaccuracies are of no concern to his grandson, Mark Johnson, Kenner, Louisiana. He knows his grandfather, of the Choctaw Indian heritage, was a loyal and reliable member of the 36th Division from Oklahoma and Texas. More importantly, his grandfather was assigned to the 142nd Infantry Regiment which fought in some of the fiercest battles the AEF participated in during the war.

However, the only thing he remembers his grandfather actually saying about the war were two remarks: "All he had to eat was horses and mules" and he "walked across France."

Back to another mystery. The name "Ed"was one of four or five "Eds" or "Eddies" with the surname of Johnson listed in the Dawes Final Rolls of 1902. The Dawes was an official listing of Citizens and Freedmen of the Five Civilized Tribes in Indian Territory. This listing began in 1898 and was completed by 1906 and included members who volunteered their information and were from the Choctaw, Cherokee, Chickasaw, Creek, and Seminole tribes. An act of Congress in 1906 began a gradual transition to citizenship for all Indians, but that process was not concluded until 1924.

The Ed Johnson assumed to be the relative of Mark Johnson, Kenner, Louisiana, was listed as a "Freedmen," meaning a former slave of the five tribes and their descendants, His draft registration lists his color as "black." According to his grandson, Ed was dark skinned because "he worked outside most the time." Ed listed his occupation both before and after the war as "laborer." Photographs show a man more Caucasian looking than either Indian or African-American.

Ed is believed to have joined the 1st Oklahoma Infantry Regiment which had existed as a National Guard unit since the Spanish-American War. It was consolidated with a Texas unit during the summer of 1917, and a few months later was officially renamed the 142nd Infantry. More changes with the unit numbers occurred when the 142nd became part of the 71st Infantry Brigade to comprise a large enough unit to send to France. More changes in unit numbers were required once they arrived in France. The 71st Infantry Brigade joined ranks with the French 4th Army which supported the AEF Second Division, and included the 141st and 142nd regiments. As part of their training, the raw American recruits usually were integrated into French or British forces before going into battle. With Ed's unit, however, the 142nd bypassed the training and took positions near St. Etienne, only 100 yards from German lines. The Germans had retreated from the once "unconquerable" Hindenburg Line but were well entrenched.

Therefore, from October 2-13, the Germans were able to make a ferocious assault on the 142nd with massive attacks of artillery shelling, gas attacks, and the rapid firing of the deadly machine gun. But the 142nd fought their way to Hill 160 near St. Etienne, their immediate goal. The next night the badly wounded 142nd and 141st regiments reorganized. They had taken 1600 casualties in the two day fight. Two soldiers from the regiments were awarded the Congressional Medal of Honor for their courageous actions. Another award four men received was the Croix de Guerre from the French. Some others were given the "Church War Cross for Gallantry." (Note: The author was unable to find a reference to the origin for this latter award.)

The losses were significant, but more casualties would come on October 12 and 13, when the regiment fought again against a well -defended German site near the Aisne River. This time they wiped out the German salient south of the Aisne. It was during this campaign that the idea came to use Choctaws to communicate messages from one AEF unit to another. Some 18-20 Choctaws were identified as the Code Talkers, but Ed's name does not appear among them. It is possible that he did not know Choctaw and may not have been eligible to carry out this responsibility.

One version of the story reads like this:
"Within two days the 36th Division was engaged in a major battle attacking the Germans in the trenches, the Americans were unprotected crossing a wide stretch of land, except for heavy artillery fire as cover from the 142nd Infantry. The artillery fire kept the Germans pinned down, allowing the Americans to kill and/or capture the Germans in their own trenches.

"Noticing German communication lines lying in the open on the ground, the Americans felt that the lines had been left behind on purpose so they would be used and the messages could be intercepted. Messengers were sent out from one company to another, but one out of four of these messengers was captured by the German troops. The Germans knew the messengers were coming because they had decoded all transmitted messages up to this point in the war."

It was then that Col. A.W. Bloor, commander of the 142nd infantry Regiment, sent a memo to Headquarters with this discovery. He suggested that since his regiment had Indians who spoke 26 different languages or dialects, some of them should be selected to communicate with each other in their company using a chosen dialect. This idea was adopted and 18 Choctaw men from the 142nd who knew each other and two from the 143rd were trained, with one man placed in each company to provide the translating and sending and receiving that were needed.

This worked well with one exception. The Choctaw language did not have words for all the military terms necessary, so they used Choctaw words describing the military word. For example,

"Big Gun" meant "artillery" and "Little gun shoot fast" meant "machine gun."

Within 24 hours after the Code Talkers began their work, the Allies were successful in their attacks on the German line. The war was over in a month, but the success of the Choctaw Code Talkers established a precedent for the use of Native American speakers and their languages in World War II in the Pacific theater, with outstanding results.

As a result of this fighting, the two regiments suffered a loss of 70% of the officers and 57% of the enlisted men, either killed or wounded. Their service had been "magnificent," declared Maj. General William Smith, Commander of the 36th Division.

Mark Johnson is proud of his grandfather, Ed Johnson, even though he had four other "namesakes." He is especially proud of the fact that his grandfather, an American Indian, who had been deprived of citizenship until 1924, fought bravely for his country. This grandfather endured hardships such as marching long distances across France, being gassed and suffering the lifelong effects of the gas, and finally being wounded in the thigh.

Ed Johnson, a combat member of the 142nd Infantry Regiment, victim of a gunshot wound and poison gas as well as other American Indians who wore the AEF uniform in wartime, were finally granted the right to citizenship in the United States of America in 1924. (World War I Choctaw Indian Code Talkers). There were more than 12,000 American Indians, with 600 from Oklahoma, who served in World War I. The citizenship privileges were extended to all Indians, perhaps partially due to the valiant actions of their soldiers.

The official record naming Choctaw Code Talkers includes these from the 142nd Infantry Regiment: Billy Albert, Bob Mitchell, George E. Davenport, Joseph H. Davenport, James M. Edwards, Tobias W. Frazier, Benjamin W. Hampton, Noel Johnson, Otis Leader, Solomon B. Louis (Lewis), Jeff Nelson, Robert Taylor, Walter Veach, and Calvin (Cabin) Wilson. All are believed to have been from Oklahoma. From the 143rd Infantry Regiment the Code Talkers included Victor Brown and Joseph Oklahombi (Oklahambi). (Choctaw Code Talkers Association).

The shoulder patch of the 36th Division, Ed's original unit, displays a light blue Indian arrow head on a round khaki patch, superimposed with a dark khaki "T." It is sometimes called the "Lone Star" or the "Panther Division." Good names for the fearless men who served in the ranks of this division. The regimental crest depicts the ruined church tower of St. Etienne, France. (Texas Military Forever Regiment)

Ed died April 1, 1969, at the Veterans Administration Hospital in Oklahoma City, Oklahoma. He was buried in the Denison Cemetery in McCurtain County, Oklahoma. His life which started out with some mysteries proved him to be a man of courage and dedication to his country despite the denial of citizenship at the time.

AND THEN THERE WERE...

Clarence W.M. "Dinty" Moore, Warren County, Illinois, was called back into military duty before war was actually declared by Congress on April 6, 1917. Moore and other members of Company H, Sixth Illinois Regiment were sent to the Rock Island Arsenal for guard duty on March 26, 1917. The Arsenal was a large manufacturer of artillery carriages on which the gun and fire control equipment are mounted. The Arsenal also supplied auxiliary equipment. At this time the Americans were fearful of German sabotage, and such vital production facilities were placed under guard by National Guard units.

The Regiment, like many state regiments, was officially mustered into national service on April 10, 1917. It assembled at Springfield, Illinois before being transferred to Houston, Texas, where it became the 123rd Field Artillery assigned to the 33rd Division, originating with men mostly from the former Illinois State Guard. The last units of the Division arrived in France by June, 11, 1918, and were immediately dispatched to the Amiens sector to be trained by the English. The 33rd Division continued to serve in combat during the major battles of Verdun, St. Mihiel and Meuse-Argonne sectors.

The Division, bearing the nickname of "Prairie Division," received many medals. Its soldiers were awarded eight Congressional Medals of Honor and 134 Congressional Distinguished Service Crosses, plus nearly 100 medals from other nations. Sadly, these medals were achieved at the high cost of nearly 3,000 dead, 11,000 wounded and 156 taken prisoner by the time the war ended. Signing the Armistice did not mean an immediate home coming for the 33rd. Its members became part of the 250,000 soldiers assigned to the AOG in Rhineland Germany. Moore's story and photo were provided by Mary Reed, Gladstone, Illinois, a granddaughter of "Dinty."

MEMBER OF THE 88TH DIVISION ESCAPES THE FLU

Brian Sweeney, who came from south of St. Louis, Missouri, was one of the fortunate soldiers in the 88th division who escaped the symptoms of the influenza that afflicted one-third of the division. Brian was a member of the 339th Field Artillery which was sent to the
south of France for training upon arrival in that country on September 9, 1918, and did not rejoin the rest of the division until after the Armistice. So it is possible that the artillery unit missed most of the final action of the war. They were sent home and discharged in January, 1919.

COULD HE LIVE LIFE AS A "DEVIL DOG"?

Croix de Guerre medal with oak clusters awarded to members of the 5th and 6th Marine Regiments.

Cecil Archie Ireland

Le Fouregerre, also awarded, is worn over the left shoulder

Cecil Archie Ireland, age 18 when he signed up for the Marines on May 21, 1918, was choosing a life he thought might supply the excitement and adventure that many young men were looking for. The Marines were known as the toughest, roughest of the ranks and "no one messed with them." They were assigned to all parts of the world, making naval landings in "trouble spots" and in guarding the United States Embassies in foreign countries.

If this was what he sought, his first few months of battle in the Aisne sector, which came after victories at Belleau Wood and Chateau-Thierry, may have given him second thoughts. In the fiercest of the German attacks and counterattacks, he was gassed and perhaps otherwise wounded. As thorough as the Marine musters are, somehow these

details are missing. They record him being taken to the first hospital near the front lines, the SOS hospital, where he probably received triage treatment; and then was sent on to a base hospital, where a full line of specialists and methods of treatment were available. It appears he spent about three months here, so his wounding must have been serious. For the actions of the Fifth and Sixth Regiments, part of the Marine Fourth Brigade, the Marines received several of France's highest decorations: the Croix de Guerre with two oak leaves; and "le fourgerre", a braided cord of various colors which is worn wrapped around the left arm. More important though is that these awards are hereditary, meaning that all men of those two regiments even today are allowed to wear them on their dress uniform.

His grandson, the Rev. Bradford Bray, Blue Springs, Missouri, remembers his grandfather many times bleeding continuously from his ears and nose. Those are significant systems of a serious exposure to gas and may have been the cause of his death in 1953 at age 53. However, his condition either wasn't that serious or considered unusual enough for a medical discharge or disability pay for he spent almost five years in the Marines, re-enlisting about every two years. A few months after his first discharge in summer, 1919, the unit was deactivated in August, then re-activated in September.

Cecil didn't re-enlist until several months later. Perhaps he was unable to find or keep a job. His grandson recalls his grandfather working at gas stations, even managing one, after he completed his second tour of duty in 1922. He met Elsie Searcy and they were married on March 14, 1923. They had one child together, Betsie born in 1925, who was mother of Reverend Bradford.

The last information available about Cecil is from the 1940 census in which he reveals for the first time that he had one year of high school, and had worked for himself 98 hours the previous week at the service station which he owned.

This Marine, highly decorated, but suffering the physical effects of war wounds, had his ups and downs in both his military and private life. But the ups consisted of Excellent Character commendations and several promotions to Private First Class, and eventually owning his own service station. He died of an unstated cause and is buried in Floral Hills Cemetery in Kansas City, Missouri.

(In Volume I is the story of another young 6th Regiment Marine, Victor Candlin, who fought the earlier battles at Belleau Wood, Chateau-Thierry, and was wounded at Sommepye. He unfortunately died almost two weeks later of those wounds and is buried in Meuse-Argonne Cemetery.)

PERHAPS HIS POST CARD COLLECTION TELLS HIS STORY OF WAR

Among the AEF troops was a private whose vast collection of French and German post cards survives today, in the care of his great niece, Joyce Kuechler, Overland Park, Kansas. This collection remains intact despite his many changes of scenery in his fighting with the 354th Infantry, part of the famed 89th Division which participated in many major battles. After the war ended, the 89th was assigned to the 250,000 AEF soldiers who went into Germany to the guard the population and maintain order. He had enlisted October 4, 1917, from his home in Columbia, Missouri, and it would be nearly two years later before he would return. The AEF along with other Allied armies' presence assured that Germany was demilitarized and stripped of all means to launch another invasion of French territory.

This extra time in Germany allowed him time to collect post cards that reflected some of his harrowing experiences as an advanced scout for the 354th. The choices of some of his post cards and his cryptic comments seem to reveal his thoughts and activities. His great niece, Joyce Kuechler, tells her uncle's story.

Private Shannon Alvin Prather had served as an advanced scout with Company I in Belgium and France. Perhaps it was his many days of hunting back home in Missouri that made him especially skilled with the rifle. A scout worked alone or with one other man. They proceeded in advance of their units, reconnoitering potentially dangerous situations, such as machine gun nests and snipers hidden in tall trees.

Shannon Alvin Prather
All cards are Courtesy Joyce Keucher

It was often a lonely experience, one full of apprehension. He constantly had to be alert and cautious, ready for any possibility of danger. His comments on many cards reflected his feelings about those scouting experiences. Blunt and brief words often made up the entire message. At other times his words were ambiguous. The words may express his feelings of disillusionment with the war.

"This is three Huns in a wheat field in this picture. It is not a very pleasant feeling some distance in front of the troops, whith (sic) only three or four soldiers, fore (sic) I have been there myself."

Of one card Shannon wrote he knew how the four Germans hiding in a wheat field must have felt. "It is not a very pleasant feeling. I have been there myself." (Underlining his.) Other cards show devastated battle fields in the Argonne where he spent a month fighting and killing. Those memories he could not forget. A card of two doughboys walking down a road lined with denuded tree trunks, was identified by Shannon as the "Road to Montfaucon," where his division had fought a bloody battle with high casualties.

Soldier riding long barrel of Big Bertha, German's 2ⁿᵈ largest gun.

Montfaucon had been a fort for nearly 2000 years atop of the now almost denuded mountain, making any approach deadly. Its' importance as a military site dates back to Roman times, and must have been the scene of the deaths of thousands of warriors in the intervening years. (Mead)

"The battle field of the Argonn (sic) was awful, the 3rd Division spent almost one month and I will remember the time."

Another card of two soldiers crouching in a tree house fifty feet or higher and camouflaged by surrounding tree trunks, brought this comment: "This is the way we were put (on) outpost, day or night, to locate the enemy position." One wonders what he must have been feeling in a situation that made him almost helpless. On another card showing an anti-aircraft gun, Shannon inscribed: "Believe me, they (the guns) make it mighty hot for (enemy planes.)" A body lying on a muddy field was described simply, "A dead Englishman somewhere on the battle field."

A card depicting a lone German airplane was referred to as, "The bird that sailed around and droped (sic) the large bombs, on the enemy country." The famous Big Bertha gun was shown with a soldier sitting on top of the gun mounted on a train flat bed. The gun was so

"I well remember Montfakon(sic) for sure was a hot place, you can imagine that the way the trees look along side the road."

heavy that the only way it could be transported was on a train car. Shannon commented, "This is the largest gun the Germans had… the Huns shelled Paris some distance away. " (Note: Range of the Paris gun was 91 miles and Big Bertha abut 80 miles.)

Other cards depicted tanks blown up; piles of battered and discarded artillery; scenes of a victory parade in Paris after the Armistice; collapsed trenches; a German balloon that landed in some tree tops; and sandbagged dugouts where soldiers desperately sought shelter. It seems Shannon tried to find cards showing the dangerous parts of the war. Was this an effort at catharsis? Perhaps it was his way to rid himself of his intense feelings about the horror and wantonness of the mass slaughter he had encountered on the battle field.

"This is the way we would often be put out, on outpost for the day or night to locate the enemy position. "

But Shannon seemed to have also found people engaged in day-to-day activities of pre-war times. There were photos of beautiful structures not damaged by bombs or shells. Other cards showed European cities and elegant buildings he visited in Brussels and Boppard, both in Belgium. He was stationed in the hub city of

Koblenz, Germany, a beautiful picturesque medieval city. Koblenz is located in the southwestern part of Germany near the French border. Serene rivers glide through cities and countrysides, elegant hotels and sidewalk cafes exist. There is even a postcard of the American YMCA building in Brussels where he stayed.

Among the writing that survives, he made only one complaint and that was about the long march to Andernach in northern Germany, his last station where he arrived on March 9, 1919. His unit had marched 250 miles in less than 30 days. They trod over good roads in France; walked on battle scarred roads in Belgium; and tramped on the poorly maintained roads in Germany. Along the way they had a few days to rest, clean equipment, and replace worn out clothing. But for this 29-year-old soldier, the 250 mile journey was enough walking for a long time, and he said so emphatically on a post card.

He was discharged from the Army on August 25, 1919, and returned to Columbia, Missouri. He married his sweetheart and took a job with Wells Fargo in Columbia. He and his wife, Margie, had one daughter, who tragically was mentally ill and had to be hospitalized. She later died.

For his great niece, Joyce, and other relatives, the collection is priceless. It reveals almost one and a half years of their relative's life in The Great War. He lived to come home despite the dangers of his assignment as company scout. If he chose to talk about it, he could have. But, as with many other veterans, Shannon, avoided telling his family about his horrendous experiences in World War I.

Joyce has decided: What he could not discuss, the pictures on his post cards spoke for him.

"This is one of the tanks that was often used, they have machine guns insides and no damage can be done, except when a direct hit by a large shell. Then the cake is all dough."

Ruined farmhouse
(All photos above are courtesy of Joyce Kuecher and belonged to Shannon Prather.)

German soldiers looking at dead bodies, probably Russians as this was taken on the Eastern front
(Courtesy of Ghent Oertel Family)

German soldiers relaxing in front of medical aid station, somewhere on the Eastern Front. Arrow probably indicates his father who was a German army medic.
(Courtesy Ghent Oertel Family)

THE MEUSE ARGONNE — THE BATTLE THAT ENDED THE WAR

The first large battle in which only American soldiers were the main participants was at St. Mihiel. Although it engaged 550,000 combatants, along with tanks, airplanes and artillery, the fighting at St. Mihiel did not prepare the inexperienced AEF for the aggressiveness they would encounter in the Meuse-Argonne. The terrain was different, composed of heavily forested areas and rough uneven hilly ground. The goal was the city of Sedan, an important railroad hub. The Germans had occupied the area for four years and had masterfully prepared it with machine gun emplacements, heavy artillery, and ground positions favorable to their defense. The huge losses incurred at St. Mihiel would be vastly overshadowed by the following two campaigns at Meuse-Argonne and Verdun. Those campaigns challenged the ability of some inexperienced high ranking officers to make the serious decisions required, and some were not up to the task. They were quickly relieved of their command by General Pershing.

By late September, 1918, almost two million enthusiastic and inadequately trained American soldiers had reached camps in France. They were in various stages of training. The first group, now called the First Division, had accompanied General Pershing in May, 1917. Now they were veterans with a year of fighting at Cambrai, Belleau Wood, Aisne River and the Marne to their credit.

The morale of the latest group to step off the ships had not been deterred by the bleak newspaper reports of AEF losses, nor by losses suffered by other armies, friendly or enemy. The AEF soldiers were in that early stage of denial that anything could or would go wrong. Little did they realize that the German army at that time consisted of troops who were desperately staging a last ditch fight for their lives. However, a large number of other German soldiers were demoralized enough to allow themselves to be captured as a prisoners of war, and taken to camps where they would receive a decent meal with no more fighting expected from them.

There was a third group of other Germans, the Landstum of older men, who were retreating either under orders or of their own decision. The German Navy meantime had gone on strike and refused to take any further action in the war. (Gilbert) German morale was at its lowest in the war.

On September 26, 1918, the series of offensives began. There were 92 divisions of British, Belgian, French and AEF forces stretched across most of the Western Front. In the center of the sector, 15 American and 22 French Divisions were stationed. The sector was named for the Meuse River that flowed to the right, and the forest on the left that was deemed so thick as to be almost impenetrable.

The American troops were assigned to the lower part of the sector in what was to become a "slaughterhouse." On the opening day of the attack, all men were in position by 1:30 A.M. Two hours later a tremendous artillery barrage began, and at 5:30 A.M. soldiers from the 35th Division began an advance that captured three villages. Each day the 110th Engineers went forward, preparing more trenches and protection from the gas shells the Germans were firing. Fortunately, the weather had turned cold, which kept the gas close to the ground. The soldiers who knew this could avoid exposure and take control of more villages. Still, many were trapped in the woods and had to wear masks continuously. On October 3, the 109th Infantry relieved the weary 110th. By now the Germans were counterattacking and inflicting huge losses on the AEF.

Detected by German spotters in airplanes, the engineers and 128th Machine Gun Battalion were hard hit. It was here that Captain Harry Truman, commander of Battery D, sent his shells into another sector, the 28th, knocking out two batteries and disabling a third. He expected to be court martialed for firing out of his assigned sector, but his action had saved the 28th battery and the court martial was never brought up. (Lengel) In the German counterattack, many Americans lost their leaders due to gun fire. Leaderless, they were disoriented as to what to do next. Captain Ralph Truman, Harry's cousin, "waved his pistol and threatened to shoot anyone who tried to retreat." That worked, and the men were reorganized and sent back to their units. (Lengel)

Heavy barrages, unexpected counterattacks, and lack of knowledge of how to re-organize when the men had to fall back, briefly described the actions of the AEF from time to time. The ferocity of the fighting by the 109th at Apremont made that village's name known to the rest of the world. The 28th Division was relieved by the 82nd Division, having lost 168 men killed; 977 wounded; and 130 listed as missing. A total of about 1.2 million Americans fought in this action, taking losses of almost 18,000 troops in the three-week offensive. (Ellis, Wright)

These three weeks saw the heaviest loss of American lives in the war. The soldiers made mistakes in their enthusiastic fighting by using tactics which were doomed to fail. These included the previously well known almost "suicide charge" such as advancing with forewarned knowledge of well hidden German machine gun nests. This particular maneuver had resulted in huge fatalities for the entire four years of the war. But some obstinate officers never learned the futility of such a charge nor accepted what would be the cost in lives. General Pershing early recognized the mistake of the frontal charge and rarely ordered it.

Nevertheless, despite the strategic errors of the AEF, the Germans retreated in the largest numbers since the First Battle of the Marne in September, 1914. In addition, parts of the German navy mutinied on October 27, refusing to make a "final desperate attack on the British fleet." (Gilbert) The Germans were in trouble on land and on sea.

A unique aspect to the success at The First Marne in 1915 was General Foch commandeering all the Parisian taxi cabs available, more than 500, to move troops to bolster a besieged French division. The result was a badly needed victory for the Allies, halting the surging German advance on Paris. The action was repeated again as the French who, now using trucks, transferred men from the AEF's 35th Division held in reserve at St. Mihiel to the area of Grange-le-Conte. There, it is said, "the greatest battle in American military history, the battle of the Argonne Forest, commenced."(Pypes family history)

These troops saw the action first : First Army Corps; 28th Division of Pennsylvania National Guard; 77th Division, 35th; and 33rd Illinois Division. The troops considered "perhaps best troops of the AEF were held in reserve:" the 1st, 2nd, 3rd, 26th, 32nd, and 42nd. Later, the actions of the 77th, 78th, 79th, 80th, 82nd, 89th, 90th, and 91st Divisions deserved a special commendation from General Pershing after the war, for their bravery and heroism. (Pershing) Col. George C. Marshall planned and directed all the logistics, and much credit for the action's success goes to him. (Meuse-Argonne Offensive Overview)

The AEF faced German soldiers from the First Guard Division, considered the best among the German fighters; and the Second Landwehr, composed of experienced but older men 35 years or older. The Germans had established four defensive lines; the Hindenburg in two parts; the Kriemhilde Stellung; and the unfinished Freya Stellung.

The AEF's 69th Brigade led the attack with columns of brigades to join in. An advance of about three miles was made by day's end. On the second day the 60th Field Artillery Brigade was hindered by the deluge of rain which made progress minimal. They were unable to take their position due to the almost impassable muddy roads.

Day Three was cold with a fine mist. The 139th and 137th Infantries were in action most the time. They encountered fierce German machine gun fire and shelling by artillery, so the AEF could not achieve their objective of capturing and holding Montrebeau Woods.

Gassing was reported, and the men were ordered to fall back from Montrebeau Woods to where the 110th Engineer Regiment was quickly preparing defenses and trenches. It was noted that the weather had turned cold again which was a relief because it kept the gas down on the ground. Late that afternoon the 35th was relieved by the First Division, who found it necessary to wear gas masks making it difficult to see because the eyeglasses fogged up.

After a few days of rest, some divisions were reassigned until November 6. The 35th was assigned to the Second Army which was planning the next great offensive on Metz, France. But the signing of the Armistice fortunately put an end to those plans.

HOW AND WHEN DID THE BATTLE AND THE WAR COME TO AN END

Meanwhile the war was slowly coming to an end. The Bulgarians signed surrender terms in September. The British controlled the Belgian coast in September. A mutiny in the Austrian army took place on October 23. Although the Allies offensive in Italy on October 24 could not break the Austrian line of defense, finally the Austrians sought an Armistice to be effective November 4. The defeated troops continued retreating from the Piave with British planes bombing the long line of retreating soldiers. On October 26 the Turks talked of armistice. The German High Seas Fleet refused an order on October 27 to fight. There was a possibility that Roumania might not supply oil to Germany, who had only six week supply. Rumors, newspaper headlines, daily steadily pronounced an quick end to the war. Meanwhile, the Allies planned a November 14 assault into Lorraine and an offensive move to capture Metz starting November 12. They thought they could not afford to believe unfounded but hopeful rumors.

Those days became ones of confusion, mistakes, chaos and shortages. Lack of horses resulted in men being hitched to wagons of supplies to pull them to the front. German General Groener, after spending four days surveying the front, warned the Kaiser on November 6 that the armistice must be signed by the 9th, at the latest. "The fleet was in mutiny, revolution was imminent, and the Government's authority had fallen so low that troops would refuse to fire on the revolutionaries." (Gilbert)

On November 7, a misled newspaper correspondent wired the *San Diego Sun* that the armistice had been signed in Cuba. America went wild with joy and celebration. Then the reporter received a wire from Paris that it was all a mistake. Fighting continued. Patrols from the 42nd Division met stiff resistance as they entered villages across the river from Sedan. On November 8 the Kaiser heard news he had never expected to hear: "his beloved navy no longer would obey his orders." (Gilbert)

The Kaiser on November 10, with revolutionaries (Bolsheviks) holding nearby towns and blockading the roads, accepted the inevitable and abdicated, resigning himself to exile in nearby Holland.

He did not apprise himself of his losses which in the last 100 days of the Allied campaign, beginning in August, resulted in 363,000 Germans taken prisoner along with 6,400 artillery guns. The Kaiser, fearing the revolutionaries might attack his train, left by car and travelled the back roads to exile.

As for AEF losses in the Meuse-Argonne campaign, official reports showed 1,480 deaths; 6,001 wounded; 10,605 replacements; and 167 captured. Though not considered "excessive," they were sustained mostly in the one battle of the Argonne, where all units suffered heavy losses. Historians are still debating the cause of these losses. Was it due to poor leadership? Or was it lack of training and the inexperience of the men? There is no debating the gallantry of the Americans fighting there. They can rightfully be proud of their accomplishments, despite the controversies that have existed for years. (Pypes family) Many Congressional Medals of Honor were earned in these battles. The 89th received the most with nine medals of honor.

Gilbert quotes a conversation in his book:" One soldier asks another quizzically, 'What's an armistice, mate?'… 'Time to bury the dead,' replied another."And this was true for the Americans after the end of the Meuse-Argonne campaign.

BUILDER OF HOSPITALS

An Englishman, Herbert Costa, made the dangerous crossing of the English Channel back and forth to Ostend, Belgium, probably a hundred times during World War I. His job for the Allies was to design and construct desperately needed hospitals for wounded Allied soldiers. His story is related here by his granddaughter, Monique Lewis, Raymore, Missouri.

Mr. Costa had been trained as an architect and engineer in England. He was contracted by the Allies to go to Ostend and convert luxury hotels into hospitals. Ostend had famous beaches where years earlier Europe's royalty and wealthy citizens spent their summers. They had stayed in large beautiful hotels, which in wartime were ideal for converting into hospitals for wounded or sick soldiers.

The streets formerly were filled with luxurious carriages pulled by well bred horses. Now the streets swarmed with army trucks, and caissons and guns pulled by mules or horses. Throngs of soldiers, usually mud covered and filthy, replaced the handsomely dressed and fashionably attired society that used to stroll on the promenades. World War I changed the picture.

From Ostend the wounded were sent to England, or to "Blighty," the nickname used. The English Channel was packed with German U-boats located at the huge submarine base along the Kiel Canal in northern Germany. The British managed to drive the German soldiers out of Ostend and take over the city. Still there were the menacing U-boats patrolling the Channel. The swift British destroyers and small water craft provided a new type of protection for troopships carrying the wounded. Early in the war, the English ships had not devised this type of protection and consequently there were great losses of ships and men.

Costa and his builders completed the construction just as the hospitals in France were filled to capacity by the influenza epidemic. The flu reached epic proportions starting in September, 1918, when vast numbers of American soldiers landed in France. It peaked about December, 1918, as the numbers of infected troops began to drop.

Meanwhile, Monique's maternal grandparents operated a restaurant in a hotel in Tervuren, near Brussels in Flanders. Because her grandmother talked little about the German occupation of Belgium during World War I, Monique lacks any direct knowledge of what her grandmother's life was then. Somehow, grandmother, her mother and the rest of the family survived the food shortages, German brutality and deprivations caused by the occupation. This was when Monique's mother, Bertha, was a young girl and unmarried.

One day her mother met Herbert Costa's son, who was named after his father. He was 17 or 18 and occasionally accompanied his father on his trips to Ostend. Bertha and young Herbert were immediately attracted to each other, despite one obstacle. Herbert spoke no French or Flemish, and Bertha spoke no English. They quickly overcame that obstacle and proved that love had its own language. They were later married. Monique has an aging photograph of her father's English home.

The family had named it "The White House" after the mansion in the United States.

Fate intervened in the lives of Belgians when in 1940 German forces led by Hitler and the Nazis again invaded Belgium. This time the Costas, unable to endure another German occupation, packed up and left Belgium. Monique, her mother, and her sister fled to London. They thought they would be safer there. Then came the "Blitz," nine months of almost nightly German air raids on London. Monique's mother refused to go to an air raid shelter. One night during a bombing raid, the ceiling of their apartment fell in on them.

This changed her mother's mind, and the family decided London was no longer a safe place in which to live. They moved to the small town of Watford, located at the end of the underground (subway.) They managed to find a council house (low rental) and stayed there for a year until the Germans stopped the raids. Because of the housing shortage, they had to share the house with two other families. It was close living quarters, but at least they were safe from the bombing raids.

The Blitz lasted from September 7, 1940, to May, 1941. More than 28,000 Londoners were killed, with 25,000 wounded. The undaunted spirit of the English people is one to be admired. They endured the terrifying and deadly almost nightly bombings. Many of their houses were destroyed with all their belongings. Businesses, like houses, were burned to the ground. All the furnishings and sales stock were lost.

Every evening the English prepared to hear the noise of German bombers coming with their destructive bombs. They shared a common fear of having to spend the night again in an uncomfortable, crowded air raid shelter. Somehow, the English attitude of maintaining a "stiff upper lip," and the inspiring radio talks by Prime Minister Winston Churchill, carried the civilians through those perilous times.

During the years of peace before World War II, Monique's father had developed a successful factory. The factory made straight pins used for sewing which were sold all around the world. This ended when the Germans again in 1939 entered Belgium, which by international law was neutral and supposed to be free from invading forces.* The Germans confiscated the factory and converted it to make war products.

After the war ended in 1945, the factory still existed. One of Herbert's partners had kept it running. Herbert and his partner converted it back into a pin factory, operating it until they retired and sold the company in the late 1960s.

Life for civilians during this second occupation by the enemy also was difficult. Civilians again endured the scarcity of food, clothing and medicines. They lost their property and belongings when the Germans confiscated them. They were exposed to unannounced raids on their homes by the Germans. Hundreds, probably thousands, of atrocities have been documented. People living near battlefields often faced death or being wounded the same as the soldiers who fought there.

Sometimes the people were forced to evacuate their farms and homes. They packed up what few possessions they could carry on a cart or wagon, and moved to an unfamiliar town or village.

Often they had no friends or family in the new place. They became strangers in their own land.

Like most Belgian people, Monique's family, in their lifetime, experienced two great wars, just 20 years apart. Additionally, there was the threat of loss of life or injury from the Blitz in England. Despite all these almost unsurmountable difficulties, they struggled to survive. They triumphed over the tragedies of war.

They became the victors, not the conquered.

* (Note: Belgium had become an independent neutral nation in 1830 in a treaty signed by all the Great Powers of Europe, including Prussia. Along with other Germanic states, powerful Prussia was incorporated into a nation state called Germany in 1871. But just as the Germans had ignored international law and invaded Belgium in World War I, they again in 1940 violated Belgium's neutrality. This path was deemed a faster means to enter and conquer France. The Germans caused great damage to Belgian cities and towns and committed brutal acts and atrocities toward its civilians, even worse than in World War I.)

MEDICAL PROFESSIONALS RESPOND QUICKLY TO URGENT NEEDS OF AEF

The medical profession, months before the United States declared war on Germany, had determined that their help was going to be needed soon in Europe and began making plans for base hospitals. The Red Cross organized the first one in Philadelphia as early as October, 1916. A base hospital was a huge endeavor, almost a small town. It needed "beds, war furniture, touring-cars, motor-trucks, a complete x-ray plant, refrigerating and laundry equipment as well as all types of medical supplies." The cost then was $75,000 or in today's dollars about four million dollars. (Davidson)

The British requested five base hospitals in 1917 and within the year, the Red Cross managed to assemble and ship 17 more. Winter in France that year was severe with many troops dying of pneumonia and meningitis. There was a scarcity of doctors and nurses in France, as well as in the States where many sick troops also required care.

Letters from nurses who were overseas give a picture of the unexpected trials and experiences they endured: "We were the first groups of nurses that ever crossed these grounds...nothing was ready for us...There was no privacy (in the dormitory)... no water nearby, only rough wooden shelves and nails on which to hang their clothes... the shrapnel fell all around us and hit on the tin roofs like big hail."

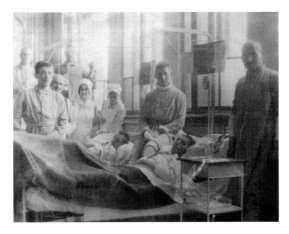 

Medical patients and press in Vienna and outside convalescing
(Courtesy Archives of NWWIMM)

The 200 beds of the hospital filled quickly and 2000 more were added. Huge numbers of wounded arrived on each train with a capacity of 600 soldiers. The letter continues: "We received the wounded from the battlefields about 12 hours after they were hurt, all in need of operation. This kept up for days; it just made my heart ache to see them coming in in such terrible condition… they lay for hours on the floor or on stretchers…so tired, hungry, sleeping or suffering, that they didn't care what happened to them…The first week of the big rush we worked eighteen or twenty hours a day. I would be in bed about three hours before I would be called again. I never felt tired, nor did I want to go to bed… We had an air raid every night… and two nights they were right over our heads…" (Davidson) Air raids on a hospital marked with the red cross were a violation of the international laws, but the Germans bombed hospitals and aid stations time after time.

During an infrequent lull in arrival of victims, the nurses provided services for French babies, such as bathing them and teaching hygienic methods to the mothers. They also administered to the tubercular, and explained good diets for old men. The next night they might be called to action, riding a truck to rescue wounded at Beauvais; or assisting with operations taking place in the dark using only flashlights for light.

The Red Cross also provided supplies of shoes, medical items, and tobacco to be distributed around the civilians in various countries. More than one million "pounds" of men's shoes were shipped to France, Roumania, and Serbia, while 150,000 pair of men's shoes went to Czecho-Slovak soldiers who were in Vladivostok, Siberia. Cigarette smoking was acceptable then and widespread especially among soldiers, so a shipment of 280,000,000 individual cigarettes made its way overseas every three months. Soap in the amount of 320 tons meant a lot of individual bars for soldiers, and 48 tons of slippers covered many feet.

Imagine how much cotton had to be raised in the United States to provide these medical supplies, including: 237 tons of bandages, 209 tons of absorbent cotton, 274 tons of sheeting, 32 tons of pillow cases, and 20 tons of towels. In addition, there were less common items consisting of 40 tons of yardsticks and 170 tons of surveyors' instruments. Image the surprise of troops in France opening boxes of chewing gum that weighed 63 tons total. In all, 13 countries were asked to make storage space for foodstuffs for civilians. Switzerland and Denmark had boxes earmarked for the Allied prisoners of war held in those countries. The American Red Cross joined with the Red Cross organizations in other countries, if there was one. The organization provided aid to:

ROUMANIA (Romania) – When this country made a separate peace with Germany, the organization was required to withdraw. Items left behind for distribution hopefully to the 2,000 earmarked people, were enough foods for three months, and large amounts of bandages, medicines, and clothing.

SERBIA – It was 1927 until the Red Cross was able to enter Serbia and that was on a long strip of land along the Greek border south of Monastir, Serbia, a scene of a large battle in 1915. The Bulgarians who had attacked the Serbians and defeated them, had stripped all of the food and livestock from the Serbs, leaving 50,000 people destitute and homeless. They were dependent upon charitable offerings. Seed and farming implements were sent to this once fertile area along with experts to assist in the planting. Hospital and dental equipment was sent to aid the Serbian prisoners in Bulgaria. In addition, there was a cash contribution of $50,000 to the Serbian Red Cross to enable it to regain its footing in the war torn country.

RUSSIA – This vast country was a large recipient of Red Cross aid which included an ambulance unit of 125 cars; 450,000 cans of condensed milk for 25,000 babies; clothing; food and the usual medical supplies. Even in the far northern region of Archangel, the Red Cross, helped by an AEF surgeon, set up and operated a 100 bed hospital. Russia which had by far the largest number of people in need, received much of the other kinds of aid also extended to all countries. But the difficulties in delivering the aid were the same as in Siberia.

SIBERIA – Just as it was difficult to extend aid to the scattered regions of Russia, so it was a hardship trying to send the aid needed for various groups such as the Czech-Slovak Army, especially the wounded who flooded Vladivostok and needed immediate medical care. Further challenges were caused by the number of different languages spoken, the lack of railroad transportation, the extremely cold temperatures, and the various forms of currencies the people used.

But the facts speak for themselves. Thousands of people in different parts of the globe were helped medically, economically, and morally, by the Red Cross and its international partners – who numbered in the thousands, and braved physical and mental hazards to supply help to the helpless. The peoples of the world generously financed these activities and they are to be thanked also. As terrible as the war was, without this help from those who wore the Red Cross armbands, the fate of thousands would have been unbearable.

PNEUMONIA CLAIMS AN EARLY VICTIM

Death by pneumonia was a commonplace event during World War I. This was especially true of servicemen who had been gassed or sick with the "Spanish flu." But neither condition explains the death of William Henry Waggoner, Jr., son of Mr. and Mrs. W.H. Waggoner of the Waggoner Milling Company in Independence, Missouri. He died on September 23, 1917.

The story of William Jr. dying is made more tragic because his mother had gone to the Chicago area to visit him where he was stationed in the United States Navy. Sadly, he became infected with the pneumonia microbe, and he died before she could reach the isolation camp where he was a patient. Mrs. Waggoner was visiting her daughter, Mrs. J.E. Fenn, in Chicago when she learned of her son's death. This information was sent by the Navy to Independence by telegram, and Mrs. Waggoner was informed by a telephone call from the Waggoner home.

She accompanied the body home by train. His was an early death in the war and by the war's end, about 500 men from Kansas City, Missouri, had died. Through the AEF, about 20,000 deaths resulted from pneumonia out of the 53,000 soldiers diagnosed with the disease.

Certificate from French Government honoring William Henry Waggoner's death from pneumonia while in the U.S. Navy
(Courtesy Bingham-Waggoner Historical Society; and the Kansas City Public Library Missouri Valley Special Collections)

William had worked in the paymaster's department at the Great Lakes Naval Training Station for six weeks, a position he had been well suited for in civilian life. Before he enlisted, he was vice-president of the historic milling company, the Waggoner-Gates, which his father had begun. William was 30 years old at his death, and the funeral was held at his parents' home on September 26, 1917. A certificate of merit signed by President Poincare of France hangs in the former Waggoner home, now called the Bingham-Waggoner Home.

The certificate is written in French but a simplified translation reads:
To the memory
of William Henry Waggoner
U.S. Navy
of the United States of America
who died for Liberty
during the Great War
Honored by France (Signed) President Poincare

P.S. The home and estate now has been voted "Best Historic Home Tour in the Midwest." The Victorian furnishings and décor of the house the Waggoners bought in 1879, bring life to that famous family who resided there until 1976. The house also once had artist George Caleb Bingham as a resident for six years until 1870. Still the certificate reminds the visitor of special memories and sacrifice the Waggoner family left behind.

THE ROLE OF A STRETCHER BEARER

Carrying wounded or dying men from the front lines or from "No Man's Land," even closer to an enemy sniper or machine gun nest, required a man to be strong of body and nerve.

Four stretcher bearers
(Public Domaine)

It was one of a soldier's most dangerous assignments. Bearers risked their lives every time when under fire they rescued a man. Usually two or four men were required to carry one casualty on a stretcher depending upon the condition of the field. But sometimes the fields were so muddy that even with six men, three on each side of the stretcher, their job was almost impossible.

Yet these men went out night after night across wet or dry ground, in bright moonlight or total darkness. Sometimes that darkness became like daylight when either side sent up flares or shelling continued. It was the bearers' task to find the man who had called "medic!" At times dogs were used to help locate the wounded, who might lie for hours or several days until help came. One story tells of a man who, shot in the chest, had to wait for 11 days before he was rescued. Another man with a broken thigh dragged himself backwards for two days to the safety of his trenches. (Spartacus Educational) Once the medics reached the injured man, they applied basic first aid and medication including morphine to relieve pain. Then began the jolting walking trip on a stretcher as the wounded man was carried back to the ambulance or horse drawn wagon.

Sometimes the pain from broken bones rubbing against each other was so severe, the agonized man went into shock. Shock could cause a premature death, and this was the dread of each bearer. Rescue work during daylight hours was done by using horses and buggies only in the most critical cases. Otherwise, because the wounded soldier often lay only a few hundred yards from the front lines or in "No Man's Land," he might suffer for hours from the agony of pain, injury, or thirst, often resulting in death.

Removal by horse drawn ambulance was done in most cases as the scarce automotive ambulances were expensive and hard to replace. The ambulances were used mostly at night and without any lights to avoid being spotted enemy snipers of overhead airplanes. There were many reports of stretcher bearers and their injured man being bombed deliberately by an enemy plane.

Although occasionally volunteers signed for this job, it was often filled by Conscientious Objectors, who chose this alternative to avoid being sent to prison for their beliefs. Stretcher bearers were not allowed to carry or use a gun. This is because they wore an armband with the Red Cross signifying their job was that of rescuing, not fighting. Also they were not assigned sentry duty and other jobs where they might be in danger and would need to use a gun. One journey with a stretcher could take as long as four hours to reach the aid station. One crew, the 109th Ambulance, reported 30 casualties – gassed, dead, and wounded, 30% out of the 100 men who were assigned to man the front line.

Nothing was cowardly about men who often struggled through ankle deep mud four or more hours to bring back just one soldier. It was not a pleasant sight for the bearers if the wounded man had lost limbs, had huge gaping holes in his body, or his face was half shot away. Sometimes only parts of the body remained as a result of shelling, and the graves registration squad had the job of bringing back these body parts.

Being a stretcher bearer required stamina, a strong stomach, and compassion for a fellow soldier who was severely wounded or dying. Many soldiers rescued by these men considered the bearers to be the real heroes of the front lines.

MAIL CARRIER TO MEDIC

In civilian life John Meade Hunter served as a rural mail carrier before and after the Great War. He probably wore the traditional postal uniform of the times or even just ordinary civilian clothes. Certainly nothing fancy or classy looking.

But once he became an American soldier, he was issued a distinguished looking uniform. In addition to the Army's regulation khaki breeches and shirt, John wore a cape with a special collar insignia designed for the medical corps. Called a "caduceus," the insignia is a round piece of brass

Caduceus insignia
(Public Domaine)

embossed with a staff on which two snakes are entwined. On the top of the staff is a pair of wings. Earlier in life John had wanted to be a doctor and would have worn such an insignia on his doctor's traditional white coat.

He probably was puzzled about his duties with the 88th Division. Would he be an engineer or a medic? He quickly learned the Medical Depot designation indicated he would be a medic riding trains carrying ammunition, an inviting target for enemy artillery. His job was potentially a dangerous one.

There was always the chance that German pilots, when spotting the trains, would drop bombs by hand over the side of their planes. Though this method was extremely inaccurate, there were times if the target was big enough, or the pilot was lucky, one or more bombs would find their target. Terrible injuries, even deaths, often resulted from the exploding ammunition. Medics were needed immediately to help the wounded.

Each division had its own railroad medics assigned to accompany loaded trains when they left ammunition dumps. This was also true with truck companies transporting the same dangerous material for artillery and or machine guns. John's primary job as a medic was to administer aid to any soldier wounded while working or in combat, or personnel on the train. John even occasionally had to assist with removal of the dead.

For a period of three or four weeks, beginning August 6, 1918, when John began his departure from training camp to an overseas assignment, he kept a small red leather covered diary in which he wrote daily. His first entry concerned his orders to join the 313th Engineers Medical Depot at Camp Mills, Long Island, New York. His unit rode the train day and night to meet their arrival time in New York scheduled for August 13, 1918. The diary and other souvenirs belong to his daughter, Marion Shippee, Kansas City, Missouri. This is the story as she knows it.

That first entry said the journey by train was expected to take one week. During the trip, John kept careful notes of every town the train passed through. In Dubuque, Iowa, the train's first stop, the Red Cross met them with ice cream, candy, and "smokes," the customary way the Red Cross regularly welcomed troops in transit to France.

Sometimes, as in Detroit, John wrote, they stopped at the train station and "took exercise," probably calisthenics to relax their bodies from sitting on the train for hours at a time. There again, Red Cross volunteers served refreshments. "Good people," John wrote, but he didn't specify what the refreshments were. Perhaps not noteworthy enough compared to Dubuque's ice cream.

On Friday they arrived several days early at Camp Mills near New York City. The camp was the large embarkation port to which thousands of AEF soldiers were sent. There he discovered, to his dismay, that they were to be quartered in tents. Greatly disappointed, he didn't want to share a tent with 19 other men, after several nights of sleeping on the train with other soldiers. However, he soon was to become accustomed to having multiple tent mates during the rest of the war. That night he and other soldiers went to New York's Coney Island, found some girls, and had "eats with them."

He had been issued a new uniform and "didn't like the suit, but guess it will do," he commented in his diary. He spent the last night at camp all alone. He doesn't say where his buddies went or why he failed to go along. The next day, en route to his ship, he saw many troop ships in New York City harbor. John didn't record what his feelings in his diary. Was he anxious? worried? excited? Probably all these thoughts were running through his head, as well as the heads of the several thousand soldiers boarding the ship.

HMHS Plassy was the name of the ship (as John spelled it), and he wrote, "It was one hell of a fine ship." Was this praise, or was it sarcasm? They were sleeping on bunks in crowded quarters, with August heat warming the below deck to uncomfortable temperatures, relieved only when they were allowed on deck. Crossing the Atlantic he saw whales and smaller fish. On August 21, he noted that "Jack Smith made me put on my life {belt}," not just for the frequently practiced lifeboat drills, but anytime a sub was spotted. Lookouts were always alert to a hidden pack of German submarines, and all portholes were covered at night to block any lights that might betray the presence of their ship.

Ships carrying American soldiers were carefully guarded by escorts of destroyers and other swift craft. These ships were rigged to drop depth charges and did not hesitate to do so. Although official records report that no AEF soldiers were lost at sea to the German subs, on February 5, 1918, submarines torpedoed and sank the steamship *SS Tuscania* with a loss over more than AEF 200 soldiers. This was only a few miles off the Irish coast. (Gilbert) There is a beautiful memorial there to mark the loss.

Soon there was a drastic reduction in the sinking of ships by U-boats, whether the ships were military or passenger, an Allied country or neutral. The name, U-boats, as noted elsewhere, originated from the German word "unterseeboot," meaning an underwater boat. After the United States declared war on the Central Powers, American ships with their numerous destroyers and sub chasers also protected Allied merchant ships as well as troop transports.

Losses dropped to 5% per month average, from the incredibly high destruction rate of 95% in losses earlier in the war. There were a total sinking of 16 hospital ships during the war, the most recent one being the *HMHS Llandovery Castle* with a loss of about one hundred lives. This was an inexcusable illegal action because the ship was clearly marked as a Red Cross vessel. (Gilbert)

It was three weeks after leaving Camp Dodge, Iowa, when the *HMHS Plassy* finally landed in Liverpool, England, on August 28. After unloading, John wrote, they marched to "Knot ash (illegible) Queen Rd." It was at these facilities that he had his first bath since leaving Iowa. He mentioned having seen both Ireland and Scotland, so it was possible their ship had to detour from its usual route to avoid submarines. John commented about young people he saw. There were many girls, but to him, they all seemed to have their teeth out. About England, he wrote,"Poor England she looks very bad." Sleeping in a tent again that night, and on subsequent nights, he usually had 19 assigned roommates, regardless of the size of the tent.

The next day he shaved and washed and "entrained at Nott…. ash." He listed about a dozen towns the train passed through. John showed a great curiosity in what he observed, jotting it down

Post cards of church and of village with hand written notations; temporary grave of Lt. Quentin Roosevelt, fourth son of former President Theodore Roosevelt. The son was buried where his plane was shot down.
(Courtesy Marion Shippee)

in his little red diary. All along the train route, the English came out to greet them. He wrote that the English Channel "is some fine riding, a little rough." They departed from a harbor across which a submarine net was stretched. They arrived at France late that evening, staying on board until the next morning. Then they marched to Rest Camp No. 1 at the port town of LeHavre. "My first French town," he remarked. "Had drinks in town, then were loaded into box cars in groups of 24 men."

On September 2, they reached Les Saumes, (his spelling), staying again in tents. The next day the men were billeted in a barn at Villa des Fleurs (rest of address is blurred.) "Had lots of wine," so a crowded barn may not have seemed too unpleasant that night. The next day, September 4, is his last entry. "Walked ¾ mile, 16 men were put in a store room to sleep on the floor. Not too bad." Perhaps he had become used to makeshift quarters and numerous roommates. He took a hike the next day and saw a monument of Napoleon and some marker that was established in 1715. John wrote that the inscription was for Rousseau, (a famous French philosopher during the Enlightenment.)

John appeared to have a good foundation of general knowledge; perhaps he was self-taught or had read many books. He was observant, knew some history, and his spelling was nearly always accurate, even names of foreign towns. His unit ended in the Alsace-Lorraine sector, which the French in 1918, assisted by the Americans, recovered from the Germans. This valuable coal area, which for centuries had belonged to France, and then was lost to Germany in 1870 in the Franco-Prussian war, became a French province again.

Since the Franco-Prussian war of 1870, for 35 years the province had been occupied by the Germans, as one of the prize spoils of the German victory. It was a rich industrialized region in addition to the vast quantities of coal, and the loss of the town of Sedan was a national disgrace.

Frenchmen cringed or became angry at the mention of "Sedan," and though they often denied it, the recovery of Alsace-Lorraine had become a chief objective of the French army in World War I.

Once the Armistice was signed, and he was granted leave time, John took advantage of being stationed in Europe for several more months and traveled extensively, including Italy.

Among the keepsakes his daughter has are a bar receipt from "restaurant Maginta" (his spelling) and a guide book to Nice, France. He also accumulated many post cards of his travels to Belfort, France; Monte Carlo; and Bordighero, Italy. On January 8, 1919, his pay record showed that he received a bonus of $60.00. Monthly pay for a private started at $30.00, so he had the money he needed for travelling.

Most cards had no writing on them, and only two had messages sent to his family. John kept the others as a private collection which was passed down to his daughter. One card to his mother told her the place "is beautiful," and he wished she could see it. The other one was to his father, saying that he, John, had hiked 12 miles that day. Some cards were the usual photos saved by the Americans, but John also collected some unusual ones. A card printed on photography paper shows two men in baseball uniforms and caps, crouching in position waiting for a ball to be thrown. A card with a touch of poignancy shows the original wooden cross on 1st Lt. Quentin Roosevelt's grave. Quentin, one of the sons of former President Theodore Roosevelt, had been shot down in his airplane in July, 1918. His body remained buried on French soil among his fellow airmen until World War II when his brother, Theodore, Jr. was killed. Quentin's body was then moved to lie by his brother in Normandy.

On another card of a small town of Marson, John put an X indicating the upper window of the house where "I sleep, eat and wash ?" (Note: He added the ?) Another card from the same village shows the upper part of the street where several civilians stand. One woman has an X on her skirt with the explanation she sold him the cards. A small child sits atop a pillar and several hay wagons line the dirt street, named the "Grand rue."

Finally, one card with Kaiser Wilhelm astride a prancing horse in a German city square bears this message from John: "This was the way the statue looked before the Armistice was signed." It is from the French city of Metz, which was planned to be the site of the Allies' next campaign had the Armistice not been signed.

At some time in his life, Marion says, her father changed the order of his name from John Mead Hunter to Mead John Hunter. He said there were too many men named "John." But both cards sent to his parents are signed "John." He was born in 1890 in Bowling Green, Missouri, and enlisted in May, 1918, a month after the United States declared war on Germany. He was 27 years old and single.

John died at age 55 and was buried in Bowling Green. Because he had fought in areas often gassed by the Germans, it is possible he had been exposed to gas. Many soldiers' discharge papers did not mention "being gassed," even though it is noted in medical or other military records.

Because doctors did not yet know the long term effects of being exposed to gas, they often assumed if the soldier lived, he had not been seriously harmed. This was a false assumption, as many soldiers developed asthma or other lung and breathing diseases.

There is one more intriguing entry midway in his little red book. It is a list of medical terms entitled, "Symptoms of a Fracture" and "Reasons for applying a splint." These entries must have been from the medical training he had received in his assignment as a medic. But for whatever reasons after his discharge, perhaps even financial, he decided to abandon, once and for all, his dream of becoming a doctor.

Marion does not recall her father talking about having an unfulfilled career. Perhaps carrying mail suited his needs, both financially and intellectually. Possibly in the war he had seen enough damaged bodies in need of medical care to satisfy him for a lifetime. Carrying mail and visiting with his customers may have been a good alternative and satisfied him.

According to his daughter, he led a pleasant life, but never talked about the war.

AMERICAN RED CROSS PROVIDES WORLD WIDE HELP DURING WAR

Americans supported their Red Cross organization with an unbelievable outpouring of money and millions of hours of service. The volunteering hours of eight million women, and donations of $400,000,000 in cash (in 1919 dollars which in today's money would be $91 billion) were just the beginning of American aid. The paid membership of 17,000,000 was the highest number to date. In addition, nine million school children in the Junior Red Cross joined in the effort to stand behind their soldiers.(Davis)

Red Cross services were rendered not only to American servicemen in France, but to French civilians as well as French soldiers. The numerous services included first aid training, hospital and convalescent home visits, distribution of clothing and comfort articles. In the U.S. Red Cross workers helped American people find jobs suitable to their needs; moved families to better housing; furnished legal advice; and helped with insurance forms and delayed or missing military allowances. One especially welcomed service was to assist in finding information about a soldier the family thought might be missing or dead.

The Bureau of Medical Service organized 47 ambulance companies to serve in France, and organized and equipped 50 base hospitals which they transferred to the military medical

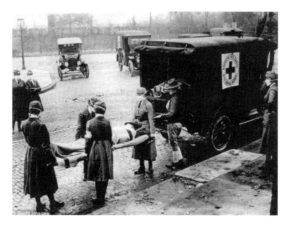

American Red Cross workers in London transferring influenza cases (note their masks) to a hospital.
(from "The American Red Cross in the Great War.")

Salvation Army women did not let German bombing stop their making of doughnuts for soldiers.
(From The American Red Cross in the Great War)

departments. In New York City an institute for the treatment of crippled veterans was established, where it rehabilitated hundreds of men. Other areas of concern addressed were sanitary conditions at the building of cantonments and other military housing; and establishing more than 700 canteens staffed with 55,000 volunteer canteen workers. (Davis) These women often met troop trains at railway stations and offered refreshments and smiles. The soldiers were being transported from camp to camp or more often, to the east coast where they would board ships to France. Letters exist in which the soldiers comment on the quality or quantity of refreshments. Ice cream was usually the most popular.

Perhaps the largest and most important of all their services was in the area of nursing. The calls for nurses recruited more than 30,000 registered nurses. These nurses had to meet high standards of professionalism and training, and their services were extended to counties other than France, including Russia, Great Britain, Roumania, Serbia, Belgium, Italy, Palestine, Switzerland, Greece and others. Their work was divided between soldiers and civilians.(Ellis)

Perhaps one of the best known posters of World War I was the smiling face of the Red Cross Nurse with the red badge blazing on her left arm. Of the 19,877 nurses who served overseas, 198 died in giving that service. (Sasse)

The Red Cross organization in England had begun before the Great War started and was active in 23 Territorial Hospitals in Great Britain. The women workers were called Voluntary Aid Detachments (VAD) and were not required to have completed full training as nurses. Usually a staff of 90 VADs were required to provide the assistance necessary per hospital. (Billington)

Equally interesting was the formation of the St. John Ambulance Association which required special training of all the stretcher bearers, orderlies and nurses. The name comes from a phrase in a message to the Knights of St. John of encouragement at the time of the Crusaders. The St. John personnel were trained to handle combat cases as well as those of civilians in distress. Sometimes the situation might be an extremely serious civilian disaster such as when an ammunition factory

American Red Cross photos: Bathing and Disinfecting Plant in England (From "The American Red Cross in the Great War")

At work in the laboratory of a British Base Hospital (from "The American Red Cross in the Great War")

exploded killing several hundred workers. Or the Gretna Green train collision in Scotland when nearly 300 soldiers died on their way to the front. The St. John Ambulances members gained widespread recognition with their work in the South African War.(Military History Forum)

Emergencies created innovative ways to solve problems. One problem was the massive number of wounded from Egypt and South Africa coming to St. Thomas's Hospital in London and how to get the huge numbers of ambulances through London's crowded streets. The solution: build a railway extension that ran into the middle of the hospital. Some trains were specially built to enable men on stretchers to be boarded without severe straining by orderlies in lifting them through windows on the train, or causing more pain to the injured.

Meanwhile, back in America hundreds of thousands of knitting needles were clicking as their owners knit enough socks, mufflers, wristlets or sweaters to fill barrels for their loved ones in France. These items knitted with love in every stitch could not begin to compare to the hundreds of thousands of clothing that were distributed among the 1,726 ,354 refugees from France, Roumania, Russia, the Balkans, Palestine, and Siberia.

The figures of aid extended generously would look like a large corporation's accounting, with foodstuffs valued at nearly ten million dollars; blankets at $3.5 million; hospital supplies, more than one million dollars; and motor vehicles and machines costing more than two million dollars. The total value shipped overseas by February, 1919 amounted to more than 31 million dollars. Without such aid, the refugees would have succumbed to disease including large number of tuberculosis cases and starvation.

Nearly 90,000 French families were recipients of aid in all forms including cash. For many their homes, farms, and way of life had been destroyed. In addition, the Red Cross cooperated with the military in operating 24 hospitals with 91,356 patients admitted. Only a small percentage, 1,457 died. Fifteen carloads of surgical dressings and front line packages were sent to the front on one day alone. That was when the St. Mihiel offensive began.

Children at school knitting socks for soldiers in a Red Cross program. Non-English speaking soldiers learn rudiments of English in classes taught by Red Cross volunteers.
(Courtesy of "The American Red Cross in the Great War")

Y.M.C.A. hut in one of the camps.
(Courtesy of "The American Red Cross in the Great War")

Other supplies such as oxygen and nitrous oxide in the millions of gallons reached the hospitals. At that time nitrous oxide had begun to be used on patients too weak to use ether. For severely disfigured soldiers, 94 portrait masks were made; and 2,284 artificial limb apparatus were distributed to the 39,000 men who were instructed in the use of them. This is the first time in war that modern surgery and invention of prostheses had been available to the wounded veteran. There were an estimated 600,000 French disabled soldiers alone; no numbers are accurate on veterans of all other nations involved in the war.

The Red Cross was known in America for the quantity and quality of its canteens, and this was true in France. At the railroad lines connecting main cities, there were 75 canteens for American and Allied soldiers traveling to other bases. Included in the services were facilities for bathing, food, sleeping, and refreshments. More than 2.3 million meals were served at a nominal charge. All other services were at no cost to the serviceman.

Another service, unknown to most Americans, was the grave photography work done solely by the Red Cross. If the grave was distinguishable enough, it was photographed and the picture sent home to the family. Most bodies were buried temporarily until some years later when the United States established official cemeteries in which to bury the bodies of their soldiers. It must have been a relief for the family to see the grave, however, crudely made, and to know their son or husband had his own identified burial place. Unfortunately there were about 3,000,000 bodies unidentified and buried without a name on the headstone.

To partially remedy this, beautiful chapels bear the names of the unknown engraved in gold on their walls. An especially impressive burial place exists at Yenin Gate, Ypres, Belgium, where more than unknown 54,000 men of the British Dominion are honored with their names carved onto the walls.

The work of the Red Cross was organized, efficient, swift to answer, and compassionate to friend or foe alike. Its work in World War I set a model for future volunteer organizations to meet and exceed.

AN ESSENTIAL ORGANIZATION — MORE ABOUT THE RED CROSS IN WORLD WAR I

Before World War I the Red Cross was an active voluntary group whose mission was to provide general relief services to civilians. With the onset of the War, however, its mission changed to make professional nursing care available on a vast scale for the wounded in battles. With help from the Red Cross, the number of doctors, nurses, and medics quickly increased by more than 400%.

The United States declared war in April, 1917, and the need for trained medical personnel was critical. There were only 750 officers, 393 nurses, and 6,619 enlisted men in the Medical Department of the military. However, the call for qualified persons was quickly answered, so that by the end of the war, those numbers had multiplied exponentially. There were 39,363 officers, 21,344 nurses and 245,652 trained enlisted men available in Europe to assist the 755,354 soldiers of many nationalities being treated in French hospitals. (Sasse) In the United States nearly 1.5 million military patients required medical care.

The Red Cross symbol, when worn on an armband or painted on the top of a hospital, building, train or ship, is recognized worldwide as designating a medic or health worker, or a place where wounded soldiers and civilians are being treated. Its display requires that the safety of inhabitants be honored and they may not harmed by military means.

Unfortunately this has not always the case. One of the greatest tragedies of World War I occurred when a hospital ship, the *HMHS Llandovery Castle*, was torpedoed and sunk on June 27, 1918. Its decks had been clearly marked with huge Red Cross symbols and the sides brightly lighted, but the Germans chose to ignore the ship's markings. The submarine torpedoed the ship which began to sink immediately, leaving its 258 passengers and crew in great peril.

Showing calmness, all the passengers abandoned the ship. However, many were not able to get into lifeboats and helplessly clung to bits of floating wreckage. The captain's boat rescued eleven persons from the water just as the U-boat emerged. The German officer on the U-boat ordered the captain to stop rescuing the drowning and to come over to the U-boat. Those who disobeyed his orders were shot at. The captain of the *HMHS Llandovery Castle* was taken on board and treated roughly while questioned about the eight American flying officers supposedly on board.

After other Canadian ship officers were questioned and released, the submarine attempted to ram the lifeboat but missed. A nightmarish period of 36 hours followed until the survivors were rescued 41 miles from the Irish coast by a torpedo-boat destroyer. Only one lifeboat survived, the other life boats having been fired upon by the submarine crew. The surviving lifeboat sailed or rowed over 70 miles to safety.

At least 14 nursing sisters died in the sinking and nearly 40 of the crew were lost to the disaster. It was believed by the 24 survivors, that after sinking the ship, the Germans wanted to destroy all survivors as witnesses to any evidence of torpedoing. Their actions were in clear violation of international shipping rules. (Sinking of the Llandovery Castle.)

ORGANIZING MEDICAL CARE FOR OVERSEAS

Hospital No. 4 was the first to leave the States on May 17, 1917, followed by five others requested by the British Medical Service. In the following seven months, 17 other base hospitals speedily embarked for France. The winter of 1917 was the most severe in many years, resulting in the deaths of many soldiers from pneumonia and meningitis. Nurses and doctors were scarce. This situation was true also in the States, so medical personnel were sent in small numbers as quickly as possible to the training camps and cantonments across the United States, where there were desperately sick soldiers.

Stories and letters survive from nurses who were overseas. For most of them, this was their first experience with battle wounds, and the sounds, sights and smells of the fighting. One army nurse wrote: "… we were the first groups of nurses that ever crossed these grounds… nothing was ready for us… we were not expected so soon." With typical efficiency the nurses readied their own barracks, then toured the hospital which occupied 62 acres. It had 32 wards with the building of more in progress. "…the first impression was daunting…" of the dormitory where she and 50 other nurses were to be housed. "There was no privacy… no water nearby, only rough wooden shelves and nails on which to hang their clothes right over our heads; the shrapnel fell all around us and hit on the tin roofs like big hail."(Davison)

Although the hospital contained 200 beds, this was soon proved to be inadequate, and the building of an additional 2000 more was ordered. Another nurse recorded this description upon receiving massive numbers of the wounded on trains (each train could carry up to 600 casualties) from an unnamed battle front:
"We received the wounded from the battlefields about 12 hours after they were hurt, all in need of operations. This kept up for days; it just made my heart ache to see them coming in in such terrible condition…they lay for hours on the floor or on stretchers for hours…" "so tired, hungry, sleeping, or suffering that they didn't care what happened to them."(Davison)

During an infrequent lull in the arrival of victims, the nurses provided services for French babies, such as bathing them and teaching hygienic methods to the mothers. They also administered to the tubercular, and explained what food was good for the health of elderly men. The next night they might be called to action, riding a truck to rescue wounded at Beauvais; or assisting with operations which took place in the dark using only flashlights for light. (Davison)

The Red Cross also provided supplies of shoes, medical items, and tobacco to be distributed among the civilians in various countries. More than one million "pounds" of men's shoes were shipped to France, Roumania, and Serbia, while 150,000 pairs of men's shoes went to Czech soldiers who were in Vladivostok. Cigarette smoking was acceptable then and widespread, especially among soldiers, so a shipment of 280,000,000 individual cigarettes made its way overseas every three months. Soap in the amount of 320 tons meant a lot of individual bars and clean soldiers; and 48 tons of slippers covered many feet.(Barker)

Imagine the amount of cotton that must be raised in the United States to provide these medical supplies: 237 tons of bandages, 209 tons of absorbent cotton, 274 tons of sheeting, 32 tons of pillow cases, and 20 tons of towels.In addition there were less common items such as 40 tons of yardsticks and 170 tons of surveyors' instruments. On top of all of this, there were boxes of chewing gum that weighed 63 tons. In all, 13 countries were asked to make storage space for foodstuffs for civilians. Switzerland and Denmark had boxes earmarked for the Allied prisoners of war held in those countries.(Barker)

The American Red Cross joined with the International Red Cross organization to furnish these items:

Roumania (Romania) – When this country made a separate peace with Germany, the organization was required to withdraw. Items left behind for distribution, hopefully to the 2,000 persons earmarked, included enough foods for three months, and large amounts of bandages, medicines and clothing.

Serbia – It was not until 1917 when the Red Cross was able to enter Serbia. The only part they could occupy was a long strip of land along the Greek border south of Monastir, scene of a large battle in 1915. The Bulgarians had stripped the land of all foods and livestock, leaving 50,000 Serbians destitute, homeless and dependent upon charitable offerings. Seed and farming implements were supplied to this once fertile area, along with experts to assist in the planting. Hospital and dental equipment aided the Serbian Army, and Serbian prisoners in Bulgaria received supplies also. In addition, there was a cash contribution of $50,000 to the Serbian Red Cross to enable it to re-establish itself in the war torn country.

Russia – This country was a large recipient of Red Cross aid which included an ambulance unit of 125 cars; 450,000 cans of condensed milk for 25,000 babies, clothing, food and the usual medical supplies. Even in the far northern region of Archangel, the Red Cross, helped by an AEF surgeon, set up and operated a 100 bed hospital. The Russians, by far the largest number of people in need, received much of the other kinds of aid extended to all countries. But the difficulties in delivering the aid to the scattered regions of Russia delayed much help that was desperately needed. Also the fighting created by the Civil War hindered the distribution of personnel services and other aids.

Siberia – Just as it was difficult to extend aid in Russia, it was equally challenging to send the aid needed to such various groups as the Czech-Slovak troops. Especially desperate were the wounded who flooded Vladivostok needing immediate medical care. Further obstacles included understanding the multiple languages spoken, the lack of railroad transportation, the extremely cold temperatures, and the various forms of currencies used by the people.

About the only criticism voiced by writers of the various books the author consulted, was about the Red Cross lack of advance planning to handle the large numbers of prisoners of war who were released by the Germans when the Armistice was signed. Hordes of ragged, ill, half-starved and diseased prisoners were released with no transportation to their homes or any means for them to obtain the food and medical care they needed at the time. The Red Cross was overwhelmed when thousands of the former POWs reached the French borders. Still, acting as quickly as they could, they set up canteens and provided medical care, either on site or in Paris.

Another handicap faced by the organization was the secrecy of the negotiations with the Germans for surrendering that began in October, allowing little time for the Red Cross to prepare properly for the aftermath of the end of fighting. (Harrison)

However, the United States had done some advance planning for the return of thousands of injured soldiers after the war, and established treatment and rehabilitation centers for five forms of disability: 1) Surgical including loss of one or more limbs 2) Blindness 3) Shell-shock including the various phases of "psychoneuorsis 4) Tuberculosis and 5) Deafness. (Davison) One can say though, that treatment for what we now call PTSD was generally primitive and limited in effectiveness.

The World War I stretched the limits of the International branches of the Red Cross and provided its greatest challenge to that date. It had been founded by a nurse, Clara Barton, to assist with the medical needs of soldiers in the American Civil War, about half a century before. She personally participated in three more wars in her working lifetime. They were the Franco-German War of 1870-71; the Second Boer War of 1899-1902; and the Spanish-American War of 1916.

Today, the Red Cross, with its many International branches, is one of the most active worldwide organizations providing help in all kinds of disasters to any country in need. But in World War I, without the help of the Red Cross, the Salvation Army, the YMCA, and other charitable groups, the lives of many soldiers and civilians would have been ones of an unnecessary tragedy.

FROM VETERANS TO VOLUNTEERS

The life of Harold Herman Hall resembles in so many ways that of his father-in-law, Kenny Tebow, that with one exception, the two lives could be carbon copies. The exception is in which areas of the world they served their country in war. Kenny signed up on August, 1918, for the army but never served overseas, because the war ended three months later, and he was discharged soon after on February 4, 1919. Harold, however, enlisted a generation later in World War II and fought in the Pacific theater for two years. This story is told by Harold Hall. So where does the resemblance lie? In addition to both of them serving their country, it is in how they lived their lives after being discharged from the services. This is how Harold, the son-in-law, tells their story.

Kenny, the father-in-law, was an excellent musician with a fine tenor voice. The army asked him to establish a band for his military unit, as every unit needed to have its own band. Kenny came from a musical family of four siblings. One brother played a trombone, another the trumpet, and the third brother, a violin. Their sister, Mary Ellen, who later became Harold's wife, played the organ, violin, and piano. The family lived in Maryville, Missouri, when the children were growing up ,and to add to the finances and the family enjoyment, they offered room and board to music students from the nearby teachers' college. "It was a fine orchestra they had at times," Harold recalls, "especially when there was a boarder who played the harp."

Harold Hall, volunteer for National World War I Museum and Memorial.
(Photo by author)

Harold almost missed his chance to become a member of the Tebow family. But not being "a nervous man," he claims, he took the necessary action to make Mary Ellen his bride. His physique belies his spirit, for Harold is 5 feet 7 inches if he stretches, and 120 pounds if soaking wet.

It seems the oldest Tebow son had invited Harold over to sing in the family's Sunday afternoon musical program and he accepted. He wanted to see Mary Ellen, but she was out of town. Not being bashful, he made up for missing Mary Ellen at the concert by telephoning and asking her to go to a movie. That was the beginning of 65 years of a happy relationship.

Kenny was pleased with his new son-in-law. One day after seeing a pencil sketch Harold had made of Mary Ellen, Kenny decided Harold was ready for some art instruction. He brought out a new set of oil paints and a still life for Harold to copy. From there they advanced to acrylics and other media. Once Harold's talent as an artist was secured, Kenny introduced Harold to woodworking.

In the meantime, Harold was teaching music in school systems in northern Missouri. His father-in-law had his own interior decorating business and spent the rest of his long life decorating houses and churches with beautiful wood carvings. He made communion rails, music stands, and other church items. Harold soon also learned the "ins and outs" from a master wood carver.

Harold has no idea how many paintings he has made and given away, as well as wood carvings. He, like his father-in-law, took on too many projects to bother counting them. Harold's projects included piecing stained glass, playing string bass in seven different orchestras, and rounding out the choir's bass section at St. John's Methodist Church in Kansas City, Missouri, his home.

Did anyone mention that Harold does weekly volunteering at two important institutions in Kansas City? Harold is a valued volunteer with six years' experience at the National World War I Museum and Memorial, where he volunteers a full day once a week. He devotes another full day to volunteering at Union Station, the vast building built in 1914, which was a transit point for 70% of all AEF soldiers being transported in all directions during the war.

Harold credits his spirit of volunteering and learning different art forms to his talented father-in-law who inspired him to take on yet another project. Kenny, a World War I veteran and army band leader, served as a role model for Harold, by devoting his life to music, the arts, and helping others. He once gave Harold a Bible inscribed with the words, "To a man of truth." Harold says that describes perfectly his father-in-law, Kenny Tebow. But maybe it describes both men.

Both were veterans, both were musicians, and both were family men. Most importantly, both valued volunteering as a way to help others. Kenny Tebow was born in 1899 in Ravenwood, Missouri, and died at age 85. His son-in-law, Harold, at age 91, is still going strong.

A glance at these two men and their life achievements, convinces one that there must something after all to a "life of volunteering, of patriotism, and devotion to the arts."

25 CENT SAVINGS STAMPS HELP FINANCE THE WAR

American children helped the war effort in numerous ways, and one of the most popular was by purchasing 25-cent Liberty Stamps. In buying these stamps, which often took them several weeks to save the money, the children believed they were doing their duty for the war. Their parents and school teachers believed that the children were learning the virtues of both thriftiness and patriotism.

Once the child bought 8 stamps, a card was needed on which to paste the stamps. This card cost an extra 12 cents. The reward (and money) could be exchanged in the year 1922, only a few years away. This paid the buyer an interest rate, starting at first at 3.5% then rising later to as much as 4.2 5% .To encourage the stamp purchases, children were shown a list of items used by soldiers and their cost. The child then imagined that his quarters were providing a soldier in the front lines with some necessary item: a pair of gloves, a cap, or even a rifle that might save his life. This propaganda campaign, with its emphasis on providing the needs of a soldier while saving money for the future, worked with amazing success.

Such monies obtained from the sale of Liberty Stamps were only a small portion of the revenue the government needed. Money was necessary to make loans to other countries; purchase military equipment; and fund the monthly payroll for four million AEF soldiers.

As a way of attracting adults to purchase a $50.00 Liberty Bond, this same technique was also successful with lists showing more costly items that the bond could provide.

One $50.00 bond could buy 18 gas masks, or four of the 6 inch shells for an artillery gun, or even purchase a sailor's uniform outfit. One such bond also could pay for enough coal to fuel a destroyer for sailing 120 miles. A surprising sum of more than $21.3 billion dollars was raised through four separate Liberty Stamp and Bond drives, money that would make a big dent in the costs of war. (Ellis)

This successful program encouraging American citizens was also initiated in World War II, but the stamps then were only 10 cents each. A more affordable price, one would think and one more practical for a child's allowance.

THE SATC, ROTC, BA, BS, OR GI BILL?

Paul Wilde of Warrenton, Missouri, became a college student and a private in the United States Army simultaneously when he signed Army enlistment papers on October 1, 1918. He was 18 and one-half years old and had just enrolled at the University of Missouri, Columbia, Missouri, as well as with the 4th Company of the Students Army Training Corps. He was on the path to earn a Bachelor of Arts (B.A.) or Bachelor of Science (B.S.) degree in the brand new SATC program.

This program was offered nationwide in more than 600 different types of advanced schooling. One type was designated Collegiate and called "A" Section. The other was termed "B" Section for vocational or technical schools. The Army realized that educated manpower would be needed to fill military positions which required more schooling than high school, and consequently developed this program. In Missouri 18 schools offered advanced training in academics, dentistry and polytechnics.

This program was expected to provide educated men with some military training to prepare them to fill officer positions. Also needed would be men capable of performing the polytechnic demands of an increasingly mechanical age. Usually the candidate had a choice of which section and which branch of the service he wanted to enter, but that option was also determined by where the military need existed. The entering rank in the SATC was that of a private. If, however, their school records were not satisfactory, they could be transferred to a vocational school or to a cantonment for army duty, as an actual private performing only military duties.

Members of both sections received from 11 to 15 ½ hours military training per week, and they attended courses on the "Issues of War." Completion of a degree or certificate would depend upon their competency with the prescribed curricula, as well as the needs of the army for additional manpower.

The program continued briefly after the war ended, then was closed. It was the precursor of the ROTC college officer preparatory program, although the latter had been experimentally started earlier in 1916 when President Wilson signed the National Defense Act of 1916. (History of Army ROTC). However, by far the best college education plan was the GI Bill of Rights adopted during 1944 for World War II veterans, offering millions of ex-soldiers an opportunity to obtain a college education or attend a trade school. This was an important step in helping to create the huge middle class of the 1940's to the1970's.

Because of its short history of availability and lack of publicity, the SATC program attracted only 3,411 students, with 106 candidates being sent to Officer's Training Schools by the time the armistice took place. For a small number of men this program offered an opportunity they most likely would have never experienced. Most emphatically, it provided a precedent for one of the most successful post war programs for veterans ever. That was the Servicemen's Readjustment Act, or more simply known as the GI Bill of Rights. (World War I in the University Archives)

THE DIARY OF PRIVATE SAM KAISER HINES

The lengthy diary kept by Private Samuel Kaiser Hines, of Company F, 1st Kansas Infantry, provides a detailed, personal description of almost two years in the army from his enlistment on June 15, 1917, only 10 days after he registered for the draft, to his discharge in May, 1919.

He was one of the early recruits to sign up after the draft was first conducted on June 5, 1917, in Kansas, and he was assigned to a National Guard unit, the 1st Kansas Infantry. Later when the guard units were combined with draftees, his unit became known as the 35th Division which was made up mostly of Kansas, Missouri and other Midwestern recruits. This diary was submitted by his grandson, Mike Hicks of Olathe, Kansas.

After training for about six weeks at Camp Morrell in Hiawatha, KS, he "and the boys" paid a last visit home to see the folks before going to Fort Sill, Oklahoma (probably Camp Doniphan). He arrived at Ft. Sill on October 1 and "It was the most dreary place I ever saw and came nearer being home sick that day than ever before in my life."

The diary's next entry is not made until March 5-10, 1918, when the troops were making hikes of six days and drilling in the trenches at various sites nearby including Signal Mt. Medicine Bluffs. Then one day his jowls felt swollen. He ended up in the hospital on March 18 with a case of the mumps. He laments he "had to leave father who was there visiting me."

It was not unusual for the soldiers to contract contagious diseases such as mumps, measles and chicken pox because they had never lived with large groups of men and were not exposed to the germs. They would have lived a more isolated life on a farm or in a small town. Now they being crowded into large barracks which was the reason the influenza struck down so many men at one time. Private Hines was released from quarantine on April 2, healthy in time for him to make the journey to the east coast and then to France beginning on April 14, 1918. He records that the train passed through Kansas City, Eldon and St. Louis, where they stopped and exercised, a usual activity to ease the stiffness of sitting long hours on the train.

He notes the train's route included Buffalo, N.Y. and Wilborough reaching Jersey City on April 18 where they took a ferry to Long Island City, and then another train to Camp Mike (not identified.) He and a buddy named Secher evidently had two days leave and visited "Minola, Hempstead, Jamaico, and then N.Y. City."

A week later the unit marched aboard the *RMS Mauretania*, and the ship steamed out of the harbor. It was a short voyage, however, "for it broke down and had to be towed back to dock." The soldiers spent the next two days on the disabled ship until the *Aeneas* arrived to take the troops overseas. Sam took his turn standing duty as Submarine Guard, but no subs were sighted until May 6, when near Ireland they saw a sunken sub. They spent a few days at a camp with the quaint name of Flowerdown near Winchester, England, then crossed the channel to France and started on the road to the Grande le Compte sector.

On May 11, 1918, they joined up with the "35th National Guard of Kansas and Missouri, in the North Sector of Wesserling sector Vasages (Vosges) one Brig (69)th." He was probably referring to the new 35th Division which initially trained in the Vosges Mountains near Gerardmer, to which the 69th Regiment also was assigned.

The Division spent the summer marching and training in a number of places Sam spells by sound, not knowing the correct French spelling. Of one march he boldly declares, "God know where, passed through edge of Paris hit Versailles and Gironcourt. (These last two names are spelled correctly.) Here the diary resumes with more details about their arrival in France. The men are hiking, riding trains "entrained for God knows wher(e)…" to the Alasa hill (Alsace?) at Kruth then on to trenches. They crossed over the highest Pt. (point) in France at Pt. Hoeneck (?) to more trenches. There "Jerry opened with some big ones on G.C.-2, where one man had been buried alive, but dug himself out." By then, Sam had been awake for 36-48 hours, but he stood guard over his Lieutenant Hughes, who was sick and slept through the trip.

From August 14 to September 2 they participated in the "Arogonne-Merial (Argonne-Meuse) at the Grangh-de-Comte sector" (Grange le Compte), a preliminary battle to the final attack in the Argonne. On September 26, "The Big Game" started at 2 A.M. with the usual artillery barrage.

Enlisted men and officers got separated from their units in the ferocity of the artillery firing and the attempts of the troops to advance. Rapid firing machine guns added to the chaos, and at times, officers gathered up troops who had lost their units, and organized them into fighting squads or companies and headed in the general direction of the enemy. When it was over, and all soldiers accounted for, Sam's company had lost 40 men dead and wounded out of a company of 200. That is 20% casualties in one battle.

His entry on Sept. 27 was a typical description of the rainy season in France when he wrote: "Slept last night between two raincoats some bed believe me. The next day their machine gun Co. broke up a counterattack by the Bosh. Lost quite a few men and the Capt." The night of Sept. 28 "Lt. Hughes and myself slept or rather tried to sleep in a (wbs) (?)hole about 6 in. deep. That night it rained most of the night "so our hole was full of water before morning (.) Our helmet under us kept us out of part of the water." (What did he mean by that?)

Sept. 29 -"Advanced again lost more men backed up to top of hill, dug in,..had no more than got our holes dug when Maj O'Conner started to hollower 'all 137th (Infantry Regiment) down to the edge of the woods'... our own artillery fired upon us – one 6 in. shell come near getting me while I was trying to signal to an aviator. We withdrew at dark and took up a position that the Engineers had prepared for us."

Sam perhaps was trying to signal their location to the aviator. Both armies had scout planes trying to locate troops and their artillery. The importance of having a good company of engineers was once again illustrated by this story.

The Germans were surrendering in large groups. As the prisoners were sent back to reserve areas, the AEF officer in charge had to be given a receipt for each prisoner. At one time, the capture of so many German prisoners interfered with the AEF being able to advance in the battle. Despite this, the 35th Division advanced 12.5 kilometers or about 7.5 miles on the front lines.

Sam breaks off his tale of fighting and hiking to insert information about the division's insignia. It is "the Santa Fe Cross within two circles of varying colors," chosen because the Santa Fe Trail started westward from a point near the town of Kansas City. Then he returns to his narrative to tell of "a Heavy bombardment on the front north of us" that turned out to be "the St. Mihill front we are in support of." Then there were three days bouncing around miserably in 200 trucks and more hiking to the Meuse-Argonne sector. His Battalion "got lost & we could not find our Co. {company} so went into the trenches with part of the 4th platoon and part of Headquarters. (This frequently happened in the chaos of thousands of troops, guns and trucks all trying to use the only three roads available which panicked civilians also crowded in fleeing from the fighting.)

On September 30 orders came "to hold our position of last night to last man. 82nd Division came through our lines about 4 o'clock, they bunched up in front of our lines while trying to cut through the wire, a bosh shell got 5 or 6 of the men."

He described several episodes of heavy artillery and machine gun fire with subsequent loss of

American soldiers and officers. To complicate the situation, it began to rain, hampering the actions of the AEF airplanes which were trying to send valuable information on numbers and formations of the enemy. Meanwhile, their ranks of the 35th had been broken when the 82nd Division came through, then later the 1st Division arrived, relieving the 35th. The 35th hiked to Auzeville, where the Division camped and completed reorganization of their troops.

Sam noticed it was October 25, which meant they had been overseas for six months, They were proud because the new red service stripe they sewed on their sleeve meant six months of overseas duty. Sam wonders," How long will it be before we see the Statue of Liberty again – if ever."

A few days later Sam got word that he was promoted to a corporal in October while he was in reserve. But it was still regular duty for him: digging trenches, standing guard duty; and slogging it out in the rain and mud like the privates. On Oct. 25 he makes one of his strongest comments: "Went into trenches at Verennes (?) and a hell of a day it is."

The next day wasn't much better for Sam and some men who went on patrol that night and ran into a "Bosh patrol. One man didn't come back. The next day, however, the fellow dragged himself into the trenches with six wounds. Sam and Luke carried the wounded man out of the trenches and over to the ration detail which had brought in the nightly meal. The detail took the wounded man to the nearest aid station. "Weeks wanted me to go with him, but of course that is impossible." Sam wondered again, "Will we ever see the Statue of Liberty again- and when."

He may have become discouraged by now, especially with the fierceness of the fighting, for until Nov. 7 their unit was in the thick of the fighting in the Meuse-Argonne campaign. When it ended, the 35th Division had captured 13 officers, 768 men and guns, 24 pieces of artillery, and 85 machine guns. These statistics would have been something to write home about if the censorship would have permitted, so it was Sam's diary that preserved some of the facts.

Finally, 11/11/11 arrived. The time and date of the Armistice. The fighting and killing stopped. "Church bells started and rang for two hours. American and French flags hung most everywhere. Our Reg. {regimental} Flag hung between the French flags from the upstairs of the Marie," (the Mayor's office).

From now on it was routine army life for Sam and his company. He missed the good Thanksgiving dinner at home, thinking, "Well the War is over so we ought to be thankful for that." "Finally some order was returning to the ranks," he decided, "when 2100 enlisted men and 5000 officers were picked up lately who were not with their organization, dodging the front lines. Stragglers, possibly; lost, maybe; just plain terrified, probably." Sam makes no more judgments on these men. Let the Army deal with them, he must have decided.

The diary continued with entries every few days describing drills, cootie baths, inspections, parades, entertainment, visits to the dentist, another 3 in 1 typhus shot. Hiking to see Mt. Sech, one of the National Fortresses of France with the remains of an old Roman fort supposedly built by Caesar. Sight seeing for Sam and buddies was common, while YMCA parties where officers and men were equal and dressed alike were a rare occasion. Regiments played occasional football games among themselves, held competition drills, "several Y minstrel shows, and a review by General Pershing and the Prince of Wales."

Family of Sam Hines: he is in the center wearing overalls with finger touching his face. Others include Cousin Rex, Mom, unidentified, Sam, Uncle Bill, Aunt Ardena Hines Henning, and Cousin Renee.
(Courtesy of Mike Hicks)

Sam noted that "Gen. Pershing is a big fine looking man a fine type of an American." His opinion of the Prince was less flattering. He commented "…He is a mere kid and I suppose is typical of English Nobility, spindle legs pale face,.. does not look Blue Blood." To top off the day of the review, the men had to hike 34 kilos both ways (20.5 miles), "walking through water almost up to our knees at one place…They had fires for us when we got back. Men fell like flies while we were standing at attention."

Feb. 4 (1919) was a special day. He wrote, "Took our first bath in the new bath house."

Mar. 17 – "St. Patrick's Day I wonder how many will be drunk tonight. I hope not any more than Saturday night." More days of rain and snow.

Mar 30 – There was a parade before Maj. Gen. Wright, "our colors were decorated and 17 men were recommended for DSC {Distinguished Service Cross} and presentation made. Message from Gen. Pershing was 'we should go home with a sense of duty well done.' "

More drills, cootie and teeth inspections, and ball games. Charlie Chaplin entertained the unit on one special night. This was how the 137th spent the endless days and nights until their names came up on the list of those to be sent home. For Sam that day was April 11, 1919, when he "loaded on the Good ship *SS Manchuria* for U.S.A. from France."

He made special note of having "my first ice cream in more than a year… Had Post Toasties this morning…"on April 24, 1919.

Finally on May 10, 1919, he was discharged, and "took car to Manhattan, train to Topeka and then Home. Mr. Bach met the train."

Sam was home once again. He closes his diary with a single word:

"Finish"

"MISS LOUIE", A MIDWESTERN SCHOOL TEACHER, EXPERIENCES WORLD WAR I

Miss Louie's diary, written almost 100 years old, gives a precise description of how she and her Midwestern farm family coped with the added problems of war, as well as the familiar daily ones encountered by farmers of that time. Her full name was Louise Alveda Thompson Allaman, after her marriage.

Few diaries by women from that time period have been published telling their stories, which were made all the more difficult and challenging by the absence of their men. Although farm women were usually considered to be hearty in physique and had the moral courage to make decisions when required, the diary reminds us that the

Miss Louie as a school teacher and brother, William, newly enlisted
(Courtesy John Allaman)

man was still the head of the household. His approval was necessary, and his word generally was obeyed.

However, in wartime, there were situations that even the head of the household could not always control, rendering his decision to little importance. This included the price of the farm products he raised, the hogs he took to Chicago, lack of wood and coal for heating, and shortages of gasoline and certain foods.

All these problems are mentioned in Miss Louie's diary in her usual brief, impersonal style. Examples of this might read: The death of a community member rated the same importance as the number of children she taught at school that day. The nearby town of Monmouth had over 1000 cases of flu. On December 13, the landing of President Wilson at Brest, France, (to discuss the treaty ending the war) competed with news about Papa shipping out pigs because they had the flu. It was foggy, Cecil Waugh came home from Camp Bradley, and Wm. (a brother) went to Mon. to bring him home. (Abbreviations are Miss Louie's.)

The importance of getting some kind of work done regardless of how she felt physically was emphasized in this entry of December 12, 1918: " I was sick all week, so did not accomplish much. I wrote the three verses for my Christmas booklet."

Here, in the abridged "Diary of Louie (Louise) Allaman," as transcribed by her son, John Allaman, Overland Park, Kansas, in 1996 and 1997, are some answers to those questions and more. Her diary refered to shortages or rationing of sugar, gasoline, and coal. The women and children worked diligently to fill or exceed Red Cross quotas to provide surgical packings, knitted goods and medical bandages. Miss Louie helped raise hundreds of dollars for Liberty bonds in a small Illinois town, near Monmouth and Oquakwa, on the eastern Iowa border.

Crowd at Oquawka Station sending draftees off to war.
(Courtesy John Allaman)

The persons mentioned in the diary are her father (Papa); Auntie (her father's unmarried sister who lived with the family); William and Frank, brothers to Miss Louie, and Gladys, her younger sister. Their mother had died several years previously.

Miss Louie, age 31, starting kept a detailed dairy, dated January 3, 1918, about daily activities of their lives, the weather, her position as a school teacher, and community events including illnesses and deaths. She wrote briefly and soberly, and was not given to expressing her emotions. She saw her role to be a recorder and used abbreviations when possible.

One of her frequent subjects was the weather and how it affected daily life. It was January and in that section of the Midwest, the weather was an important part of their lives, whether it was freezing cold or scorching hot. The roads to the school were primitive dirt paths, so her father would sometimes drive her and others in a sleigh, stopping occasionally to shovel out a path. At other times school and community events would be cancelled, so the telephone system must have been working. She mentioned the directors calling school off for various reasons, including (see later) the influenza.

The little town of Oquawka, Illinois, had a movie house which they frequented. Friends came to Miss Louie's house to sew, while the men helped each other butcher pigs. Miss Louie was prone to sickness of an unknown nature in her back, and she spent several days in bed from time to time. On January 5, Auntie went alone to the all day Red Cross Meeting at the Baptist Church, something Miss Louie always enjoyed. Fortunately that day's meeting was successful, for on the next day, January 6, 1918, "the worst storm is on that we have had for years…No services held at either the Methodist or Baptist Church."

January 8 they had school with only five of the 17 students present. But work at home continued, despite the storm. Folks were rendering lard, butchering more hogs, making sausage and 70 quarts of kraut. More storms for almost a week kept temperatures falling to 24 degrees below zero at 10:30 P.M. on January 12. In an effort to keep warm "The boys slept on cots in the furnace room and Papa had the lounge over the library register. Auntie, Margaret and Miss Louie shared Papa's room."

The next day the CB& Q train did not run, church was cancelled, and mail delivery stopped. When school resumed, Miss Louie explained "Thrift Certificates" to the children. The men shoveled neighbors out of drifts and took a team with ropes to get Lou Hanna out of a ditch. On January 22 they were not sure if they could have school because of the Coal Conservation order, so the men had a "wood-sawing" today. (The government had ordered conservation of coal and gasoline with "Gasoline Sundays.")

A break in the weather on January 26 allowed Miss Louie and Auntie to attend another all day Red Cross meeting at the Baptist Church, where they made 61 of the 9x9 compresses required by the Red Cross. "Cakes are conspicuous nowadays by their absence and we get along just as well without them," she piously wrote.

Events that might cause great newspaper headlines in newspapers rated a single comment such as: "The Catholic Church of Monmouth burned down today. Auntie ran the sewing machine needle thru the end of her finger. Frank received a notice to appear next Wed. for physical examination. In early February Gladys came home for the rest of the week as the Monmouth schools were out of coal. After going to school several times in a sleigh, on February 7th she went in a "storm buggy" (an enclosed buggy). The ladies served lunch at Dave Cowden's sale and cleared something over $60.00. Mrs. Barr died this morning."

Frank "passed the examination on February 11 but does not know when he will be called." There was no school so Miss Louie and helpers washed lamps at the one room school house and oiled half the floor. Miss Louie later made new curtains for the windows and took her Teacher's Extension Lesson. Only five more lessons to go {and she would receive her certification}. Also more cold temperatures and children sick with tonsillitis. The men finished shucking corn on February 23, and Papa planted radish and lettuce seeds. A Red Cross meeting with another lunch at a sale which brought in only $18.00."

Papa and the boys cleaned out the cistern at the Barr place on February 25. The Red Cross met the next day and the ladies made 530 mouth wipes, 2 comfort pillows and 3 tray cloths. A siege of measles hit the community in March causing all church services to be cancelled. Eleven of the Red Cross ladies met at the school, where they children finished the 1000 mouth wipes they had been assigned to make. Miss Louie sent money with Frank to buy two War Savings Stamps costing $4.14 each when he reported in Oquawka on the Petit Jury.

More cases of the measles with Edward Nicols dying from "the effects." Miss Louie suffered several days with a severe headache. Auntie made soap. One day it rained, filling the cistern with soft water. The ladies quilted. On March 21 it was reported the big German drive is on in France. "16,000 Allies reported as captured."(This was the final desperate German push called Big Michael in some notices.)

"Oranges are now $1.00 to $1.20 per dozen, apples 6 for a quarter, and red bananas 50 cents a dozen. The third Liberty Loan is to start Saturday. Three billion dollars are wanted this time."They practiced for the patriotic meeting to be held at the Baptist Church. On March 31 was the first day under 'War Time.' All clocks are advanced one hour."(The United States was adopting England's practice of changing the clocks to give an extra working hour.) Daylight Saving Time is now almost 100 years old.

And so the year continued with births and deaths; funerals, Liberty Bond drives. Fuel was needed at the school house and Frank went to basic training camp. Miss Louie and her father took the train to New York City later to see him off to Europe. William was classified 1-A; the oats were cut; a war lecturer spoke harshly of the Germans. Pat O'Brien, the aviator who escaped from a German prison camp gave a "grand lecture," closing the annual Chautauqua. Strawberries were picked. Mrs. Will Woods was killed in an auto accident.

On October 18, a telegram cancelled William's basic training because of the influenza outbreak. That same month the clocks went back to "good old 'Sun Time.' A few days after Bulgaria signs peace terms, the country of Turkey surrendered, while Carrie Moore is home from Camp Grant, Illinois, after having a siege of Pneumonia Influenza."

November 3 is marked with a large X. "Today is my 31st birthday and I have celebrated by being sick a-bed all day. Two letters came soon afterwards from Frank. On November 7 word had spread that Germany surrendered. People are going wild in the towns and are ringing bells. We finished the Red Cross Scrap Books, and exceeded our quota of $16,932.19 with the generous amount of $28,550.00.

In her usual non-committal way, Miss Louie related that she received a letter from the War Department on November 19 saying her application to volunteer for war work in France was rejected, now that the war was over. There had been a call for 2,000 women volunteers to do clerical work, and she had "been watching ever since the war began to find some work I felt I would be able to do." So after receiving permission from her father and Auntie, she applied. "I am much disappointed that I did not get across in time to do my bit." This is the first time she expresses her feelings in her diary.

Her last entry posted December 15 reflects the year's contents: "This has been a lovely day. Cecil Waugh was here… Gladys did not come home again…"

This diary of Miss Louie, unmarried school teacher, intelligent, sensitive, hard working and giving of herself, provides an interesting look at the life of a Midwestern spinster school teacher. She eventually marries and raises a family. She fulfilled the traditional role of an American woman with the high moral and religious values, that, together with hard work, helped make our country great.

SOS MEANT "HELP," AS WELL AS SERVICE OF SUPPLY

The men behind the men with the guns provided services that enabled those guns to be fired. The soldiers had to be re-supplied with ammunition, food, water, clothing, gas masks, as well as with the multitude of items that men required stationed on the front lines. Providing these necessities was the job of thousands of men called "stevedores," whose strong arms and backs were employed daily to unload the innumerable tons of supplies from ships that crowded the harbors of France.

Service of Supply insignia
(Public Domaine)

These members of the Service of Supply included thousands of African-Americans, Chinese, German prisoners, white soldiers, and natives from Africa and Asiatic countries. These stevedores carried heavy boxes containing everything from saddles and harnesses to huge bales of forage for the animals; to containers of lard, tins of gasoline, and even cartons of matches and cigarettes which were in great demand by soldiers. The harbors of Brest, St. Nazaire, Bordeaux, Havre, and Marseilles bristled with ships arriving safely with the convoy system that the United States set into motion once they declared war.

A lack of officers from the ranks of the "colored," the term was used at the time, led the Army to provide brief officer training for noncombatant "colored" officers of at least one month's duration. This allowed opportunities for the African-Americans to command their men. The different stevedore units, once they learned the routines for unloading the various supplies off the ships, often competed with other units to see who could unload the fastest. One group unloaded 1200 tons of flour in 9 ½ hours, a record never broken in the war.

The same pride and competitiveness extended to building railroads for American trains which were of a different gauge track than the French. The use of rail transport sped up the process of transferring goods to storage depots located nearer the front. One storage depot was built that covered six square miles. All supplies except artillery, heavy ammunition and airplane products, were shipped by American trains on the proper sized rail to the depots.

Those large items had a special depot that was diamond shaped with 140 miles of interior railroad lines concentrated in the area. The United States shipped overseas nearly 2000 locomotives, with 650 of them already set up on their own wheels. The other trains had to be assembled upon arrival. Because the setup locomotives had never been shipped before, special ships had to be refitted for the planned 200 locomotives to be shipped each month.

In addition, the Army also transported to France nearly 27,000 freight cars as well as 47,000 trucks. Not forgetting the valuable four legged power source, nearly 69,000 horses and mules were loaded into ships, accompanied by veterinarians and medics plus tons of forage.

The morale of the stevedores usually was high, partially due to their competitiveness but also to their practice of singing and joking as they worked. (Scott) This eased the drudgery, dullness and monotony of labor, commented a Dr. Ferguson, when speaking at one of the YMCA canteens built for the African-Americans. Segregation of the troops was still the practice in the army and did not end until years later when President Harry S. Truman issued an executive order in July, 1948, terminating it in the military service.

There was some relief from the monotony of labor when the YMCA offered the same kind of services for the African-American troops as for the white troops. These included entertainment, movies, circulating libraries, classes in reading and arithmetic for men whose education had been limited, and lessons in the French language. Addressing other needs of the men, the YMCA offered religious services, classes and lectures as well as athletic events. African-American secretaries were there to offer refreshments as well as help with letter writing.

E.J. Scott has said that in addition to the experiences of traveling abroad and meeting people from other countries, the stevedores learned the practical side of their job. He pointed to "Lessons in self -control, cleanliness, promptness, obedience, efficiency and the value of time." Another commenter was Ralph W. Tyler, an official U.S. observer, who concluded, "The colored stevedore has greater endurance than the others." He also complimented them for increasing by 10% the goods handled in September, 1918, over what had been unloaded in August. This amounted to a daily amount of 25,588 tons unloaded and shipped out.

All in all, the United States shipped the almost inconceivable amount of 7,500,000 tons of cargo to Europe by April, 1919. That required a "Lot Of Lifting" by thousands of SOS stevedores and laborers on the other side of the Atlantic.

In addition, there was a forward section of the SOS which had responsibility for:

- Motor vehicle overhaul parks
- Bakeries with daily products of about one million pounds
- Laundries built in at least eight towns which washed and cleaned one million pieces of clothing per month
- Mills providing lumber for the immense AEF construction projects
- Construction of barracks, hospitals, water supply lines and storage tanks, and refrigeration plants

It has been said an army marches on its stomach (full or empty). It may limp along in worn-out boots, and its cartridge belt maybe almost empty, but this was rarely the plight of the AEF during World War I. The excellent support service supplied by the men of the SOS made possible the supplies that enabled the American foot soldier to bring about a victorious conclusion to the war.

The 366th Infantry Regiment was cited for bravery by both American and French officers. Nine individuals in the regiment were awarded the Distinguished Service Cross.

Source: *They Came to Fight!* by Joelouis Mattox, 2008

(Mr. Mattox is a local historian who attended Lincoln University, Jefferson City, Missouri, studying history. He serves as an independent scholar at the Bruce R. Watkins Cultural Heritage Center in Kansas City. He also is a member of the boards of two community organizations and has published numerous magazine and newspaper articles. He is active community affairs and a leader of the African-American genealogy society, M.A.G.I.C., and advocates for African-American veterans around the United States, as well as African-Americans in general.)

FACTS AND FIGURES ABOUT AFRICAN-AMERICAN SOLDIERS IN WORLD WAR 1

Black, nation-wide, all services   Between 370,000 and 400,000

Black draftees   367,710

Commissioned officers   1,400

TWO DIVISIONS, all Black:

92nd – Shoulder patch: Charging Buffalo
93rd – Shoulder patch: French Hadrian Helmet

Famous Infantry Regiments:

92nd Division – 366th and 367th Regiments
93rd Division – 369th and 370th Regiments

Estimated number of Blacks from Kansas City in war   600
Number of Blacks from Kansas City who died in war   21
(Mattox)

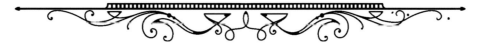

Private Joseph Blount of Montmorenci, South Carolina, was one of the thousands of men who had the back breaking task of unloading hundreds of tons of military equipment daily so the front line was adequately supplied. He volunteered on October 5, 1917, at age 26 and trained briefly at Camp Hill, Virginia. Later his unit was moved to Hoboken, New Jersey. Hoboken was one of the main ports of departure ports for AEF troops heading to France. Upon his arrival in France he was one of the earliest groups of American soldiers to reach France. (Order of Battle of the United States Land Forces in the World War 1917-1919) He served in Company B and then D of the 302nd Stevedore Regiment until Feb. 16, 1918. His story is told by Bernard Harris, a great-nephew, who lives in Leavenworth, Kansas.

Photo of Private Joseph Blount
(Courtesy of Bernard Harris)
and Buffalo shoulder patch,
(Public Domaine)

The 302nd Stevedore Regiment was part of the Quartermaster Corps which was organized under the Service of Supply. (SOS) (see story p. 123) The SOS headquarters was based in Tours, France, and provided logistics support for all the AEF units overseas. (Order of Battle of the United States Land Forces in the World War {1917-1919) Afterward in February, Private Blount's regiment was transferred to the Transportation Corps in September, 1918, having previously been transferred to Company G until July 13, 1918. (Center of Military History)

There were four separately designated Stevedore Regiments, the 301, 303rd, and 304th, and the 302nd to which Joseph was assigned. These regiments were separate units and were not assigned to an infantry regiment or division. Their work required them to be based mostly at the ports on the southwest coast of France. The northern ports were reserved for British use.

At the time of the Americans' arrival in 1917, the French ports were small and in poor condition. One of the first tasks assigned to the stevedores was to improve the ports at Brest, Bordeaux, Havre, Marseille and St. Nazaire so they could store and ship supplies to the front lines. In addition, some men were used to build storage depots and ammunition dumps near the front lines. It is not known the exact work to which Joseph was assigned, but African-American stevedores sometimes worked 24 hour shifts non-stop to get ships off-loaded. They followed a tight time schedule for supplies to be transferred to trucks taking badly needed supplies to the storage facilities.

Documents indicate that a Baptist minister by the name of Julian L. Brown, provided religious services and cared for the needs of the 302nd Regiment. (Emmett) There were more than 60 African-American ministers of various denominations who volunteered to service the religious needs of their members at home and in France. Documents also show a Private First Class Herman Johns of Wilmington, Clinton, Ohio, who also was a member of the 302nd. It is not known if Johns and Blount knew each other. (ancestry)

The stevedore regiments were part of the Service of Supply that was based in Tour. To encourage the men to work hard, various competitions were held to see which group could break records of the time required for unloading a certain ship. As an inducement to the working men, different bands played musical programs, and a contest, called "A Race to Berlin," was created to encourage record breaking efforts at the docks and storage places.(Sweeney)

Some of the stevedores in Joseph's 302nd regiment were credited with operating a consolidated mess kitchen at Rest Camp Number 4 in Bassin, France, beginning June 10, 1918. There is no evidence however that Private Blount was involved in that kitchen, but he was served food from this kitchen. Joseph's unit mostly operated in and around the port city of Bordeaux, France, in the southwestern coast in Base Section Number 2. The port of Bordeaux maintained several Quartermaster warehouses that provided laundries; salvage depots for clothing; horse harnesses; metal; typewriters; bakeries; and storage space. (Huston & Johnson)

At Bordeaux the stevedores did the mammoth job of unloading 800,000 tons of material in September, 1918, an average of 25,000 tons per day. (Barbeau & Henri) To obtain these amounts and weight, they unloaded everything from bales of hay to 90-ton naval guns, often singing while they worked. African American "pacesetters" established a fast tempo with the song leaders maintaining it. African-American men called "jolliers" kept the men laughing as they sang. (Barbeau

& Henri) It was also reported that at times some stevedores worked without wearing their shoes, and that in cold weather they handled cold pieces of iron and steel without any gloves. Again, it is not known if Private Blount worked under these conditions. (Hunton & Johnson)

In October, 1918, Joseph was transferred one last time to the 831st Company of the Transportation Corps. With all these transfers, his family must have had great difficulty trying to send and receive mail from him. (Center of Military History)

The military camps around the port of Bordeaux also supported YMCA troop morale and welfare facilities. Joseph may have been given leave to rest in one of these YMCA facilities and may have met Mrs. James L. Curtis, one of only three African-American women to serve initially in France with the YMCA. She was a great favorite with all the men. Not only did she make the highly desired ice cream and other "goodies," she was described as letting "the troops open their hearts to her." She was never forgotten by the men of the Bordeaux camps where she worked. In 1919 sixteen additional African-American women arrived to help the YMCA.

After the Armistice, Joseph was one of the stevedores assigned to serve in the Army of Occupation of Germany, so he was not shipped home and discharged until July 7, 1919. As to be expected from the tenor of the times, the African-- American stevedores often experienced the same racial discrimination in France as they did in the States, but it must be noted this was not by the French people. This was from other Americans soldiers the stevedores served with. The stevedores had hoped they had left discrimination and bigotry behind, but it followed them across the ocean. The hard physical labor often without the assistance of heavy equipment echoed back to the days of slavery. The French respected the African Americans because they were used to dealing with Africans from their French colonies in Africa.

A poem written by the then wellknown white American poet, Ella Wheeler Wilcox, in 1917 while entertaining soldiers at the SOS bases, of which Bordeaux was part, honored those hard working stevedores for their hard work and sacrifice:

> "We are the army stevedores, lusty and virile and strong,
> We are given the hardest work of the war and the hours are long.
> We handle the heavy boxes and shovel the dirty coal;
> While soldiers and sailors work in the light, we burrow below in the hole.
> But somebody has to do this work, or the soldiers could not fight
> And whatever work is given a man, is good if he does it right.
>
> "We are the army stevedores, and we are volunteers,
> We did not wait for the draft to come, to put aside our fears.
> We flung them away on the wings of fate, at the very first call of our land,
> And each of us offered a willing heart, and the strength of a brawny hand.
> We are the stevedores and work as we must and may.
> The cross of honor will never be ours to proudly wear away.

"But the men at the front could not be there,
And the battles could not be won
If the stevedores stopped in their dull routine,
Somebody has to do this work, be glad that it isn't you,
We are the army stevedores ---- give us our due!"

by Ella Wheeler Wilcox

Inspiration. Hope. Pride in their work and in themselves. Just what the stevedore needed. "We are the army stevedores—give us our due!"

(Note: Mr. Harris' grandmother, Mrs.Oliver, told him that Joseph had difficulty breathing and that Joseph attributed this problem to having been gassed. There are no known records indicating how he may have been exposed to gas, but accidents on the docks loading and unloading dangerous materials happened frequently. Joseph may have been exposed to friendly chemical munitions being unloaded from the States for use on the front lines. In addition, unless the gas caused a serious injury, it usually was not reported on the discharge paper of Joseph's, a copy of which is not available.) (Ellis)

B-B-B ROOM, WATCH OUT! HERE COME THE MOTORCYCLES!!!

An almost unknown job performed by non-combatants, especially by the African-Americans, was the exciting but dangerous assignment of serving as motorcycle messengers during World War I. As couriers, it was their job to deliver messages at any time of night or day from the command posts or headquarters to the front lines. Many times they carried officers in sidecars, roaring along damaged French roads at speeds up to 65 miles per hour. And they drove without headlights, if night had fallen.

AEF Motorcycle couriers await orders at Headquarters, Lagney, near Toul, France. November 22, 1918. (Public Domaine)

The drivers had to quickly learn the paths the roads took, the turnoffs, forks, and locations of military outposts. As they sped along, often

German artillery was firing overhead, or a sniper might be posted in a tree high above the ground, alert to the noise of the oncoming motorcycle. E.J. Scott commented upon his several rides with one of the more than 70 drivers in the African-American unit.

"He (the driver) was indifferent to American anti-aircraft shells aimed at the Boche airplane in the sky above us; he was oblivious to the thunder of the German cannon…to our right; he merely had his mind, as he kept his eyes to the front, on getting me back to the point which we had left a few hours before, a distance of five miles, in ten minutes."

Scott concluded that "when the history of this war is written… the bravery, daring and speed of the colored motorcycle riders…" must be told with all its details, emphasizing the amazing skill of these fellows."(Scott)

WHAT NEXT? WILL WOMEN BE WEARING TROUSERS INSTEAD OF SKIRTS?

Women in the Navy? Impossible, Never work out. Nothin' doin'. Such were the reactions to a proposal made by the Secretary of the Navy Josephus Daniels in a letter on March 19, 1917, to all Commandants of Naval Districts, informing them "that women may be enrolled in this class of the Naval Reserve Force." A section of the Naval Reserve Act of 1916, in referring to recruiting, failed to specify "males," instead, using the word, "persons." To Secretary Daniels that included women.

Kansas City had at least one young lady who joined the Yeomanettes, as they came to be called. Marjorie Lewis was born in 1895, according to the 1910 United States Census, and attended Garfield School in the Kansas City School District. It was one of the largest and most innovative of its time. On July 27,1918, she joined the military and served for two years, being discharged in 1920. She was one of the women who were allowed to leave the services early, although about half of them served their four years, sometimes in a government civilian status. She lived a long life, dying on Feb. 26, 1981.

Secretary Daniels suspected that the United States would soon be involved in the European War or The Great War, and later to be called "World War I," and Daniels tallied up the number of naval personnel under his direction. Discovering that there were only 53,000 sailors wearing the United States uniform, he thought of a new form of replacements for all the desk bound sailors who could be released for duty on ships. Great Britain was the acknowledged leading naval power, and Germany was close behind due to an accelerated warships --building program over the past dozen or so years.

The United States needed to speed up its Naval building program. So the recruiting doors were open to young women who would fill dozens of jobs, mostly clerical, but who would also serve as translators, draftsmen, fingerprint experts, even camouflage designers and recruiting agents.

About 200 young women between the ages of 18 to 35 rushed to the recruiting offices the first month. They signed up for the standard four years as did their male counterparts, although it was assumed that they would not need to serve the entire time. Once the commandants and officers of lesser ranks accepted the inevitability of women in the Navy, probably after some complaining from the lowest to highest ranks, the Navy settled down to solve some basic but essential problems. (Guthrie)

Women in the Navy were called "Yeomanettes." They had to buy or make their uniforms and served mostly in office or clerical positions.
(Public Domaine.)

The first problem encountering the Navy Department was the issue of what women's uniform would be. It was unthinkable then for a woman to wear anything but a dress or a skirt with a hem line four inches above the ankle. They compromised by raising the hem to eight inches. At first, women either made their own uniforms or bought ready made and a white or blue single breasted jacket. Hats usually were stiff felt with brims. The main complaint from the ladies was that the white shirts had a tight fitting collar which resulted in "ring around the collar," meaning washing a shirt every night. By the end of the war, the Navy had decided upon other essential items as gloves, handkerchiefs, and the actual design of jackets and skirts.(Patch)

Not all problems were solved as easily. For example, what would be their rank? How would it be indicated and what noun described their status? After much debate, it was decided they would be called "Yeomanette" with a beginning rank of "Yeoman (F)"and, believe it or not, with the same pay as a sailor. Their pay was $28.75 per month with daily subsistence pay of $1.50, later raised to $1.75 for their room and board. The latter was not furnished by the Navy although a uniform allowance, medical and war risk insurance were made the same as the men had.

Once these problems were solved, there remained one that worried the Yeomanettes the most. There was no government housing available or barracks as were provided for the men. The women had to find their own housing by renting a room from a friendly family, or a sharing a house with three or four women, or even staying in hotels. Their daily living allowance often did not cover expenses. The Navy recognized that the housing problem was one the military had to step in and solve. One way was to add a housing and food allowance.

One big difference was in punishment. The Yeoman (F) did not serve time in the brig for offenses but loss of pay or liberty was substituted for infraction of rules. (American Women in World War One)

The young women came from all social classes, mostly middle class, but also from wealthy families, daughters of legislators, and all sections of the United States and Alaska. Two families in Massachusetts, each sent their four daughters, one of the most unusual recruitment situations for either female or male. Preferably, most were high school graduates with some office or business experience, but all that was actually required was to pass the physical examination and several tests involving office skills and language usage. In addition, it helped if they were good looking and mannerly.

By the time of the Armistice signing, a total of 11,275 Yeomanettes or Yeoman (F) had been signed up, undergone the briefest of training procedures, learned to march in order for the many Liberty bonds parades they participated in, and to start pounding the typewriter or other office machines to which they were assigned. Some few had more challenging jobs such as being assigned to Office of Naval Intelligence in Puerto Rico, while a few drew a ticket for berths to Guam, Hawaii and the Panama Canal Zone. (Patch) No sluggards were among them as they usually worked six days a week, 10 hours a day, while the long parades marching in leather pumps made their feet ache like that of the Yank in Europe. Granted, the streets of America were in considerably better condition than French roads.

The Marines, not to be outdone by the Navy, also created a program in which they enrolled 300 "marinettes" in the Marine Corps.

One job that some Yeomanettes enjoyed was raising money for the war effort from the audience during the intermission at the movies. Surely the women had been given a free pass to the movie also.

Just like their civilian sisters, a number of Yeomanettes experienced personal tragedy. One, Alice Regina Costello, within a period of six months, received reports of the deaths of three brothers. Still, she carried on in the proud Navy tradition, perhaps thinking that by her working on land, she was freeing up someone else's brother who would come home safely.

The women marched often in parades. One type of parade that stood out was a "military funeral" procession of women. Marching in front of the flag covered coffin were a group of women in the uniform of the American Navy. Sailors marched alongside and behind the coffin. The whole experience, wrote one onlooker, "seems strange and unusual, and somehow very, very sad." (American Women of War)

Although only a few troopships were hit by the Germans, a story that shocked the whole world was the attack in September, 1918, on the *Mount Vernon*, a troop transport ship torpedoed by a German sub off the French coast. The torpedo hit the boiler, and 35 men were killed immediately. Every survivor rushed to his post and the ships' guns spoke back. The ship barely made it into the French port of Brest but every sailor who was still capable, was performing his job.

The outcome of the Yeomanette program led to the formation of the WAVES in World War II. At that time there were 112 former Yeoman (F) still working in the Navy Bureau of Supplies and Accounts. New jobs assigned to them included torpedo assemblers, telegraphers, librarians, and commissary stewards.

Other tragic incidences occurred, including 51 who reportedly died of the flu. It was estimated that 548,000 American citizens died of the flu, which was nearly twice the number of soldiers who died and were wounded in combat. While some women were discharged before their four years of duty expired, many stayed on with the service that allowed them to wear their unique uniforms.

One very special person in the program was Loretta P. Walsh, who became the first woman Navy petty officer on March 21, 1917, when she received the rank of Chief Yeoman. She completed her four-year enlistment, then left the navy, and unfortunately died of August 6, 1925 of tuberculosis. She is buried in Elyphant, Pennsylvania, near her home town of Philadelphia. (Stevens – Find a Grave)

This program is another one of the "firsts" that reflect the importance of World War I as an agent of change in the history of the 20th century. It was quite an adventure for the young women and their families; assuredly, some several mothers wept as profusely when their daughter joined up, as when their son joined the colors. The Yeoman (F) contributions ranged from the most routine clerical jobs to ones such as the one held by Ann Dunn, who was "keeper of the logs," requiring her to work all day in a locked room on the third floor of the Navy Building in Washington, D.C. The room contained 14,000 volumes of naval history as far back as 1861. The logs contained routine information but also stories of heroism, conquests and daily combat at sea. (American Women in WWI)

As for this program's effect on women, it reached beyond replacing men in office and shipyard assignments. Naval officers, and even the sailors, began to recognize the previously unknown and unacknowledged abilities of women working outside the home. Two other consequences can be identified. One was the influence on the passing of the 19th amendment which gave women the right to vote, and the other was the precedent for creating the WAVES program. (Women Accepted for Volunteer Emergency Service) in World War II. (Patch)

THE MENNONITES
THEIR RELIGIOUS BELIEFS CHALLENGED THE RULES OF WARTIME

The fall of 1917 saw the beginning of an enlistment problem the Army had not anticipated, or at least, had hoped it would be able to avoid. The problem arose when about 130 to 150 Mennonite draftees arrived at Camp Funston, Kansas, for basic training. Because of their strong religious belief about "nonresistance," which they interpreted to mean that they would not respond to violence in any manner, they were to provoke what became a national problem among conscientious objectors. The Army had to determine how to handle recruits whose personal religious beliefs conflicted with their military duties. "Nonresistance" was a fundamental tenet of their religion, and in their 300 -year history, they had fled their homelands rather than to take up arms when required by law.

Some men refused to wear the Army uniform and wore civilian clothes instead.
(Courtesy of the Mennonite Library and Archives, Bethel College.)

They refused to participate in any manner to perform military duties or services that they believed might aid the war effort, such as carrying rocks to make a road, or assisting with sanitary work of removing trash and garbage. Their resistance frustrated junior officers who had no training on how to discipline such behavior, other than use physical punishment or incarceration. The senior officers encouraged the use of humane methods including persuasion and attempts to reason with those who displayed obstinate behavior. The problem, while not affecting large numbers of recruits nationwide, was baffling enough at Camp Funston to cause irritation and often angry responses from the junior officers. While physical punishment was frowned upon, there were a few cases when a riding crop was used in an effort to curb the lack of cooperation by the draftee.

Mennonite Conscientious objectors at Camp Funston are sent to bring back rocks from a nearby field. They will crush these rocks to make roads for the camp. While some of the COs agreed to do this, others refused, saying they would be helping the war effort by improving camp conditions.
(Courtesy of the Mennonite Library and Archives, Bethel College.)

Despite many efforts to offer other duties that the military deemed not in the usual line of duty, such as working in the quartermaster corps or medical corps, these approaches often failed. Eventually the matter rose through the various levels of military authority until it landed on the desk of the War Department, where a humane definition of appropriate duties for conscientious objectors had to be determined and written. Such duties had to be compatible with the Mennonites' religious beliefs and the demands of society that all capable men serve their country in time of war.

Mennonites at Camp Funston, KS. peeling potatoes, as a noncombative duty.
(Courtesy of the Mennonite Library and Archives, Bethel College.)

The Mennonites and a small group of Hutterites had a long history of fleeing their homelands when pressured to perform military duty rather than concede. They had emigrated to America as early as 1683, although most came in 1873 from Russia to escape military conscription. These German speaking men were viewed with suspicion and hostility by the officers and service men because of their refusal to wear a uniform, carry a rifle, or perform any duty slightly relating to the military. While there were conscientious objectors of other beliefs throughout the United States, this band of Mennonites was one of the largest groups confronting the military.

Camp Funston, Kansas, was where the army was faced with the need to determine what were humane and legal ways to discipline and deal with the Mennonites. These problems eventually made their way to the desk of President Wilson, who on March 23, 1918, tried to define "noncombatant service." He admitted that even his words were vague and unsatisfactory, although his definition included service in the medical corps at home and abroad; service in the quartermaster corps in both theaters; engineer service in the States; and in the rear of operations in the war theater. Still the President realized that this definition was limited, and would not satisfy the needs of both military and the religious objectors.

In the interim, at Camp Funston, Major General Leonard Wood handled the situations as best as he could, considering his own biases toward the recruits who were German speaking, usually unkempt in appearance, and held rigid beliefs. There was to be no physical punishments, no withholding of food or life necessities. No harassment or disciplinary actions. These restrictions created more frustration and confusion among the junior officers who had to deal with the Mennonites on a daily basis.

For example, it was ordered that they carry rocks to lay roads and paths on the newly built camp grounds or to work in the kitchen, the hospital, or quartermaster corps. These tasks were acceptable to a number of the Mennonites at first, with only five refusing to work. However, over time, this number, for various reasons, grew to 21 refusals on January 28, 1918. On March 4, 1918, there were 119 refusals. Clearly the policy was not working. Eventually, eight men who previously

Some conscientious objectors at Fort Riley, Kansas, await their turn for a hearing before the Board of Inquiry. On the far right and left stand some military guards.
(Courtesy of the Mennonite Library and Archives, Bethel College.)

Mennonite reading newspaper to other Mennonites at Camp Funston, KS. 1918
(Courtesy of Bethel College Mennonite Library and Archives)

had cooperated, but now resisted, were arrested, tried, and found guilty enough to spend time at Fort Leavenworth Federal Prison.

Other forms of discipline included threats and psychological persuasion which had the effect of making the group even more cohesive. There is a report of at least two Hutterites dying from maltreatment (Stoltzfus) but no similar incidents were confirmed at Camp Funston, although recent evidence seems to contradict that conclusion. (Stoltzfus) The Mennonites had ways to report abuse and grievances through the local clergy and the National Civil Liberties Union. Of the 450 who were court martialed, 113 of this number were released by the board of inquiry in January, 1919.

Fortunately for all involved, the problem which had existed for ten months, was eliminated when November 11, 1918, arrived and the Armistice was signed. The Mennonites were discharged from the army with a paper that was neither an honorable or dishonorable discharge. The blue sheet said, "This is a conscientious objector who has done no military duty whatsoever and refused to wear a uniform." (Capozzola) President Wilson later in 1920 granted amnesty to most of the objectors.

The problem which had plagued the administration of Newton D. Baker, Secretary of the War Department, was eventually translated into a situation resolved by the war coming to an end.

One may note that among the eight men, whose disobedience brought prison terms at Fort Leavenworth, Kansas, one man died of illness. There also were dozens of others Mennonites, who served as "object lessons" in their refusal to compromise their religious beliefs, despite the societal expectations of defense in time of war by able bodied men.

Conscientious objection would remain a difficult issue in times of war, but a variety of precedents had been set.

(This story is a condensation of a study by Sarah D. Shields, "The Treatment of Conscientious Objectors During World War I: Mennonites at Camp Funston."

THE DENTIST AND THE FIRE TRUCK

He gave five-year-old Hank Riffe a toy fire engine and later a bicycle. That's how Hank remembers the World War I veteran who was gassed in France. That veteran was Dr. Ralph Albertson, a dentist and a family friend who lived in Sioux Falls, South Dakota, where Hank's grandparents had property. Hank visited his grandparents in the summers, and often spent long hours in Dr. Albertson's company. This story is told by Hank, a resident of Overland Park, Kansas.

Dr. Albertson's assignment as an Army dentist, was to teach 40 to 50 other military dentists, often from England and France as well as the AEF, how to make dentures. Shrapnel shells, which split into sharp pieces of metal when exploding and were embedded in the head, caused soldiers to suffer terrible, disfiguring facial wounds. Often dentures were required to replace lost teeth. When the recruit entered the army, he was subjected to a thorough dental check by the two dozen or more dentists. Emergency calls can be made but usually the dentist worked on an appointment basis, much like in civilian practice.

While in boot camp, regular inspections were held every two months in which the mouth and teeth are inspected. Although the dentist has less time per patient, still badly diseased teeth are extracted and fillings made of amalgam (silver) were used. Bridge and plate work were done when necessary for the man to eat properly. Otherwise, temporary measures were made.(Sasse)

After the war, Dr. Albertson returned to the States and became a traveling dentist. He drove from state to state sharing his skills in making dentures. There were 4,620 dentists in the army that served in France.

Dr. Albertson was born in 1895 and lived until the 1980's, dying of a mysterious kidney failure. Whether it was related to his being gassed in the war is a matter of speculation. Although he has been gone more than 20 years, he still lives in Hank Riffe's mind. For Hank he was always the adult friend who gave Hank wonderful childhood toys, and created the precious memories Hank recalls today.

ARROWHEADS TO SOLDIERING — AN UNUSUAL FAMILY

How would the Army have met its quota in World War I without families who had brothers like the Rodewald family? First it was George, then Harry, Frank, and lastly, Howard. All followed George to the recruiter's office once their draft notices appeared. This story, as related by a great niece, Nancy Turner, of Dearborn, Missouri, is mostly about Howard, who served in the Company B, 140th Regiment of the 354th Infantry Division. This finally became a part of the 35th Division. Of the 156,232 Missourians on duty with the Army, one-half of them went overseas. However, Howard was the only one of the Rodewald brothers who served in France.

Rodewalds: Great Uncle George, Grandma, Great-Uncle Harry, and Great-Uncle Howard (Courtesy of Nancy Turner)

He was inducted on September 20, 1917, at Fulton, Missouri, where most of his brothers joined up. He probably received basic training either at Camp Funston, Kansas, or Camp Doniphan, Oklahoma, where most Midwest men were sent. He was 25 years and one month old, according to the way the army recorded age. Howard was among the earliest AEF soldiers to arrive in France, landing there on April 25, 1918.

A copy of one of Howard's letters, dated Feb. 23rd, 1919, and with A.P.O "Pont sur Meuse" or Meuse Bridge, remains in his great niece's collection. It is written on Knights of Columbus OVERSEAS SERVICE letterhead. In it Howard tells of receiving a picture of his brother George "coming on deck in his greasy clothes; he does not look natural in them." He tells about going to the abandoned German trenches about 6 or 7 miles from his location, looking for souvenirs. It was useless as "everything is torn up by shells and bombs or 'pigs' from trench mortars" (named because of their large round size). "The wire entanglements are all torn up and it is hard to walk through it and the brush too."

He recollects it was here the Americans started the "great St. Mihiel drive that you have probably heard about. Our division was held in reserve on that drive." He concludes that the Germans "were prepared to stay there a long time." (It was noted that the Germans had well prepared trenches with many conveniences.)

He goes on to defend the 35th Division's combat action and its huge number of casualties. "…the 35th div. being shot up so bad; there was other outfits that were in more fights than us; I don't like for them to carry on about us that way, as it will do no good." The controversy about the leadership of the 35th continued after the war when Congress and the Army investigated the staff's decisions as to whether negligence and poor judgment were involved. Howard concludes by describing the Division review held recently with General Pershing and the Prince of Wales in attendance. He comments, "A division sure makes a big bunch of men." An American division consisted of about 25,000 men of fighting strength plus 2,000 men in support. He concludes by saying there are large numbers of German prisoners where he is located, but he can't say anything more because of censorship.

The fighting at St. Mihiel and the Argonne Forest was where many soldiers were gassed. It is not known if Howard was gassed but the large number of casualties were recorded with 7,047 casualties including 1,516 killed, 5,513 wounded, and 18 missing and presumed dead. Many of the seriously wounded were sent to Base Hospital 28, which was financed and organized by a group of Kansas City doctors. (Ellis)

He mentions the Kansas City Base Hospital Unit, No. 28 as one of two cited as having one of the best records for treatment. Only 69 soldiers died out of the 10,000 treated in that hospital. Another Missouri hospital was Base Hospital No. 21, sponsored by Washington University and Barnes Hospital in St. Louis. But evidently Howard returned home without any serious injury, as being gassed was not considered important enough to be noted on the discharge paper. Doctors did not realize the long term effects it could have on the lungs.

Howard was familiar with the horses and mules used to provide the pulling power for the army. Many childhood experiences had taught him the hard way. He had emphatically told Nancy, as a young child, "to never put your feet in the stirrups." He had been dragged by a mule on the farm and kept yelling "Whoa!" until the mule stopped on his own accord. Nancy Turner obeys her great uncle's command to this day. She is an accomplished rider but never uses stirrups unless required to.

Brother Harry had a different story about his service in the army. He was inducted almost a year later on September 5, 1918, also in Fulton, Missouri. He was about 21 years old and was sent to an infantry replacement and training camp at Camp McArthur, Texas, where he remained only a few months until the Armistice was signed on November 11, 1918.

As for George, he took to the sea, serving in the U.S. Navy as a Fireman, 3rd Class on the *USS West Loquassuck*, a ship commissioned just before the war ended. It was used for a transport ship during the time George was aboard. He was the first one to enlist on June 17, 1917, and the oldest of the brothers at age 31 years, 4 months. He signed up in Kansas City, Missouri, and served until his discharge more than two years later on July 5, 1919, in St. Louis, MO with the rating of Fireman 1st Class.

There are no military records available for Frank. Perhaps they may have been destroyed in the accidental fire in 1973 at the St. Louis Federal Archives. Personnel are still trying to reconstruct the vast number of army service records that were lost.

Nancy tells an illustrative story about her ancestors and their personalities. The German grandparents of these four men had married and immigrated to America, despite their parental opposition. Great-grandfather, Lewis Rodewald, was supposedly from an impoverished but High German speaking family, probably living in Prussia. He fell in love with a girl, Emma, who had some Irish ancestry in her family. That meant she wasn't pure German and not a likely candidate as his bride, according to customs of the time. Love won over parental disapproval and once they were married, they immigrated, and settled in Fulton, Missouri, a thriving German town.

The area around Fulton, being populated with German families, called for a general store. Not being a farmer, great- grandfather opened a dry goods store. As their children grew old enough to help, they worked in the store. Anna was the only daughter, and later married Ed Anderson and had six children of her own. However, Anna, as a child, had to contend with the antics of four rambunctious brothers. In addition, she overheard her grandparents' loudly expressed disagreements, all of which perpetuated the usual confusion and noise of many loud voices in the large household. For Nancy, it became too noisy at times. Still they somehow managed to live together peacefully, if noisily.

A lifelong hobby of four of the uncles was hunting for Indian arrowheads. Howard specialized in finding stones shaped to use for axes. He lived in Rulo, Nebraska, which had been a camp site for Indians years ago. Arrowheads of all sizes and descriptions kept turning up after heavy rains or after plowing. Uncle Harry's speciality was making small windmills and Ferris wheels, and he covered his yard with them. The brothers kept antiques, stuffing the barns with all manner of chairs, tables, dressers and other old furniture.

Because Uncle Howard never learned to drive, Nancy and her sister. Linda, about once a month, took groceries to him to supplement the meat he got by hunting. He raised his own vegetables. One of his more eccentric behaviors was to hide cash in the barn. When he died in 1972, he had left Nancy and her sister each $1800.00 in cash that had been found in the barn. That was quite a sum in those days. In his hunting, he was said to walk many miles every day to check his traps.

Uncle Harry had a "cool" car, according to Nancy. She doesn't remember the make, but she and her sister proudly rode around town with their Uncle Harry, showing off the car. Harry lived in Falls City, Nebraska. Howard lived in a rural area in a little house without indoor plumbing. She recalls the outhouse with its important Sears, Roebuck catalog. Howard was a carpenter and would stay at people's houses until he finished his job. That was customary in those days, especially when the jobs were away from home.

Only two of the Rodewald brothers married, while the other two lived separately from each other. Nancy also has an unmarried uncle on her maternal side who lived with his parents and served in World War I. Guess they weren't the marrying type, Nancy admits. But Frank took a wife named Mary. Neither couple had children.

Recounting the lives of her great uncles, Nancy says," Howard spent a lot of time trapping wild animals, often walking up ten miles a day. Uncle Harry drank when he wasn't doing carpenter work, so he often was dubbed an "alcoholic, whether that was true or not." George became a recluse, a hermit. Frank was deemed to be the only successful one. He became a CEO for an oil company and traveled widely.

Aunt Anna's three sons never married. One son died of appendicitis in the Navy on Christmas Eve during World War II. Her two daughters served in the Women's Army Corps in World War II, as did their cousin, Nancy's mother, who enlisted because she had no job. It was near the end of the Depression and it seemed a good way to spend part of her life. She served with distinction for ten years and later married.

Although some behaviors of the uncles could be considered odd, or beyond the ordinary, Nancy and her sister loved them, especially the times when Uncle Howard came to visit. He was "big" on education of the selftaught kind. He encouraged the girls to learn by asking questions. Despite the occasional turmoil and loud voices, they were a close family. Aunt Anna was a good cook and served tasty meals from her garden. She rode her horse astride, which shocked the local women. Married early at age 16, as was the custom of the time, Aunt Anna quoted the Bible frequently and read encyclopedias. She also urged all the children to get married. The state of matrimony must have satisfied her.

Nancy's maternal uncle, Lewis, obviously followed his cousin Anna's advice. He married and had 15 children, including two sets of twins. He expected them all to go to college. Nancy doesn't know if that happened, but she does agree she has an unusual family background. Still she is proud of all of them, especially her uncles. Recently she donated artifacts from their service to a museum for preservation and research. She is pleased that some researcher can go there and study what her uncles had collected from their days in the war, and pass on their thoughts and writing so others can learn.

THE VETERANS' BEST FRIEND

Attacking a French town with the name, "Stenay," meant a possible death sentence for the men of the 89th Division under Major General William Wright's command on the last day of fighting in World War I. One of those men was Sergeant Edward Roche of St. Louis, Missouri.

The date was November 11, 1918, the last day of the war. The Armistice was officially to be signed at 11A.M., although it had been signed earlier at 5:10 a.m. by the Germans and the Allies. All hostilities were to stop immediately at 11 a.m. Officers all over the Western Front synchronized their watches to the exact time. However, in ordering the attack, General Wright claimed he was following orders of Major General Charles P. Summerall.

Tragically, while most commanders of Allied units honored this order, there were a number of exceptions. The commanders ordered offensive movements to be made which would continue well past the 11 o'clock hour. Fortunately for thousands of troops, many officers delayed preparations for an attack if they could. But not General Wright. He ordered an attack on the small village of Stenay (population now down to 800) across the Marne River. This decision was not only unwise, it was expressly against top command orders. Most importantly, it was costly. It resulted in the loss of more than 300 American lives as well as those of unnumbered Germans. Those Germans who could escape, fled after their initial defense.

The General's explanation was that "his troops had been deprived of proper bathing facilities, and if the enemy were permitted to stay in Stenay, our troops would be deprived of the probable bathing facilities there." (Persico)

Sergeant Roche and his Company C, 314th Engineers, 89th Division, were assigned to construct a pontoon bridge over the Marne River as an initial part of the assault. This was to be built in spite of well placed enemy guns that fired on the helpless unarmed engineers. Somehow, the engineers built the bridge despite the heavy fire, and hundreds of Americans crossed the cold muddy waters of the Marne. We do not know Sergeant Roche's particular experience except that he escaped unharmed.

The 314th Engineers had previously spent several months engaged in hazardous jobs of repairing roads, placing barbed wire in front of trenches, and patrolling at night to see if the wire was still in place. These tasks were performed in the battles where high casualty rates resulted and included Alsace-Lorraine, St. Mihiel, and Grande le Courte in Argonne sector. The engineers' previous experience with German machine guns and heavy artillery taught them what to expect. This story is told by Sergeant Roche's grandson, Neil J. Bruntrager, St. Louis, Missouri.

The disaster at Stenay was one of several unfortunate situations on November 11. The 314th Engineers included Roche and several friends from St. Louis who joined with him. He was Irish, single, and 26 years old when he was drafted. It was his luck that his number was the first one to be selected in the draft.

When he received his draft notice, he told his father, who had emigrated from Ireland in 1880, that he was going to fight "the Hun." His father's only response was, "Damn Lloyd-George, why doesn't he free the Irish?" David Lloyd-George was England's prime minister and Ireland was still under English control.

The first groups of draftees departed from St. Louis with great fanfare. The streets were decorated with bunting, and martial music filled the air. The men left for basic training at Camp Funston, Kansas, which was a new camp hurriedly built to remedy the mushrooming housing needs of the Army. Training at Camp Funston was as primitive as was the housing. Men carried and trained with wooden rifles until enough real rifles were manufactured and sent to them, instead of being shipped overseas to the French and English. Since the beginning of the war, the United States had supplied billions of dollars of armaments to the Allies.

It was there that Private Roche learned the first rule for any serviceman. He shared this story with his grandson: "One day a number of soldiers were engaged in the drudgery of camp life. Jobs included peeling potatoes, cleaning latrines, and policing the grounds. A sergeant approached a group of men and said that he needed some men to help with the colonel's car. Most of these men had come from St. Louis or Kansas City and knew about repairing cars. They saw this as an opportunity to do mechanical work or perhaps even drive the automobile. It would be good work for the common foot soldier."

But the large group who volunteered and marched off with the pleased sergeant were surprised and taught a valuable lesson early in military life. They arrived at a rail line and saw a railcar full of coal. The sergeant commanded, "Grab a shovel. This is the colonel's coal car, and it needs to be unloaded." The men immediately learned: "Never volunteer for anything."

Other stories his grandson tells include one about music. As with many Irishmen, music was an essential part of Sergeant Roche's everyday life. The songs of World War I, their melodies and harmonies, were passed down by Frank Roche to his children and grandchildren. Even now, his descendants can provide a rousing rendition of "Over There" or "K-K-Katie." The singing bachelor married in 1920, later had two children, and kept on singing.

He became active in the newly formed American Legion. He decided to give politics a try, and became a Democratic committee man in St. Louis. Frank Roche also served on the committee that built the Soldiers Memorial in St. Louis. In later years he attended several National Democratic Conventions as a delegate from Missouri.

In addition, during the 1930's Frank Roche was active as head of the Works Progress Administration (WPA) in St. Louis. This was part of an important program known as "The New Deal," initiated by President Roosevelt. Roche helped veterans get jobs during slow employment times. These men became an important part of his political base. It was understood that a person voted for the man who provided jobs for them. During the Great Depression, lines of unemployed veterans would constantly file in and out of Mr. Roche's house.

The friends that Mr. Roche made in the service became his friends for life. Because there were so many from St. Louis in the 89th, it was easy to maintain these friendships. Some friendships were forged with men who otherwise had nothing in common with Mr. Roche. For instance, Hyman Shifrin, a sell educated American Jewish engineer, was highly respected and liked by Mr. Roche, an Irish Catholic with barely an eighth grade education. Mr. Roche often said that men will make the best of any difficult situation, so he never glamorized war. Instead he often spoke of how "awful the war was." He recalled the miserable life of being in the trenches.

It was a rare occasion when veterans would talk to their families or the public about their war experiences. Mr. Roche was an exception when he told about the patrols he made in the dark of "No Man's Land" to make sure the wire that protected his trenches was still in place. The Germans would constantly bomb their opponents' rolls of wire to destroy the wire, making it easier for the Germans to attack.

Destroying the barbed wire defenses before an offensive was vital to the survival of the soldiers and success of the attack. The British artillery learned a lesson they would never forget. It was about the importance of destroying the enemy's barbed wire rolls. At the first important battle at the Somme in 1916, the British artillery's aim was poorly set. Shells fell just in front of the wire, so almost none of the rolls of wire was destroyed. When the whistle was blown, the British attacked as planned. Thousands of soldiers climbed out of the trenches and went over the top. They thought the wire had been destroyed, and the path to the German trenches would be clear and fairly safe. They discovered to their horror the wire was still whole and in place.

Dead bodies fell on the wire as hidden German machine guns sprayed the oncoming troops with bullets. There was no place for the oncoming troops to hide or take shelter from the massacring guns. This crucial error cost the lives of 20,000 British soldiers that first day. Another 40,000 British were wounded. It was the worse day in all of British military history, and one that is still remembered with remorse at the unnecessary loss of life. The Americans learned to check the condition of their own defensive rolls of wire. This is what Sergeant Roche was referring to.

After the war, Mr. Roche and Warren Hearnes, future governor of Missouri, became friends in the American Legion. Mr. Roche mustered out of the reserve as a sergeant and became a Regional Commander of the American Legion. Sgt. Edward Roche passed away in 1983 at age 92 and is buried in St. Louis. He is remembered as "the veteran's best friend."

Meanwhile, "Stenay" still represents betrayal and a futile waste of 300 American lives.

SAVED BY THE TRAIN WHISTLE

Life in the army in World War I started out for William Claude Tillotson the same as for most draftees. On July 18, 1918, in Kansas City, Missouri, he took his oath of allegiance and was assigned to the 18th Recruitment Company for basic training. Then, in a surprise turn of events, his expectations and destination changed.

It all happened quickly. The train whistled once and the men and gear were all aboard, when the sergeant received an urgent message. He asked William and two others to step forward. "Forward to what?" they wondered. "Why three?" The sergeant announced they would not be going with their unit. Instead they were headed to a camp in Missouri. The Quartermaster Corps needed three good stenographers.

At first William was disappointed. He had looked forward

Pvt. William C. Tillotson
(Courtesy of Betty Tillotson)

144

to whatever their assignment would be. They had not been officially told that their destination would be Russia or Siberia yet, but President Wilson had ordered about 5000 Americans troops into northern Russia and Siberia to protect military supplies and aid those civilians that were both anti-German and anti-Bolshevik. The Americans were sometimes referred to as the "Polar Bears" or "The Forgotten Army." Later in life, William what he was to learn made him greatly relieved he had not been sent. The "Polar Bears" stayed an extra two years in Siberia after the war ended, guarding huge storehouses of arms and munitions the Czar of Russia had purchased several years ago with money loaned by American bankers. (Connaughton)

Meanwhile, back at Jefferson Barracks Military Post in St. Louis, Missouri, after a mild case of the influenza, William worked in an office, a job he loved and at which he excelled. He also ate army food of unusual tastiness, as the cook had been head chef at a famous Chicago restaurant. William's good fortune continued. He met May Tankersley, who would be his future wife. They were married November 27, 1919, six months after his discharge. Their only daughter, Betty Tillotson, Kansas City, Missouri, describes her mother from a photograph: "She was lovely in a gorgeous beige suit and matching hat. Even the winter rain and sleet didn't spoil their wedding day."

The newlyweds took the train to Holton, Kansas, to meet his parents and some townspeople, whose habits surprised May greatly. She saw little Indian boys smoking cigars. She had never seen Indians, and certainly not little boys smoking cigars. But the welcome from her new in-laws eased the strangeness, and they had baked the coconut cake she loved.

Life was good for the Tillotson family until their five year old son tragically died from an operation to correct a spinal defect. With the loss of his son, William realized he was the last of the Tillotson line. He had been spared the fighting and possible death in France, or being killed in the cold of Siberia. But he could not escape the realization that this was the end of the Tillotson's recorded history, which extended as far back at least to 1691. This was a sobering time for the family.

He ended his days in the army as a sergeant and a "crackerjack" stenographer, as the men recalled. The army needed large numbers of foot soldiers, but it also needed expert men at typewriters and file cabinets to keep track of the troops and their supplies and to be sure they were paid on time. William Claude Tillotson could proudly say he was one of those valuable men.

He was 93 years old when he died in 1985. A real "cracker Jack."

THE FORGOTTEN AMERICAN SOLDIERS — SIBERIA BOUND

Sub-zero duty: I Co. 339th Inf.,
85th Div. in North Russia.
(Courtesy of Veterans of Foreign Wars Magazine, 2004)

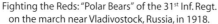

Fighting the Reds: "Polar Bears" of the 31st Inf. Regt.
on the march near Vladivostock, Russia, in 1918.

Approximately 15,000 American soldiers served almost two years from 1918-1920, in what became the Soviet Union. This was after the Armistice with the Central Powers had been signed in November, 1918. The men involved and their families often questioned this U.S. military decision. It was finally the families' constant petitioning that brought an end to the occupation. The official reasons remain obscure even now. During those years, the U.S. government did not even officially acknowledge the soldiers' presence in the lands of Siberia and Northern Russia, specifically Archangel, in the northeastern tip of Russia.

Although the AEF served under British command, and they were mixed with members of the Free Czech Army, and Canadian, Japanese, Italian and Chinese soldiers, it was not labeled an Allied cause at first. However, that is what it eventually was called. The campaign began May 24, 1918, when Allied troops occupied the city of Archangel in Russia to protect stockpiles of weapons purchased by the now deceased Czar of Russia, and to keep them from getting into the "wrong" hands. The official identity of who those hands were, was never officially or otherwise named.

But it was known that two Russian armies struggled to gain control of the government and therefore, its supplies. One force was the Bolsheviks, later called the Red Army, and the other group was the White Army, made up mostly of supporters of the czar's imperial forces.

The Allied group was reinforced by 55 in 1918 by crewmen from the U.S. cruiser, *USS Olympia*. Days later 150 Marines arrived to support the *Olympia* crew. The AEF units assigned to the intervention were the 339th Infantry Regiment, 310th Engineer Regiment (first battalion); 337th Ambulance Company; 337th Field Hospital, and 167th and 168th companies of the North Russian Transportation Corps. One dangerous incident was experienced by Company A, 31st Infantry which had camped beside the railroad to the Souchan Mine. "At dawn, several hundred partisans

The Allies, left to right: On duty in Siberia were American, Canadian, French, Japanese, Italian, Czech and Chinese (Courtesy G.O.S.)

rolled explosives into the camp and attacked. This was the bloodiest single battle of the Siberian Intervention, with 19 AEF soldiers killed and 25 wounded out of a force of 72 infantrymen."(Ron Magee)

Another incident recorded was on January 9-10, 1920, when Sgt. Carl Robbins climbed onto an enemy locomotive and threw a hand grenade. He was killed but he disabled the locomotive. His men took the train on which five Russians had been killed and one wounded, and captured one general, six officers, and 48 enlisted men. The Americans had two killed and one wounded. (Ron Magee) By the time the expedition had ended, and the men departed on June 27, 1919, they had sustained casualties of 144 killed in action; 305 wounded in action; 81 dead from disease; and 19 killed in accidents. (Graves)

On the same continent, but about 4000 miles to the east, was a Marine detachment from the *USS Brooklyn*, which landed at Vladivostok to protect the United States Consulate located there. Eventually, 9,000 AEF troops from the Philippines and a California unit arrived in August 15, 1918, to form the AEF fighting force. The first AEF casualty was Pvt. Stephen Duhart, who was wounded in action when a 40-man detachment from the 27th Infantry was ambushed by Chinese bandits.

More military action took place in June, 1919, when five AEF troops were captured by the Red Army. The Allies sent 110 men from the 31st Infantry to rescue the captives but were ambushed. The greatest loss of AEF lives occurred in Siberia when 24 men were killed by Red soldiers and bandits. The next month, joined by troops from the *USS Albany* and *USS New Orleans*, the Americans attacked Red soldiers hiding in Suchan Valley. The AEF successfully cleared the valley and occupied hostile villages, killing more than 500 enemy guerrilas in the attack.

One source of confusion and occasional irritation was the variety of groups that attacked the supply piles and the railroad blockhouses that protected them. It could be Red or White Russians or various tribes of Chinese bandits as well as Cossacks. The AEF troops were now disillusioned by the manner in which their services had been required by the Russian army and then the type of compensation.

The original British goal of protecting the stores of grain and oil to keep them out of German hands during the war, took on a new dimension after the Armistice. They were to guard the huge piles of munitions and 1,500 locomotives with 30,000 boxcars and 329 railway workers who formed the Russian Railway Service Corps. However, the civilian workers refused to stay unless an armed Allied guard was there to protect them. Various interpretations of President Wilson's orders often provided confusion as to the extent of protection the AEF was to offer. The area to be protected consisted of at least 4,126 miles along the Trans-Siberian Railway. (Work of American Red Cross)

Another source of confusion was the Japanese attempt to seize control of the Trans-Siberian railroad. A meeting of various representatives ended with the Japanese leaving the meeting in anger. As a result, various countries were in charge of different sections of the railroad. Skirmishes broke out when one country tried to exceed its authority and some fighting took place at the railroad stations.

This assignment has been called "one of the more bizarre actions in American history" by historian George Kennan. It certainly needs to be a subject of more research with the results perhaps proving to be an embarrassment and a needless tragedy for those the Allies fought there. (Magee)

On January 9, 1920, the last combat action took place at Posolskaya railroad station when a 39 man platoon from the 27th Infantry was shot at from a Cossack armored train. Two soldiers were killed and two were wounded. In April the last AEF troops left Russia, and Japanese troops took control of Vladivostok three days later.

The final toll for this expedition was 48 men killed in action and 52 were wounded. Another 122 lives were lost due to disease and mishaps. While the actual number of casualties is not proportionally high when compared to the figures from the battlegrounds of France, still, the American families must have questioned the value of these losses especially when the purpose of the venture was obscure then and remains unclear today.

However, the nearly 15,000 AEF well deserved the nickname "Polarbears," and earned the specially designed shoulder patch of a lumbering bear adding a distinctive touch to their uniform.

Surely the families of those injured or who died must have felt negative emotions toward the military that ordered their loved ones to the freezing and hazardous regions of Russia, although once that country had been part of the Allies. With their family members spending two years in those miserably cold regions for unknown goal or purpose, families asked their Congressmen in a concerted effort to have the men brought home. Perhaps it was their strong petitions that ended the expedition in Russia. (VFW Magazine, 2004)

Historian George Kennan comments, 'never, surely, in the history of American diplomacy has so much been paid for so little." M. G. Graves in his book, *America's Siberian Adventure*, admits that even though he was in charge of the AEF troops in Siberia, "I must admit, I do not know what the United States was trying to accomplish by military intervention." The episode is still being investigated.

GREAT MOMENTS IN THEIR LIVES

The military provided an unexpected turn of events in the lives of Maurice D. McDaniel, and his wife, Esteline. McDaniel, from Fortuna, Missouri, enlisted in Kansas City, Missouri, when he was 25 years old. He worked as an accountant in the army, continuing the same line of work from civilian life. The day came when his basic training was completed, and he said his farewells to his family. His unit, the 339th Infantry was leaving the States.

Loaded with over 60 pounds of gear, he climbed aboard a train. It would be a three to four day ride to the port of embarkation for overseas duty, with the final destination of Siberia. Why Siberia, when the fighting was in France?

Maurice D. McDaniel was assigned
to Jefferson Barracks, MO
(Courtesy Marian Neal)

The soldiers had almost finished boarding, when at the last minute, a call came from the Quartermaster Corps. They needed experienced office staff in the States, soldiers with up to date accounting skills. McDaniel and two others were selected. McDaniel later realized this became his greatest moment in his army service. St. Louis instead of Siberia! His story is told by his daughter, Marian Neale, Raymore, Missouri.

The new assignment changed his Army career plans completely. McDaniel unpacked his rifle and kit and sat down again at a typewriter and accounting pad. He was assigned to duty in the Quartermaster Corps at Camp Meigs after spending some time at Jefferson Barracks, near St. Louis, Missouri. He was discharged shortly after the Armistice was signed November 11, 1918. Meanwhile the troops in Siberia had to stay at their assignment for two years longer. It was not until 1920 when their units were finally recalled. Sometimes they thought they had become "The Forgotten Unit." (Ellis)

"The Polar Bear Unit," as they were also called, had a shoulder insignia showing a polar bear. They experienced a number of hardships, illnesses, and about 200 deaths from the extremely cold temperatures. Most puzzling of all, they didn't know why they were in Siberia, or why they were opposing the Bolsheviks at first, known later as the Communists, then later fighting the White Russians or the anti-Bolsheviks. (Doughboy Center) (See story, p. 145)

McDaniel learned years later the Americans had joined forces from Japan, the free Czech army, and Great Britain and other forces. All were assigned to protect great stores of munitions and armaments that had been sent from the United States to the Russian czar before he was assassinated. The czar had borrowed heavily from American bankers to pay for the materiel.

Finally, in 1921 the Bolsheviks defeated the White Russians, and all foreign troops, including the "Polar Bears," were finally dispatched home. The Bolsheviks took possession of the munitions. There is no public information about whether the American bankers were ever repaid.

McDaniel, his accounting skills in high demand by the Army, admitted many times he was lucky to have spent the war years in the States, and not in the far off, frozen land of Siberia. No "Polar Bears" for him.

Meanwhile, in 1920 Maurice, 33, and Esteline, 28, married. The time for Mrs. McDaniel to have her great moment came on November 1, 1921. It was during the dedication of the grounds of the World War I Liberty Memorial in Kansas City, Missouri. The couple had moved to Kansas City after they married, and all area servicemen and their wives were invited to the ceremony. The dignitaries were the five most famous military leaders from the war.

France's Marshal General Foch, Allied Supreme Commander, headed the list. General Jacques from Belgium stood next to Italy's reknowned General Dias. Just behind General Foch stood America's AEF commander, General John J. Pershing. The fifth dignitary was Great Britain's Admiral Beattie of the British Royal Navy.

But seeing these famous men was not the only highlight of the day. Mr. McDaniels donned his uniform again and was in the inspection parade of veterans passing in review of the military leaders. The wives of the parading veterans were later invited to a private reception to shake hands with the dignitaries. Mrs. McDaniels talked of this "handshake experience" the rest of her long life, her daughter recalls. Marian, born in 1926, was the couple's only child.

Another important time for the family, Marian remembers, was in 1936 when the Veterans' Bonus, long promised by Congress, was finally paid. Friends and neighbors all congregated on the McDaniel's porch to hear the news on the radio. They cheered so boisterously that Marian says she will never forget the night.

Both parents were active in forming the local American Legion unit and engaging in its activities. That became the center of their social life, Marian recalls. Another favorite custom was the "Last Man's Club." Veterans gathered each year to drink from a bottle, celebrating they were still alive. This was to continue until finally only one man would still be alive. He would get to keep the bottle.

Marian's father died just short of his 83rd birthday, but that was not long enough to keep the bottle. Several others outlasted him. Marian doesn't know who finally kept the bottle. She's lost track of her old life and her old friends. But she's never forgotten the stories that were the occasions of her parents' greatest moments.

PRIVATE LENTZ — A PERSHING ADMIRER

It was Private Dowell Mowery Lentz's good fortune, or bad luck, whichever way he viewed it, that his draft date came up three months before the Armistice was signed. This meant that his training would not be completed in time for him to be shipped overseas, although no one was aware the Armistice would be signed in November. He planned on a voyage to France, once his training was completed. But in early 1919 he packed away his uniform, scarcely worn. He had been drafted too late to complete his training as an artillery gunner.

He did have a big military moment, but that had to wait for three years. On November 21, 1921, a civilian again, his good fortune was to stand among the crowd of thousands from all over America for a momentous occasion. They had come to see the Allies' five most important generals conduct the dedication of the Liberty Memorial ground in Kansas City, Missouri. They were General Jacques, Belgium; General Diaz, Italy; General Foch, Supreme Commander of Allied Forces; General Pershing, United States; and Admiral Beattie, Great Britain, Navy.

Pvt. Dowell Mowery Lentz
(Courtesy of Peggy Fisher)

Private Lentz served briefly under one of those five men, General John J. Pershing, commander of the AEF forces although General Pershing was in France with the troops, while Private Lentz was still in a stateside training camp on November 11, 1918. His daughter, Peggy Smith, Independence, Missouri, says her father never talked much about the war, only about the grand inspection parades in front of the military leaders. He was "bursting at the seams" when he saw his Gen. John J. Pershing, on the inspection stand. After he finished training, as a member of Company F, 30th Field Artillery Regiment, he was scheduled to join the rest of the regiment already fighting overseas. Those men had been drafted earlier in 1918 and been trained in time to get some battlefield experience.

Lentz and others remained stateside until their discharge January 29, 1919, at Camp Funston, Kansas. It was in later years that the 30th Field Artillery again fought, in World War II, and received honors of distinction, but by then Lentz was too old to sign up. However, there were some reminders of army life that Private Lentz did not escape. One was the painful injections that protected him from several diseases after his induction in August, 1918. Another reminder were the miles and miles of march in order, to various cadences. He had sore feet on those nights.

He told his family many times that he thought "General Pershing was next to God." Five years after the dedication of the land for the memorial, still in great admiration of the general, Lentz managed to attend the dedication of the completed memorial on November 21, 1926. This time, however, it was President Calvin Coolidge who took the stage in the absence of General Pershing. A park named after the General stood near the Memorial, which Lentz's daughter, Peggy, remembers. Her father, a quiet modest man, said his few months in the Army were nothing compared to the service of the boys "who got shot at." They were the heroes, he claimed.

Lentz was born May 29, 1897, in Atchison, Kansas, and died May 21, 1968, age 71, just a few days short of being 72. He married Gladys Langer in 1926, and they had three children. He worked for the Vendo Company in Kansas City for years, and is buried beside the graves of many of his relatives. Peggy has a family genealogy dating back to 1789 when a German ancestor came to America with six of his brothers.

Her father, before being drafted in 1918, trained mules in Colorado for sale to the army. Peggy wonders if her father had been shipped to France, would he have recognized any of the mules he trained in Colorado. And would they have recognized him also? She laughs at the possibility.

THE FIRST AND LAST — LIEUTENANT FITZSIMONS & PRIVATE MINER

Pvt. Wayne Miner at left and Lt. William H. Clark at center and Lt. William A. Fitzsimons at right.
(Miner and Clark courtesy of Joelouis Mattox) (Fitzsimons Courtesy Archives NWWIMM)

"How tragic." That was the natural reaction of Kansas Citians when the Armistice was declared ending the war, only to be followed by word that an heroic Kansas City serviceman had been killed only a half hour before the deadline. Perhaps those who heard this, also recalled that a little more than a year earlier, the first American officer to be killed was also from Kansas City. Ironic. What a waste of life. This is what war is like, as many citizens learned. They were as powerless to change those outcomes, as the two soldiers could have changed the direction of the weapon that killed them.

The officer was Lt. William T. Fitzsimons, who was stationed September, 1917 at a Base Hospital in France, when he was killed by a bomb from an overhead flying machine. Some stories say Zeppelin, others say aeroplane. Private Wayne Miner, who died on Armistice Day, was a black soldier assigned to the 366th Infantry Regiment, 92nd Division, an all Black combat unit assigned to the Marbache Sector, part of the St.Mihiel campaign. Earlier that morning, Miner had been the first of four men to volunteer to carry ammunition to an outpost, an extremely dangerous mission.

His story is told in part through records compiled by 1st Lieutenant William H. Clark, Kansas City, Kansas, who commanded the unit of Company A, 1st Battalion, 366th Infantry, 92nd Division. The Division was advancing as the spearhead of the regiment's position in the Allied line of the Marlache Sector. Wayne Miner was a private in the First Platoon. Clark writes, "We were on high ground in the village of Montfaveon, overlooking the Bois Vivrotte, and our first objective was one mile away and known to be occupied by German outpost units."

Lieutenant Clark continues: "Just before time to attack, a message came requesting four men from each company to assist in carrying machine gun ammunition. This was an unwanted assignment and I always called for volunteers. I made a strong appeal but for a minute or two, no one stepped forward to accept. I told the boys they were letting me down and I would use the lottery system... Private Wayne Miner stepped forward, then another, and others... When Wayne Miner stepped out, a lump-like feeling accumulated in my throat. He was a highly cultured and courageous soldier, respected by the entire company of 250 men..."

Commenting further, Clark says, Miner had been on "every patrol I made, including one on October 16...Brigadier General Barnum praised us highly...(in a) personal eulogy (which) was my most prized possession..." When carrying the heavy ammunition, the soldier is helpless to defend himself because he has slung his rifle across his back to free his arms for carrying. Lt. Clark declared: "I never saw Wayne Miner again..." Clark was wounded in the attack and while in the hospital, he learned that bursting shrapnel had killed Miner. "I recommended him for the Distinguished Service Cross. Somehow, my captain through whom it was sent, never received it and a brave sacrificing and deserving soldier did not receive his just reward even posthumously."

Lieutenant Clark continued with his narrative about the fierceness of the ensuing attack and the deaths of other men around him. He told of mustard gas "dripping from the trees" after being exploded in such quantities. Casualties of the two platoons Clark commanded amounted to about 40%. The other platoons saw higher casualty figures. Private Wayne Miner is buried in the St. Mihiel American Cemetery along with the graves of 4,153 other Americans. His death was announced in a December 6, 1918, issue of the Kansas City STAR newspaper, along with the deaths of several other local soldiers. A memorial flag pole has been constructed at the end of a boulevard in Kansas City on a ledge. Below the flag is carved a memorial fountain to Lieutenant Fitzsimons. (Mattox)

"The First and the Last" - Lieutenant Fitzsimons and Private Miner. A Kansas City tragedy of world wide proportions.

Post Script:
Wayne Miner was born August 17, 1894, and lived his early years in Iowa. He married Belle Carter sometime between the years 1910 and 1918. He entered the army on October 16, 1917, as a volunteer and received his basic training at Camp Dodge, Iowa. He was sent to France on June 15, 1918. The year following his death saw the founding of American Legion Wayne Miner Post #149 in Kansas City. In its early years the Post founded a Ladies' Auxiliary and a Drum and Bugle Corps. The Post advocated for desegregation of veterans' hospitals and soldiers' homes. In a story about the 1919 Armistice Parade in Kansas City, it was printed that as many as 100 members of his post marched under the leadership of Lieutenant Roberts. (KC STAR) Miner was one of 21 African-Americans from Kansas City killed in the war.
In 1960 the largest housing development was named in his honor by the Housing Authority of Kansas City. (Mattox)The Kansas City CALL reported that upon enlisting, Wayne changed his name from "Wayman Minor." (KC Call Week June 3-9, 2011)

THE CLASS ASSIGNMENT TODAY:
MY GRANDFATHER, A SOLDIER IN WORLD WAR I

History teacher, Dan Nolan, decided to search his family background for a topic his high school students could study. As a result of his seminar at the National World War I Museum and Memorial during the summer of 2014, he used his research on his grandfather, Luther Clyde Williams, as the topic. Dan had learned that his grandfather had started his soldiering in 1916 or earlier, as a member of the Alabama National Guard.

Luther was 20 years old and a farm worker in Cleburne County, Alabama. One record remaining says Luther was "present 4 drills {in} Mar. 1916," and was issued from Sheffield, Alabama. Another record reveals that Luther belonged to G Company of the 4th Infantry. The Alabama troops were recalled from Mexico and the pursuit of the bandit, Pancho Villa, after the United States declared war on Germany on April 6, 1917. At that time, National Guard companies were integrated into division size units, and the 4th Infantry became part of the 167th Regiment of the famed 42nd Division.

If this was the actual situation for Luther, then he would have been among the first group of troops to be sent to France which left October 17, 1917. There they completed more up- to- date training in using trenches, grenades, and how to move over unfamiliar ground. This was the usual course of instruction for AEF troops where they finished training in France under the experienced English and French officers. The first battle the 42nd participated in was the 1918 (Second) Aisne-Marne Offensive of July 25 through August 3. The training and additional AEF troops brought about a decisive victory over the Germans. The 42nd moved on to such familiar sites as Meuse-Argonne and Verdun. It is not known if Luther's company was involved in those battles, but units from the 42nd were used from time to time, with periods of relief in between battles.

Because of the hazardous battle, the 42nd counted 2,713 dead and 13,292 wounded. For the numerous acts of bravery, 205 Distinguished Crosses, America's second highest medal, were awarded. Luther received a certificate saying: "The United States of America honors the memory of Luther Clyde Williams in 'recognition of devoted and selfless consecration to the service of our country in the Armed Forces of the United States.' " President Gerald Ford signed the long delayed document on August 31, 1970.

However, his townsmen recognized Luther's contributions much earlier by making him a lifetime member of the American Legion of the Fletcher-McCollister Post # 135 at Phenix City, Alabama. This was the tribute to a farm boy from a family of seven children, who served as one of the 5,000 National Guardsmen from Alabama early in The Great War.

His grandson, Dan, concludes by proudly saying that after his class lesson on his grandfather, "It isn't often that a class applauds the teacher at the end of the day," as his students did. Dan must be the "chip off the old block" that his grandfather, Luther Clyde Williams, personified. Luther died in 1975 at the age of 79 and was buried in Phenix City, Russel County, Alabama. Dan teaches at Norman High School, Norman, Oklahoma.

GARFIELD SCHOOL WORLD WAR I PLAQUE SPEAKS

"I can be found on a wall in Garfield School in the Old Northeast area of Kansas City, Missouri. After World War I ended, I was installed as an important reminder of how many of our Garfield students served their country when it called them. I am engraved with the names of 213 students who walked through these school halls, and later joined to fight for our country. I am proud to bear their names. Take a look. Is there a name you recognize?

"In 1886 my doors opened, making me one of the oldest ward schools in Kansas City. Children living in Ward 9 were assigned to my building. At first, I had only eight rooms, but in 1909 and 1921 many additions were made. I was a splendid looking school and attracted many students. In 1914, for example, we had a total enrollment of 552 students. As for how I was named, you probably have guessed. It was in honor of President James A. Garfield, who was assassinated in July, 1881. President Garfield's assassination came so soon after President Lincoln was shot in 1866, people everywhere were

Garfield School Plaque
(Photo by author)

shocked. Such a horrible event occurring, two of our presidents assassinated within 15 years while in office. So I felt honored to bear President Garfield's name. We already had a school named after President Lincoln.

"After World War I ended in 1918, students and parents decided to commemorate the former Garfield students who served. They collected the large sum of $1000.00 to erect my remarkable bronze plaque memorial. Six of the men were killed in the war. Their names are James W. Swofford, Jr., Robert McClelland Simpson, Harry Fenton, Stanley Willis Wood, Amos Johnson and Murray Davis. Many of the 213 students were children of immigrants from the British Isles, Germany, the Baltics and the Balkans. There were two women who also joined war organizations to help, Helen Mitchell Spencer and Marjorie Lewis.

"From the very first, Garfield School was an unusual school, experimenting with new ideas and many new subjects. In the early 1900's a group of 60 students learned the German language. They continued studying German until the war started and unfortunately, ill feelings toward the German people brought an end to the study of their language.

"Other students started the first garden in a school. Later, we introduced pre-vocational training and athletics into a school curriculum. Parents wanted their children to get a good education, and that is why they liked Garfield. These parents worked in low paying jobs under unpleasant and dangerous working conditions in the numerous factories and meat slaughtering plants near here. They knew how important a good education was, and they wanted a better life for their children.

"Then The Great War broke out in Europe in 1914. The United States did not enter the fighting until 1917, when it declared war against the Central Powers of which Germany was the leader. That was when former Garfield students volunteered or were drafted into the services. In addition to the six who died, many of the others soldiers were gassed or wounded, causing some of them to lead lives of pain and misery. A few former students were so anxious to help the Allies, they joined in the Canadian, British or French armies in 1915 and 1916.They included Captain Stanley Wood who was among the 22 from Kansas City who enlisted. A nurse from Kansas City, Loretta Hollenback, was among the first to die from the flu at Camp Funston. Everyone thinks that's where the flu originated.

156

They called it "Spanish flu" for some reason, I don't know. There were a number of families who had two or three sons who were killed in the war including some from Garfield.

"But, if asked why they served, the soldiers might have said: 'It was my duty to serve my country.' Or 'The war was terrible. We must never have another one like it again. Another would have explained, 'I'm proud to have been a soldier,' or ' I lost my best friend in a battle.' 'I fought for children who are immigrants like I was.' Maybe someone might even add, 'I died so they could have a free public education.' "

After the children left the school, the plaque started talking again. It explained, "While the background of today's students is of different origins now, such as African-American, Hispanic and Asian, the students have the same goal. They are here to get a good education so they can be loyal American citizens, like their parents." He seemed satisfied with his remarks.

Suddenly the plaque spoke up again. "Be quiet. Here they come, the six who died. Sometimes they come to visit me and tell me their war stories. Maybe they will today. Let's listen."

The six apparitions walked slowly down the empty hall. In almost inaudible words, they talked to each other. I had to strain to hear them; John Stanley Wood reminded the others of the concerts the Glee Club gave in 1913, two years before he graduated. He had been a captain in the British-Canadian service, joining in 1915, two years after he graduated and was wearing that uniform. "Unfortunately, I only served about a year when I took my last flight on June 13, 1916. That's the way it was in those early days of flying. You just took a chance, and some of us lost."

Second Lt. James Swofford, Jr. reminded the group that there were eight men from Kansas City killed on Armistice Day, 1918, but none had attended Garfield, so they had not known them. One was an African-American, Wayne Miner, who became somewhat a hero because he volunteered to carry machine gun ammunition to the unit's outpost. He and three others were killed by a German bomb blast, just minutes before the Armistice took place. He shook his head in sympathy, and added, "Guess those guys took a chance, like I did while standing in a hospital tent and lost too." Swofford had been in the medical unit attached to the 52nd Artillery.

Another apparition spoke up. "Weren't you all kinds of officers in this and that?" James smiled, "Well, someone had to fill those positions. Yes, I was class treasurer, president of the Central Webster Club, Advertising Manager for the "Luminary." I kinda liked acting so I was in the Christmas play, and won a gold medal in the Literary Contest. I graduated in 1911, so I am older than some of you guys." He grinned and patted the lapels of his AEF uniform. Turning to the figure next to him, he asked, "Why don't you ever tell us about yourself?"

The next figure to speak was Robert M. Simpson, private first class. "You all have heard about the 42nd Rainbow Division. I fought with the 117th Field Signal Battalion. I went to France early right after General Pershing did. I was killed June 20, 1918 and buried in the Meuse-Argonne Cemetery finally. Then my family had me brought back to Missouri to be buried nearer them in The East Slope Gardens at Riverside. Sure makes it easier to come back here and meet all of you. What about you, Harry?"

Harry Fenton hesitated, then said," You think you're the old man of the bunch. I was born in 1890, so I was a lot older than you when I signed up at age 24. I'd already sailed over and back on the Atlantic before the war even started. I was a consulting mining engineer in Belgium, and Belgium sure looked a lot prettier when I was there the first time." Harry paused, then began. " Right after high school I moved to Washington, D. C. in about 1909, then returned to Jackson County and in 1916, Mary Ann Redford and I married. That was shortly before I signed up as a lieutenant. When I died, I left her and my two sisters behind. Sure made me feel bad about how they were going to manage without me. But it looks like they managed, although sure was rough for them at first." He had tears in his eyes. The rest of the group looked away, all except Swafford who put a hand on his shoulder.

Some of the men remembered Marjorie Lewis who joined the Yeomanettes, the women's branch of the Navy in July 27, 1918. Few of them knew Helen M. Spencer, although she was born in 1893 and would have been their age. She had graduated from Central High School, attended the University of Missouri, later graduating from Northwestern University. She received a Master's degree at Columbia University in New York.

She taught school for about eight years before being appointed a canteen worker for the Y.M.C.A. overseas. Miss Spencer was in France for a year, then returned on the ship *SMS Kronprinz Friedrich Wilhelm*, according to a telegram her father received.

In a letter she wrote from Blois, France, where she was in charge of a YMCA Reading Hut, she commented that, "Many of the boys are marrying French girls. Many are going to stay here, and I wonder if they will be happy and contented when the others go home. The American is 'it' here… Blois is full of hospitals and men in B and C class—convalescents. The troops are passing through all the time and the 'Y' huts and hotels are packed. The pianos are rotten, but the Yanks must have music. Many of them play beautifully, and sing, too."(Kansas City Star, January 3, 1919.)

Just as they were about to break up, a new apparition appeared. He was greeted with "Hey, aren't the lawyer guy, Murray Davis , who decided a gun would defeat the Huns better than a pencil?" Murray bashfully grinned and looked down, then straightened his shoulders. "Yes, I was a major stuck in general's office while the rest of you were out taking all the Boche could throw at you. I asked for a transfer to the 140th Infantry of the 35th Division which most of you belonged to."

One of the apparitions asked, "But that was a fairly safe job, and you worked hard to rise in rank from private to major. I don't understand why you left it." Murray was silent a moment, then said, "I'm not sure I understood too. But even though I am older than even you," he turned to Robert," I guess I wanted to be one of the boys. The Argonne Forest presented my chance to see how I would react under fire. Too bad I was killed September 29 before the fighting was all over." Harry burst in," From the look of all those ribbons, you must have acted pretty darned brave before your time came." Amos spoke up, "And there's that square dedicated to you to 40th and Main. You must be a swell." "Not really," Murray hastened to explain, "That square is dedicated to all of us if you read it carefully. The people who raised much of the money just happened to know my dad. Say, it sure was good to see you guys again. We'll have to get together again. Any particular date?" Someone said," No, but you'll know. That's one of the neat things about being like we are. We know a lot in advance."

After talking briefly about some of the other names on the plaque, James Swofford looked at his watch. "Hey, fellows, our time is up. Sure was good to see you again, until next time." They all shook hands and gradually disappeared from sight. The plaque continued with a smile in his voice. "They sure are my fellows. It always makes me feel good when they make a visit. Now my time is up, also. Glad you came along today. Hope you think it was worth it." He was quiet again.

(Annals of Kansas City, Missouri. Missouri Valley Historical Society, Kansas City, Missouri, 1925-26; The Waldo Story, The Home of Friendly Merchants. LaDene Morton. Missouri Historical Review, State Historical Society of Missouri. Vol. Num. Oct.

MAIL THAT FAMILIES DREADED TO RECEIVE

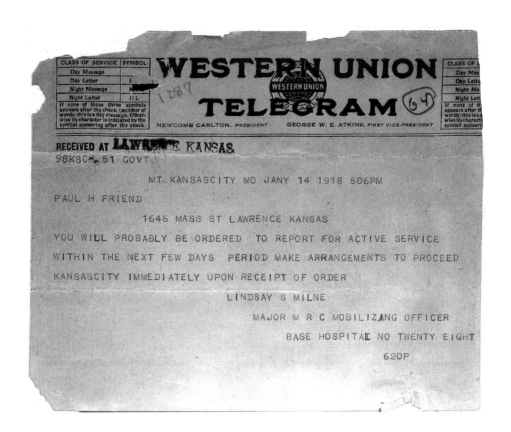

Company K 119th Infantry.
Dec. 3(?) 1918

Text of letter to Mrs. Robert (?) Hayden
            1451 N. 8th St.
            St. Louis, Mo.

Dear Mrs. Hayden:

In reply to yours of the 7th of Nov. received today, am glad to give you
the particulars of your brother's death and at the same time take the opportunity
of telling you of his glorious record as a soldier, and the noble
manner in which he made the Supreme sacrifice. He was highly thought of by his offi... (?)
and comrades; he was at all times ready to do his full duty. He died
at his post, faithful to the last.

It was in the Trenches at Ypres, Belgium, that h(?) and three others were killed
during a terrific bombardment by th(?) German Artillery. Posted as a
Sentinel, he refused to move from his post, even though he knew that death and destruction
was rai(?)ing about him. He died as he lived- faithful to the cause of Humanity,
Justice and Freedom.

I am glad to have this opportunity of expressin(?) myself to his sisters.

            Yours Very Truly,
            (signed) Robert B. Holden
            Lieut 119 Inf.

(Courtesy of the American Cemetery at Flanders, Belgium.)

Wording on telegram 12/27:

Dated: Washington, D.C. 12/27
To: Mrs.Sophie Fossum
(Words on first line are illegible)as is (35 Gov?)

Deeply regret to inform you that Private William(?) T. Fossum infantry is officially reported as killed in action about November
eleventh.

Harris
The Adjutant General

(NOTE: The year is not given, but most likely was 1918, as there were few American soldiers in France in November, 1917. Where there are question marks, it means the writing is illegible. This means her son was one of the last AEF to die.)

Wording on envelope:

From

Mrs. Wesley J. Creech	**Deceased**
Ballou, N.C.	Capt. JWJ 9/16 (18?)

       To
         Private Wesley J. Creech
         CO. C 120 Inf. 35 Division
         c/o American E. Force
         Via New York
            France

(Note: What a heartache Mrs. Creech must have felt when her letter was returned in this manner, even though she may have been notified by telegram earlier of his death.)

(Courtesy of American Flanders Field Cemetery, Flanders, Belgium)

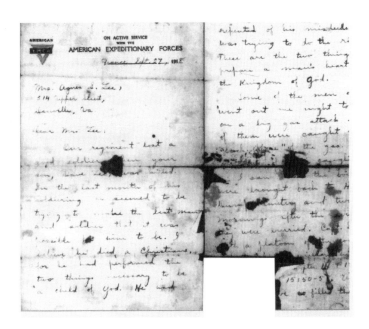

COPY OF REMNANTS OF LETTER SENT TO MOTHER OF DEAD SON

Letterhead reads:

ON ACTIVE SERVICE
WITH THE
AMERICAN EXPEDITIONARY FORCES

Mrs. Agnes S. Lee,
514 Cupper Street
Danville, VA.

Dear Mrs.Lee:

Our regiment lost a good soldier when your son, Dave Lee, was killed.
In the last months of his soldering he seemed to be trying to make the bestman and
soldier that it was possible (marked out) him to be. I believe he died a Chrisian, for he
two things necessary to be a child of God. He had repented of his misdeeds... was
trying to do the ri... These are the two things ... prepare a man's heart ... for the Kingdom
of God.
     Some of the men...l went out one night to ...on a big gas attack...of them were
caught...(illegible) of the gas. (Illegible) cauaght.
     I saw (blot) the boys... the boys were brought back to ...Dis(blot) cemetery and two
mornings after the (blot) they were buried. Capt. (illegible)

The letter has blots of ink or perhaps holes where mice or silverfish may have been chewing. It
is a comforting letter, and provides as much solicitude as can be relayed by letter. Pity the poor
mother, but also pity the officer who probably wrote many such letters to grieving parents.

(Courtesy of the American Flanders Field Cemetery, Flanders, Belgium.)

TRULY A WORLD WAR

It was estimated that more than 100 nations, principalities, dominions, territories, and concessions, and colonies participated in some manner in World War I. Here are a few of these non-European cultures, ethnic groups and nations and the role they held in the conflict of 1914-1918.

CHINA: The British recruited about 175,000 Chinese to supply their Labor Corps to dig trenches, carry supplies, cut lumber, build roads, lay railroads, and carry ammunition. A total of 50,000 Chinese and Indian laborers died in Europe, some from disease, and other from wounding directly on the front lines. There is a cemetery devoted entirely to Chinese burials. The Germans and French likewise conscripted about 150,000 Chinese each from their consignments in German Tientsin and the French in Shanghai. These, in addition to doing laboring work, also worked in factories.

VIETNAM: The French used between 94,000 and 140,000 Vietnamese, often obtaining them by harsh and repressive means. The Vietnamese responded by forming secret societies to actively resist French recruitment.

INDIA: India had a standing army of 1.4 million men who fought for the British, whose standing army was a mere pittance of 130,000 professional soldiers. The Indians paid a high price for their support, with near 114,000 dead, wounded or missing. In addition, more than half a million Indian non-combatants helped the war effort working as laborers, carriers, and railway constructors. Many historians believe the arrival of the Indian forces forestalled a quick German victory. These troops often were assigned to some of the most hazardous attacks such as the 20th Deccan Cavalry charge at High Wood and in the July, 1916, Battle of the Somme against hidden German machine guns.

For their courage and bravery the Indian soldiers won 12,455 British and 463 Allied medals and decorations, including 12 Victoria Cross awards.

JAPAN: Japanese soldiers quickly took over German island possessions in China as well as most of Germany's Pacific Island colonies. They also provided sea patrols of trade routes from Australia and New Zealand as well as from India for the Allied ships. They watched for German submarine packs and protected the Allied merchant ships.

CANADA: A dominion of Britain, the Canadian troops fought bravely at Gallipoli and other battle sites; defeated the Germans at the harshly contested Vimy Ridge, Thievpal Ridge, Passchendaele, Cambrai, Amiens, and Valenciennes. One of their privates was among the last to be killed in the war. At 10:58 a.m. on November 11, 1918, Private George Price was killed by a gunshot wound.

LATIN AMERICA: While most Latin American countries refrained from joining the war efforts for either side, four countries did make major contributions in providing supplies. They included Mexico with petroleum; Argentina, surplus wheat; Chile, nitrates and copper; and Brazil, food, especially beef, beans and sugar. They also seized German ships to be available for transport.

AFRICA: This continent played a dual role in the war by furnishing both troops to fight local battles and sending troops and laborers to serve in Europe. One dangerous job they fulfilled was as porters carrying supplies and weapons to the Allies. Often walking 14 miles a day carrying heavy loads, their paths often led them through war torn areas. Estimates of their deaths range from 200,000 to 250,000 which is more than 10 percent of the two million Africans of various countries who served in Europe. In addition to the high rate of deaths, they faced racial discrimination and mistreatment routinely in their work.

WEST AFRICA (Senegal and Morocco)- More than 135,000 men from these colonies were drafted by the French to serve in the European armies. As with other Africans, they experienced frequent discrimination, fear, difficulties and degradation. French soldiers and society segregated them, isolating them socially. In addition, the troops were used as "shock troops", leading the French in the most hazardous of battles, resulting in death rates of 25% higher than the French. However, some troops including the Moroccans in the defense of Paris, became the most highly decorated units in the French army.

AUSTRALIA: As a British colony in 1914, Australia had a population of less than five million from which an army was raised numbering almost 417,000 men. Over 330,000 served overseas. Australians are famous for their participation in the ill fated Gallipoli campaign of 1915, where they suffered untenable casualties. Of the 26,111 injured, nearly one-third of them died. The high casualties resulted with more than half dying and/or being gassed, wounded or taken prisoner of war. Even now, every year hundreds of Australians and New Zealanders make a pilgrimage to the peninsula of Gallipoli to honor their ANZAC soldiers, as they were called. Their sacrifice was not in vain, for in 1986 their countries finally became independent of Great Britain.(History Site, Schaeffer)

WAR'S DESTRUCTION, AND LESSONS LEARNED

By Niel M. Johnson, Ph.D. – Guest Commentator

New Magnitudes of Destruction:

World War I was a war of destruction, on a magnitude the world had not experienced before. The number of those killed, wounded, or died of disease--principally from a pandemic of influenza--was larger than in any previous war. In an age of expanding technology, that phenomenon was caused in part by the invention of new weapons, especially of long-range, large bore artillery and the mobile machine gun, as well as the development and use of poison gas and of armored vehicles on treads (the tank). A main contributor, too, was the unplanned need to bunker down in thousands of miles of trenches, from which infantry charges were met by lethal machine gun fire as well as by more conventional rifle fire. The use of armed aircraft, invented only a decade before, added to the carnage.

At least nine million soldiers and sailors died in combat, and two to three times that number suffered wounds. Of those captured, about ten percent died in prison camps. The global flu epidemic in 1918-19 claimed the lives, including civilians, of two to three times the number who died on the battlefield. (Weber) In addition to those numbers are the millions who died and suffered in the civil war in Russia from 1918-21, which was an outgrowth of the civil disruption triggered by the war on the Russian front. Not to be forgotten, too, is the massacre, also referred to as a genocide, of up to a million Armenians, mostly Christian, in the aftermath of the collapse of the Ottoman empire.

In monetary terms, the total direct costs of the war have been estimated at $180.5 billion, and the indirect costs at about $151.6 billion, amounting to a total of $331 billion. (Langer, Encyclopedia of World History, 976.) Another source says that England alone had spent $44 billion on the war, greater than all the British capital invested in the country's industrial and financial enterprises of the United Kingdom. Germany had expended 22 percent of its national wealth, the Italians, 26 percent, and the French, 30 percent. France depleted one half of its gold reserves. (Weber, A Modern History of Europe, 858)

Of course, it was in France and Belgium that most of the property and human destruction occurred on the western front. They had the difficult task of rebuilding their homes, businesses, and public buildings. Such expenses also had to compete with repayment of war debts. The enormous cost of rebuilding helps account for the huge and unrealistic indemnity that was imposed on Germany in the Versailles Treaty after the war ended. New states, some of which remained unstable, were also created from the remnants that remained from the destruction of the Austro-Hungarian, Russian, and Ottoman Empires. The drawing of borders of new states in the Middle East was especially problematic. The effort to provide self-determination for subject peoples was based on respect for different ethnic-cultural populations, but created new opportunities for conflict.

The provisions of this treaty and its burdens were fated to prepare the ground for an even greater conflict a generation later. The reparations bill imposed on the German government was scaled down in the 1920s from nearly 30 billion dollars to 8.5 billion in 1929 (the Young Plan) and finally to three billion German marks in 1930 to be paid over a three-year period. That amount was repudiated when the Nazis obtained power.

Meanwhile, high unemployment also resulted in the wake of the war during the time it took to convert war production back into civilian output. Germany would experience a period of hyper-inflation in the mid-1920s, as well as political instability under the Weimar Republic, where as many as thirty parties vied for influence and power. The same kind of instability afflicted Italy, preparing the ground for Mussolini's fascist movement. By the early 1920s the Bolsheviks had gained control in Russia, and were creating the Soviet Union. Adding to that was the beginning of the Great Depression in Europe and America in 1929-30. One result was the ability of Adolf Hitler and his Nazi party to gain power in Germany in 1933, followed by the government's repudiation of its war debts, and the beginnings of a massive rearmament program in Germany.

The one bright spot that appears in the dismal picture of postwar Europe and the Middle East is the emergence of Turkey as a reasonably progressive state. It was a core remnant of the Ottoman Empire. It came under the rule of Ataturk, who abolished the sultanate and brought western-style reforms to the Turkish society.

All in all, however, the First World War was a tragedy from the beginning. Moreover, the inability of the European states to deal effectively with its aftermath produced another tragedy--the march into an even greater war that lasted from 1939 to mid-1945. The United States was slow to react to this second war, but measures were taken such as the Lend-Lease program adopted in 1941 that aided the allies in their war against Nazi expansion. Only with all-out American involvement in the war after Pearl Harbor was it possible to defeat the Axis powers in Europe and Asia.

Lessons learned:

There is consolation in the fact that the lessons learned from the debacles following World War I were applied in the post-World War II period. Under American leadership, and aided by the foresight of President Truman, a new framework for peace was created, including the institution of a new United Nations organization. This was in contrast to the decision of the U.S. government to decline membership in the League of Nations after the First World War. Also, unlike the earlier example of offering only loans to European allies, the U.S. in 1947 offered outright grants of huge sums for the rebuilding of western Europe, through the Marshall Plan. This spending on production, actually an investment, also helped the U.S. avoid a postwar economic depression that the Communist world believed and hoped would weaken the capitalist countries, which actually had become mixed economies. In 1949 the United States, for the first time in peacetime, took the lead in forming an alliance with European allies, for the purpose of opposing Communist expansionism in Europe. Thus was formed the North Atlantic Treaty Organization. Meanwhile, the United States did not impose reparation payments on the defeated nations. These were lessons learned that have made Germany and Japan among our best friends overseas.

Finally, it must be recognized that the most significant costs of World War I are told in the immense casualties that were incurred by all the belligerent countries. These losses cut across the board in terms of loss of human lives, wounds resulting in physical and mental disabilities, disruption of daily life patterns, and changes in the traditional ways of conducting business.

In brief, the Great War brought great sorrow to millions of people. No price can be placed on the absence of a beloved family member.

VOLUME II GLOSSARY

AEF – name for American Expeditionary Forces who fought in World War I as opposed to the Regular Army which had existed before the war. The AEF also consisted of men from the National Guard units from different states. (See National Guard.)

ALLIES – agreed to join together and fight the Central Powers. The main ones were Great Britain, France, Russia, Belgium, Italy, and the United States with small nations consisting of 23 nations in all.

ANZAC – Soldiers from the British dominions of Australia and New Zealand who fought for the British, especially at Gallipoli.

ARMISTICE – A written agreement in which fighting ceases and a truce is called between two or more armies. It is not the same as a peace treaty.

ARTILLERY – Weapons that fired large caliber shells from a long distance.

ATTRITION – The strategy for fighting to continue until the men of one army were killed in large enough numbers they would have to surrender.

BARRAGE – A large number of guns are directed to fire into an extended line of enemy territory.

BASE HOSPITAL – A large hospital about 200 miles away from the front lines where all types of medical and surgical procedures were available. There were more than 70 such hospitals in France and England. Base Hospital # 28 came from Kansas University and #21 from Washington University, St. Louis.

BATTERY – In artillery, consisting of usually four but possible six, artillery pieces. Also included are ammunition caissons, water tank, kitchen wagon and other support. A section chief directs the activity.

BOCHE – a name of derision for the German soldier.

BOLSHEVIKS – The Russian radical activists who rebelled against the Czarist government and eventually overthrew the Czar's government and executed the Czar and his family. They were known as the Red Russians while the Czar's army was called the White Russians.

CAMPAIGN – Consists of a number of battles; sometimes grouped to achieve a larger goal.

CENTRAL POWERS – Nations who fought the Allies. They included Germany, Austria-Hungary, Turkey (the old Ottoman Empire) and Bulgaria.

COMBATANT – another name for a soldier who fights.

COMMAND POST (C.P.) – Where the commanding officers made their headquarters. It could be in a fine chateau or in a small muddy dugout.

CONSCRIPTION – Forced enrollment of men in the army, also known as draft.

CONVOY – a group of ships sailing together to provide protection from German sub attacks.

DIPLOMACY – A way of conducting international relationships to make treaties of alliances.

DOUGHBOYS – Nickname given American troops. Origin is not certain.

DRAFT – A law and procedure requiring eligible men to register for military service.

DUGOUT – A shelter dug into the ground or a hillside, with sand bags and perhaps timbers to reinforce it.

FASCISM – A form of government where a single ruler holds all authority over all matters.

FLANK – A side of a military formation; the enemy tried to find the weakest side to attack.

FRONT – The line at which two armies meet to conduct a battle.

FRITZ – Another nickname for a German soldier.

GAS CANNISTERS – Shells containing gas that were fired especially into woods and areas with gulleys, low lying spots, or marshes where the gas would remain for day, making it a long term hazard.

HORSES, A TEAM OF – Six horses were required to pull an artillery weapon. Other horses needed by an artillery battery included some to pull the water cart, the rolling kitchen, and caissons, so a minimum of 35 necessary for each gun.

HOWITZER – A short cannon with a medium muzzle which makes high arcs when firing shells especially effective against trenches.

LANDWEHR – A well trained German soldier; generally those from 17 years of age to about 23. Then transferred to the second levy until age 39; finally the LANDSTURN to age 45.

LIBERTY BONDS – Bonds issued by the U.S. Government to provide revenue for costs of war. Although many civilians and children purchased large amounts, most were bought by commercial interests because of the high interest paid and the security, especially as civilian consumption was decreasing.

MOBILIZATION – The process of organizing soldiers to prepare to fight for a nation.

MORTAR – an effective and relatively inexpensive gun which is designed to "lob" a large shell over a short distance with great destructive effect. Also known in German as "Minewerfer."

NATIONAL GUARD – A soldier who had served in the armed forces on part time duty, usually in natural disasters before the war was declared. They were trained but not as skilled or knowledgeable as the Regular Army soldier who was full time.

NON-COMBATANT – someone not a member of the armed services. He or she helped serve the soldiers as chaplains, nurses, stretcher bearers, ambulance drivers; volunteers from the YMCA, Salvation Army, Red Cross etc. They do not carry weapons and are not allowed to participate in fighting.

"NO MAN'S LAND" – the land between two facing armies; especially dangerous in trench warfare; can be as short in length as 100 feet or a mile wide.

OSSUARY – A sacred place for storage of bones from bodies. The largest one is at Duamont Cemetery, France where approximately bones from 130,000 unknown soldiers are contained.

OUTPOST – (O.P.) An observation post usually high in a tree, often camouflaged to conceal the presence of the observer or a sniper.

PROTECTIVE BARRAGE – Firing artillery shells directly in front of one's troops to guard against an enemy's advancing troops. It was essential that the troops march or walk at a certain speed to avoid being shot by their own shells.

PUTTEES – Long wraps for legs and ankles to keep water out of the books. If not wrapped properly or too tightly, trench foot" could develop or even gangrene. Worn by British and American soldiers, the word came from India. Officers were responsible to conduct regular foot inspections when the war conditions allowed, and this reduced the incidence greatly of disease.

ROLLING BARRAGE – The range is gradually increased in short periods of time in front of one's own advancing infantry. (Also called "creeping.")

ROOKIE – A new recruit or replacement in the line.

SALIENT – A U-shaped area of the battlefront extending outward into enemy territory. It could be defended on all three sides, making it difficult to attack and seize. St. Mihiel is an excellent example of a famous salient.

SHELL OR ROUND -The round or shell for the 75 mm artillery gun weights 16 lbs. and has a maximum range of 5.3 miles. It could be fired up to 20 rounds (times) a minutes by an experienced crew before the barrel became so hot it might rupture. Then it had to be cooled down with wet clothes or allowed to rest. Of a battery of four guns, usually one gun was cooling down.

SHELL SHOCK – a form of mental distress coming from a variety of reasons. It often unfortunately was interpreted as cowardice and more than 300 English troops were executed for it.

SHRAPNEL – A special artillery shell containing metal balls or pieces which explode upon impact. Small pieces are hot and sharp and can cause serious injury, decapitation of a limb, or death.

SNIPER – A rifleman with excellent aim who usually shoots from a concealed place. He may have a special sight attached to his gun which measures how far away the target is.

TANK – This vehicle was a surprise to the Germans who were unaware for the most part of its development. American engineers from tractor factories went to England to help with the design. A complete secret, it achieved its name from the box like covering when not being worked on. The box covered a "tank," it was said, and people assumed it was a water tank. However, frequent improvements were made with the design, with almost weekly reports relating the problems which could be solved quickly.

TREATY PROTECTION OF THE NEUTRALITY OF BELGIUM – A treaty signed by all major nations in April, 1839, when the nation of Belgium was formed. Germany violated its signature when its troops crossed Belgium's borders in August, 1914. This was a major cause for World War I to begin.

TRENCH – An excavation in the ground, usually in a short strip for protection of soldiers from enemy fire. They were usually six feet or more if possible in depth, sometimes with wooden planks as flooring if no planks were available. However, when raining or snowing, the ground would be extremely muddy. The trench sides were reinforced, if possible with branches, boards, sand bags or other materials. They were built in a zig zag pattern to prevent the enemy from firing straight down the line and killing many men.

TRENCH FOOT – A painful condition of the feet caused by frostbite or prolonged exposure to water or moisture from tight fitting boots. Can result in gangrene, possibly requiring amputation of toes or entire foot.

U-BOATS (SUBMARINES OR UNTERSEEBOOT) – After the Battle of Jutland in 1916 with Germany against England, the results of which were "a draw," Germany concentrated on building fleets of U-boats to attack and sink all ships, regardless of the flag they were flying, if they were headed in the direction of Britain and France carrying supplies and armaments. The submarines were successful at first in torpedoing more ships than could be built. When the United States entered the war and set up the convoy system, sinkage due to submarine attacks, dropped to a low of 5% of the highest amount.

WESTERN FRONT – Parallel lines of trenches, from 3 to six lines which began at the Belgian coast and continued to the Swiss border. It was about 460 miles long and was where most of the fighting of World War I in Belgium and France took place. (Schaeffer)

BIBLIOGRAPHY

Bridger, Geoff. *The Great War Handbook*. South Yorkshire: Pen and Sword. 2013.

Billington, Mary Frances. *The Red Cross in War*. London:Hodder and Stoughton. 1914.

Davidson, Henry P. *The American Red Cross in the Great War*. New York: The Macmillin Co.1919.

Dalessandro, Robert J. and Torrence, Gerald. *Willing Patriots, Men of Color in the First World War.* Atglen, PA: Schiffer Military History.

Drinker, Frederick E. *Our War for Human Rights*. Washington, D.C.: Austin Jenkins Co. 1917.

Eisenhower, John S.D. *Yanks. The Epic Story of the American Army in World War I.* New York: The Free Press. 2001.

Ellis, Edward S., ed. *Library of American History. America's Part in The World War.* Cincinnati Ohio: The Jones Brothers Publishing Company, 1918.

Ferrell, Robert. *America's Deadliest Battle. Meuse-Argonne, 1918.* University of Kansas Press. 2007.

Fort Leonard Wood Research Center. *Historical Outline on the 32nd Engineers, ordered December, 1917.*

Freidel, Frank. *Over There. The American Experience in World War I.* Short Hills, N.J.: Burford Books. 1964.

Fromkin, David. *A Peace to End All Peace*. New York: Holt Paperbacks. 1989.

Gray, Randall and Argyle, Christopher. *Chronicles of the First World War, Vol. 1 and 2.* Oxford: Facts of File, Ltd. 1990 and 1991.

Gilbert, Martin. *The First World War. A Complete History.* New York: Henry Holt and Company. 1994.

Harrison, Carter H., Capt. A.R.C. *With the American Red Cross in France.* 1947.

Hochschild, Adam. *To End All Wars*. New York: Houghton Mifflin Harcourt. 2011.

Hunter, Addie W., Johnson, Kathryn. *Two Colored Women With the American Expeditionary Forces.* Brooklyn Eagle Press.

Langer, William. *An Encyclopedia of Modern World History*. Boston: Houghton, Mifflin Co. 1968.

Magee, Ron, Volunteer Researcher at National World War I Museum and Memorial. *Brief Outline of the Siberian Intervention.* Kansas City, MO: 2011. (unpublished)

Mattox, Joelouis. *They Came to Fight, A Presentation for Black History Month.* Kansas City, MO: The African American History & Culture House, University of Missouri-Kansas City. 2008.

Mead, Gary. *The Doughboys. America and the First World War.* Woodstock, N.Y. The Overlook Press. Peter Mayer, Publ. 2000.

Meyer, G.J. *A World Undone. A Story of the Great War. 1914-1918.* New York: Bantam Dell. 2007.

Ovitt, S.W. 1st Lieut. A.S., editor. The BALLOON SECTION OF THE AMERICAN EXPEDITIONARY FORCES.

Perisco, Joseph E. *Eleventh Month, Eleventh Day, Eleventh Hour. Armistice Day, 1918.* New York: Random House. 2005.

Sasse, Fred A. *Rookie Days of a Soldier*. St. Paul, MN: W.G. Greene. 1924.

Schaefer, Christina. *THE GREAT WAR. A Guide to the Service Records of All The World's Fighting Men and Volunteers.* Baltimore, Md. 1998.

Schneider, Dorothy and Carl J. *Into the Breach*. New York: Viking. 1991. (Role of women in war)

Scott, E.J. The Negro in the Service of Supply. No date or publisher listed

Shields, Sarah D. *A Study: "The Treatment of Conscientious Objectors During World War I: Mennonites at Camp Funston."*

Sweeney, W. Allison. *History of the African American Soldier.* No date or publisher listed
Weber, Eugen. *A Modern History of Europe.* New York: Norton and Company, 1971.
Willmott, H.P. *World War I.* New York: DK Publishing. 2009.
Wright, William . *Meuse-Argonne Diary. A Division Commander in World War I.* Columbia, MO: The
    University of Missouri Press, 2004.
Yoder, Anne. Archivist, *World War I Conscientious Objection.* Swarthmore, PA: Swarthmore College
    Peace Collection, 2002.

INTERNET REFERENCES:

AEF Siberia, Christine L. Putnam. Doughboy Center. Presented by Worldwar1.com
American Battle Monuments Commission. www.abamc.gov
United States Army Europe. www.eur.army.mil/organization/history.htm
US Army Air Service, Doughboy Center, 43rd Balloon Co.
"Measuring Worth."http://www.measuringworth.com.uscompare/relativevalue.php.
Texas Military Forces Museum. 142nd Infantry Regiment Line
Lineage and Honors http://www.texasmilitaryforcemuseum.org/36divisionarchives/142/142lin.htm.
"World War I Choctaw Code Talkers"; www.texasmilitaryforcemuseum.org.cho
"Stretcher Bearers." Spartacus Educational.com
"Battle of the Argonne. Diary of a Waggoner." www.worldwarI.com/dbc/pierson.htm.
Role of Non-EuropeanNationalsWWI.faculty.sfhs.com/lesleymullerAP...wwwI/
    role_of_noneuro_nations.pdf.

RECOMMENDED READING: *

Addington, Scott. *5 Minute History. First World War Weapons.* The History Press: Stroud,
    Gloucestershire, GL2, 2QG. The History Press. 2014.
    ————-*5 Minute History. First World War Great Battles.* The History Press: Stroud,   Gloucestershire,
    GL2, 2QG, 2014.
Christie, Norm. *For King & Empire. The Canadians at Vimy.* CEF Books, Ottawa, Ontario.   2002.
Clark, Alan. *The Donkeys.* New York: Award Books, 1965.
Clark, Christopher. *The Sleepwalkers.* New York: Harper Perennial. 2012.
Cohen, Joseph. *Journey to the Trenches. The Life of Isaac Rosenberg, 1890-1918.*
    New York: Basic Books, Inc. 1975. .
Fisk, Robert. *The Great War for Civilization. The Conquest for the Middle East.* New York:
    Vintage Books. 2007.
Hansen, Arlen J. and Plimpton, George. *Gentlemen Volunteers. the Story of American
    Ambulance Drivers in WWI.* New York: Arcade Publ. 201 1.
Hochschild. *To End All Wars. A Story of Protest and Patriotism in the First World War.* London:
    MacMillan.2012.
Kennedy, Paul. *The Rise and Fall of the Great Powers. Economic Change and Military
    Conflict from 1500 to 2000.* New York: Random House. 1987.
Manning, Frederic. *Her Privates We.* London: Hogarth Press. 1986.
Moran, Lord. *The Anatomy of Courage. The Classic WWI Account of the Psychological Effects of War.*
    New York: Carroll & Graf Publishers. 2007.
Newton, Douglas. *The Darkest Days. The Truth Behind Britain's Rush to War, 1914.* London: Verso.
    2014.
Nelson, James Carl. *Five Lieutenants. The Heartbreaking Story of Five Harvard Men Who Led America
    to Victory in World War I.* New York: St. Martin's Press. 2012.

Nelson, Peter. *The Harlem Hellfighters' Struggle for Freedom in WWI and Equality at Home*. New York: Basic Civitas Books. 2009.

Palmer, Alan. *Victory 1918*.New York: Atlantic Monthly Press. 1998.

Phillips, David. *Lethal Warriors. When the New Band of Brothers Came Home. Uncovering the Tragic Reality of PTSD*. New York: St. Martin's Press. 2010.

Purdom, C.B., editor. *On the Front Lines. True World War I Stories*. London: Constable. 009.

Reed, Fiona. *Broken Men. Shell Shock, Treatment and Recovery in Britain 1914-30*. London: Bloomsbury, 2011

Reynolds, David. *The Long Shadow.The Legacies of the Great War in the Twentieth Century.* New York: W.W. Norton. 2014.

Rice, Eugene, Consulting Editor. *World War I: A Turning Point in Modern History*. New York: Alfred A. Knopf. 1967.

Thompson, Mark. *White War. Life and Death on the Italian Front 1915-1919*, New York: Basic Books. 2008.

Tuchman, Barbara. *Bible and Sword*. New York: Ballantine Books. 1956.(She gives an historical prospective to war, especially in the Middle East.)

Underwood, Lamar. *The Greatest War Stories Ever Told. Twenty-four Incredible Tales.* Guilford, Connecticut: The Lyons Press. 2001.

Van Emden, Richard. *The Soldier's War.* London: Bloomsbury. 2008.

Also highly recommended although they were written a few years after World War I, are these two beautifully written visions of flying and what makes man want to take to the air:

Saint-Exupery, Antoine de. *Wind, Sand and Stars*. 1939 and *Night Flight*, 1932. both are published by A Harvest Book, U.S.A. after translation from the French.

OTHER MEDIA RECOMMENDED:

1*) Passchendaele*, story of the Canadians who conquered the unconquerable battle. Excellent. DVD format from a film by Paul Gross.

2) *The First World War*. Complete series of a 4 DVD set based on the book by Hew Strachan and narrated and produced by Jonathan Lewis. Excellent also.

3) *All Quiet on the Western Front.* From best picture of 1930. DVD format of one of the finest books ever written about World War I.

4) WWI- The War to End All Wars, a 10 part comprehensive look at the war that shaped the 20th century. DVD format. (Collector's Edition)

5) *World War I: "The Great War"*- Prof. Vejas G. Liulevicius, The Teaching Company. In 3 parts with 36 lessons. One of the best and most comprehensive of all. (See if your local library has this series. Most of them do.)

*As you will notice, I have added a number of new books to this list. For one thing, many interesting books on the War are being published that deal with other topics than the history, battles, and statistics. These new topics include women's role (although I found only one good enough to recommend); shell shock; revolt against war and disagreement with why nations were going to war; and the devaluation of the individual soldier.

TABLE OF LOSSES IN COMBAT
Died in battle or died later of wounds

Germany	1,800,000	Roumania	335,000
Russia	1,700,000	Turkey	325,000
France	1,384,000	Bulgaria	90,000
Austria-Hungary	1,290,000	Canada	60,000
Britain	743,000*	Australia	59,000
Italy	615,000		

* Only men from the British Isles

MAJOR BATTLES IN WHICH MEN IN THIS VOLUME FOUGHT:

Aisne-	May 27 - June 5, 1918
Champagne-Marne	July 15 - 18, 1918
Aisne-Marne	July 18 - Aug. 6, 1918
Somme Offensive	Aug. 8 - Nov. 11, 1918
Oise-Aisne	Aug. 19 - Nov. 11, 1918
St. Mihiel	Sept. 12 -16, 1918
Meuse-Argonne	Sept. 26 - Nov. 11, 1918
Vittorio-Veneto	Oct. 24 - Nov. 4, 1918

AOG–Army of Occupation of Germany – Nov. 12, 1919 until July, 1919
Siberian–Russia Campaign 1918 – Summer, 1920
(from General Headquarters, AEF)

THE LAST WORD
by Nancy Cramer

As I interview people, research what they told me, then write their stories, I have come to envision a larger picture. That picture includes everyone who ever says, or just remembers, that they had a relative in World War I. I am urging them to jot down every little detail, bits of a story, or family lore they can recall. Then, if they don't have the opportunity to do the research themselves, the information is there for someone else to use.

Each man who wore the AEF uniform was important, regardless of his assignment or his actions. These soldiers deserve to have their stories preserved. This war was the most disastrous in history to that date. The number of deaths and wounded was enormous, and the losses in property destruction and economic dollars were colossal.

Was the war worth it? Did world leaders and their populations learn the important lessons the war offered? You decide. I know my answer, and it will be my last word. No.

ACKNOWLEDGEMENTS

Although this is not intended to be the work of a scholar, several scholars graciously gave of their time. To mention some is not meant to neglect all of them, but I will start with Doran Cart, Senior Curator, and Jonathan Casey, Archivist, at the National World War I Museum and Memorial, and the Research Center volunteers. John Thiesen, archivist at Bethel College; Joelouis Mattox, historian for American Legion Wayne Miner Post 149; and the staff at Webster Museum, Lawrence, KS, and members of the Marine Corps Archives also deserve my gratitude. State Historical Societies of Missouri, Oklahoma, Iowa and Kansas have provided valuable information.

My biggest appreciation goes to Niel Johnson, Ph.D. whose editing, writing and collaboration helped create these two volumes, honoring more than 100 World War I veterans and their families. To all, I simply say "Thank you. Your deeds speak louder than your words."

Also thanks to Ghent Oehsen for use of two of his father's photographs on page 86. His father, a medic in the German army, emigrated after the war with his family and the irreplaceable album of some 400 photographs of his service on the Eastern Front with the Germans. Ghent bequeathed the priceless album to the National World War Museum and Memorial for such research projects as this book. I was proud to have known Ghent briefly before he died in fall, 2014. The story of Ghent's father and more photographs can be found in Volume I of "Unheard Voices, Untold Stories."

CORRECTION FROM Volume I, "Unheard Voices, Untold Stories," p. 116:

The men of the 369th Regiment were stated as being assigned to the AEF 92nd Division. That is incorrect. They were members of the 93rd Division which was never fully completed, and therefore transferred by General Pershing to the 14th French Army, according to Bernard Harris, retired Army officer, who has studied thoroughly the assignments and actions of the African-American troops in France.

General Pershing was reluctant to assign AEF African-American troops to the front lines in the AEF regular divisions because of possible racial problems . However, the French army was desperate for replacements and their troops were accustomed to, in Mr. Harris' words: "working with Africans from the French colonies, so they gladly took the four regiments, 369, 370, 371, and 372, from the mostly African American 93rd incomplete Division…" "The entire 369th Regiment was kept in the French army for the duration of the war from about March, 1918 to November, 1918. .." "Because the 369th was allowed to serve as combat troops and not just as laborers, this is one reason they received so many French awards. They did not receive any American awards at the end of the war." The author appreciates Mr. Harris' careful study of the information and the correction and clarification.

The National World War I Museum and Memorial
In Kansas City, Missouri

This memorial was built by the urging of its citizens who, in two weeks after the war ended, raised $2,000,000 (today's equivalent of 40 million). Approximately 4,000 to 6,000 local men has been inducted into the various services, some as early as 1915 when the Canadian Royal Air Corps began recruiting here. The city was very patriotic minded and helped fund and establish Base Hospital No. 28 with the University of Kansas, one of the 70 or more base hospitals the United States set up in France.

The land, a bluff across from the recently built Union Station through which as many 70% of the AEF troops utilized, traveling in all directions, was purchased. A great celebration to dedicate the land was held November 11, 1921, with five of the most important Allied military leaders present. A mural in Memory Hall commemorates this occasion and depicts General Jacque, Belgium; General Dias, Italy; Supreme Commander, General Foch, France; General Pershing, AEF; and Admiral Beattie, British Isles.

The Memorial remained a symbol of the sacrifice of all American troops and honored our Allies. Then in 2000, another citizen group raised almost 21 million dollars to build the Museum. It was opened in 2006, and it and the Memorial both have attained a national status. The Museum was voted one of the best 25 museums in the United States and is the only museum in the U.S. devoted solely to World War I. Kansas City is proud to honor veterans of all services who served in any war in which the United States was involved.

THE NATIONAL WWI MUSEUM
and MEMORIAL
100 W. 26th St., Kansas City, MO 64108
Call 816.888.8100
theworldwar.org

 theworldwar

 thewwimuseum

Named one of the United States best 25 museums.